Employment Rights Act 1996

CHAPTER 18

Explanatory Notes are available separately

GRAN*GIS* UK Publishing

Adapted and published by GRANGIS (Grand Register Library).
Online: www.grangis.com
E-mail: contact@grangis.com

In this version:
ISBN: 979-8-88559-017-4

Note: This is the original version (as it was originally enacted). Title, sub-title and the generated date is as marked on the pages.

Employment Rights Act 1996

CHAPTER 18

EMPLOYMENT RIGHTS ACT 1996

PART I

EMPLOYMENT PARTICULARS

Right to statements of employment particulars

Right to itemised pay statement

Enforcement

PART II

PROTECTION OF WAGES

PART X

UNFAIR DISMISSAL

CHAPTER I

RIGHT NOT TO BE UNFAIRLY DISMISSED

The right

Dismissal

Fairness

Exclusion of right

CHAPTER II

REMEDIES FOR UNFAIR DISMISSAL

Introductory

Orders for reinstatement or re-engagement

Compensation

Supplementary

CHAPTER III

RIGHT BY REASON OF LAY-OFF OR SHORT-TIME

Lay-off and short-time

Exclusions

Supplementary

CHAPTER IV

GENERAL EXCLUSIONS FROM RIGHT

CHAPTER V

OTHER PROVISIONS ABOUT REDUNDANCY PAYMENTS

CHAPTER VI

PAYMENTS BY SECRETARY OF STATE

SCHEDULES

The New Towns (Scotland) Act 1977 (c. 16)

12 In section 3(6) of the New Towns (Scotland) Act 1977,...

The National Health Service (Scotland) Act 1978 (c. 29)

13 In section 12C(3) of the National Health Service (Scotland) Act...

The House of Commons (Administration) Act 1978 (c. 36)

14 In paragraph 1 of Schedule 2 to the House of...

The New Towns Act 1981 (c. 64)

15 In section 54(5) of the New Towns Act 1981, for...

The Wildlife and Countryside Act 1981 (c. 69)

16 In paragraph 8(4) of Schedule 13 to the Wildlife and...

The Hops Marketing Act 1982 (c. 5)

17 In section 2(7) of the Hops Marketing Act 1982, for...

The Oil and Gas (Enterprise) Act 1982 (c. 23)

18 (1) In Schedule 3 to the Oil and Gas (Enterprise)...

The Local Government Finance Act 1982 (c. 32)

19 In paragraph 8(3) of Schedule 3 to the Local Government...

The Administration of Justice Act 1982 (c. 53)

20 In section 10(d) of the Administration of Justice Act 1982—...

The Health and Social Services and Social Security Adjudications Act 1983 (c. 14)

21 In paragraph 23 of Part II of Schedule 3 to...

The National Audit Act 1983 (c. 44)

22 In paragraph 2(3) of Schedule 2 to the National Audit...

The National Heritage Act 1983 (c. 47)

23 In— (a) paragraph 5(5) of Part I of Schedule 1,...

The National Heritage (Scotland) Act 1985 (c. 16)

24 In— (a) paragraph 5(5) of Part I, and

The Prosecution of Offences Act 1985 (c. 23)

25 (1) The Prosecution of Offences Act 1985 is amended as...

The Local Government Act 1985 (c. 51)

26 (1) The Local Government Act 1985 is amended as follows....

The Trustee Savings Banks Act 1985 (c. 58)

27 In section 3(7) of the Trustee Savings Banks Act 1985,...

The Housing (Consequential Provisions) Act 1985 (c. 71)

28 In paragraph 7(2)(b) of Schedule 4 to the Housing (Consequential...

The Insolvency Act 1986 (c. 45)

29 In paragraph 13 of Schedule 6 to the Insolvency Act...

The Legal Aid (Scotland) Act 1986 (c. 47)

30 In paragraph 10(1) of Schedule 1 to the Legal Aid...

The Debtors (Scotland) Act 1987 (c. 18)

31 In section 73(3)(g) of the Debtors (Scotland) Act 1987, for...

The Pilotage Act 1987 (c. 21)

32 In section 25(6) of the Pilotage Act 1987, for “Schedule...

The Housing (Scotland) Act 1987 (c. 26)

33 In paragraph 10(2)(b) of Schedule 22 to the Housing (Scotland)...

The Consumer Protection Act 1987 (c. 43)

34 In section 22(5) of the Consumer Protection Act 1987, for...

The Income and Corporation Taxes Act 1988 (c. 1)

35 (1) The Income and Corporation Taxes Act 1988 is amended...

The Legal Aid Act 1988 (c. 34)

36 In paragraph 7(1) of Schedule 7 to the Legal Aid...

The Education Reform Act 1988 (c. 40)

37 (1) The Education Reform Act 1988 is amended as follows....

The Local Government Finance Act 1988 (c. 41)

38 In paragraph 6(4) of Schedule 11 to the Local Government...

The Housing (Scotland) Act 1988 (c. 43)

39 In paragraph 12(1) of Schedule 1 to the Housing (Scotland)...

The Health and Medicines Act 1988 (c. 49)

40 In section 18 of the Health and Medicines Act 1988,...

The Housing Act 1988 (c. 50)

41 In paragraph 10(1) of Schedule 5 to the Housing Act...

The Dock Work Act 1989 (c. 13)

42 In section 6(3) of the Dock Work Act 1989—

The Electricity Act 1989 (c. 29)

43 (1) The Electricity Act 1989 is amended as follows.

The Local Government and Housing Act 1989 (c. 42)

44 In section 10 of the Local Government and Housing Act...

The National Health Service and Community Care Act 1990 (c. 19)

45 (1) The National Health Service and Community Care Act 1990...

The Enterprise and New Towns (Scotland) Act 1990 (c. 35)

46 In paragraph 17(1) of Schedule 1 to the Enterprise and...

The Environmental Protection Act 1990 (c. 43)

47 In paragraph 15 of Schedule 10 to the Environmental Protection...

The Natural Heritage (Scotland) Act 1991 (c. 28)

48 In paragraph 4 of Schedule 4 to the Natural Heritage...

The Coal Mining Subsidence Act 1991 (c. 45)

49 In section 30(7) of the Coal Mining Subsidence Act 1991—...

The Ports Act 1991 (c. 52)

50 In section 24(8) of the Ports Act 1991, for the...

The Social Security Contributions and Benefits Act 1992 (c. 4)

51 (1) The Social Security Contributions and Benefits Act 1992 is...

The Further and Higher Education Act 1992 (c. 13)

52 (1) The Further and Higher Education Act 1992 is amended...

The Timeshare Act 1992 (c. 35)

53 In section 1 of the Timeshare Act 1992—

The Further and Higher Education (Scotland) Act 1992 (c. 37)

54 In section 33(3)(b) of the Further and Higher Education (Scotland)...

The Museums and Galleries Act 1992 (c. 44)

55 In section 1(7) of the Museums and Galleries Act 1992,...

The Trade Union and Labour Relations (Consolidation) Act 1992 (c. 52)

56 (1) The Trade Union and Labour Relations (Consolidation) Act 1992...

The Tribunals and Inquiries Act 1992 (c. 53)

57 In section 11(2) of the Tribunals and Inquiries Act 1992,...

The Social Security Act 1993 (c. 3)

58 In section 2(4)(b) of the Social Security Act 1993, for...

The Education Act 1993 (c. 35)

59 In section 305(1) of the Education Act 1993, for "the...

The Railways Act 1993 (c. 43)

60 (1) The Railways Act 1993 is amended as follows.

The Pension Schemes Act 1993 (c. 48)

61 (1) The Pension Schemes Act 1993 is amended as follows....

The Finance Act 1994 (c. 9)

62 In paragraph 27 of Schedule 24 to the Finance Act...

The Local Government (Wales) Act 1994 (c. 19)

63 (1) The Local Government (Wales) Act 1994 is amended as...

The Coal Industry Act 1994 (c. 21)

64 In paragraph 4(11) of Schedule 5 to the Coal Industry...

The Criminal Justice and Public Order Act 1994 (c. 33)

65 In section 126(2) of the Criminal Justice and Public Order...

The Local Government etc. (Scotland) Act 1994 (c. 39)

66 (1) The Local Government etc. (Scotland) Act 1994 is amended...

The Jobseekers Act 1995 (c. 18)

67 (1) The Jobseekers Act 1995 is amended as follows.

The Environment Act 1995 (c. 25)

68 In paragraph 3 of Schedule 2 to the Environment Act...

The Disability Discrimination Act 1995 (c. 50)

69 (1) The Disability Discrimination Act 1995 is amended as follows....

SCHEDULE 2 — Transitional provisions, savings and transitory provisions
Part I — TRANSITIONAL PROVISIONS AND SAVINGS

General transitionals and savings

1 The substitution of this Act for the provisions repealed or...
2 (1) Anything done, or having effect as done, (including the...
3 Any reference (express or implied) in this Act or any...

2 The following abbreviations are used in the Table— BGLA Betting,...

Employment Rights Act 1996

1996 CHAPTER 18

An Act to consolidate enactments relating to employment rights. [22nd May 1996]

Be it enacted by the Queen's most Excellent Majesty, by and with the advice and consent of the Lords Spiritual and Temporal, and Commons, in this present Parliament assembled, and by the authority of the same, as follows:—

PART I

EMPLOYMENT PARTICULARS

Right to statements of employment particulars

1 Statement of initial employment particulars

(1) Where an employee begins employment with an employer, the employer shall give to the employee a written statement of particulars of employment.

(2) The statement may (subject to section 2(4)) be given in instalments and (whether or not given in instalments) shall be given not later than two months after the beginning of the employment.

(3) The statement shall contain particulars of—

(a) the names of the employer and employee,

(b) the date when the employment began, and

(c) the date on which the employee's period of continuous employment began (taking into account any employment with a previous employer which counts towards that period).

(4) The statement shall also contain particulars, as at a specified date not more than seven days before the statement (or the instalment containing them) is given, of—

(a) the scale or rate of remuneration or the method of calculating remuneration,

(b) the intervals at which remuneration is paid (that is, weekly, monthly or other specified intervals),

(c) any terms and conditions relating to hours of work (including any terms and conditions relating to normal working hours),

(d) any terms and conditions relating to any of the following—

(i) entitlement to holidays, including public holidays, and holiday pay (the particulars given being sufficient to enable the employee's entitlement, including any entitlement to accrued holiday pay on the termination of employment, to be precisely calculated),

(ii) incapacity for work due to sickness or injury, including any provision for sick pay, and

(iii) pensions and pension schemes,

(e) the length of notice which the employee is obliged to give and entitled to receive to terminate his contract of employment,

(f) the title of the job which the employee is employed to do or a brief description of the work for which he is employed,

(g) where the employment is not intended to be permanent, the period for which it is expected to continue or, if it is for a fixed term, the date when it is to end,

(h) either the place of work or, where the employee is required or permitted to work at various places, an indication of that and of the address of the employer,

(j) any collective agreements which directly affect the terms and conditions of the employment including, where the employer is not a party, the persons by whom they were made, and

(k) where the employee is required to work outside the United Kingdom for a period of more than one month—

(i) the period for which he is to work outside the United Kingdom,

(ii) the currency in which remuneration is to be paid while he is working outside the United Kingdom,

(iii) any additional remuneration payable to him, and any benefits to be provided to or in respect of him, by reason of his being required to work outside the United Kingdom, and

(iv) any terms and conditions relating to his return to the United Kingdom.

(5) Subsection (4)(d)(iii) does not apply to an employee of a body or authority if—

(a) the employee's pension rights depend on the terms of a pension scheme established under any provision contained in or having effect under any Act, and

(b) any such provision requires the body or authority to give to a new employee information concerning the employee's pension rights or the determination of questions affecting those rights.

2 Statement of initial particulars: supplementary

(1) If, in the case of a statement under section 1, there are no particulars to be entered under any of the heads of paragraph (d) or (k) of subsection (4) of that section, or under any of the other paragraphs of subsection (3) or (4) of that section, that fact shall be stated.

(2) A statement under section 1 may refer the employee for particulars of any of the matters specified in subsection (4)(d)(ii) and (iii) of that section to the provisions of some other document which is reasonably accessible to the employee.

(3) A statement under section 1 may refer the employee for particulars of either of the matters specified in subsection (4)(e) of that section to the law or to the provisions of any collective agreement directly affecting the terms and conditions of the employment which is reasonably accessible to the employee.

(4) The particulars required by section 1(3) and (4)(a) to (c), (d)(i), (f) and (h) shall be included in a single document.

(5) Where before the end of the period of two months after the beginning of an employee's employment the employee is to begin to work outside the United Kingdom for a period of more than one month, the statement under section 1 shall be given to him not later than the time when he leaves the United Kingdom in order to begin so to work.

(6) A statement shall be given to a person under section 1 even if his employment ends before the end of the period within which the statement is required to be given.

3 Note about disciplinary procedures and pensions

(1) A statement under section 1 shall include a note—

(a) specifying any disciplinary rules applicable to the employee or referring the employee to the provisions of a document specifying such rules which is reasonably accessible to the employee,

(b) specifying (by description or otherwise)—

(i) a person to whom the employee can apply if dissatisfied with any disciplinary decision relating to him, and

(ii) a person to whom the employee can apply for the purpose of seeking redress of any grievance relating to his employment,

and the manner in which any such application should be made, and

(c) where there are further steps consequent on any such application, explaining those steps or referring to the provisions of a document explaining them which is reasonably accessible to the employee.

(2) Subsection (1) does not apply to rules, disciplinary decisions, grievances or procedures relating to health or safety at work.

(3) The note need not comply with the following provisions of subsection (1)—

(a) paragraph (a),

(b) in paragraph (b), sub-paragraph (i) and the words following sub-paragraph (ii) so far as relating to sub-paragraph (i), and

(c) paragraph (c),

if on the date when the employee's employment began the relevant number of employees was less than twenty.

(4) In subsection (3) "the relevant number of employees", in relation to an employee, means the number of employees employed by his employer added to the number of employees employed by any associated employer.

(5) The note shall also state whether there is in force a contracting-out certificate (issued in accordance with Chapter I of Part III of the Pension Schemes Act 1993) stating that the employment is contracted-out employment (for the purposes of that Part of that Act).

4 Statement of changes

(1) If, after the material date, there is a change in any of the matters particulars of which are required by sections 1 to 3 to be included or referred to in a statement under section 1, the employer shall give to the employee a written statement containing particulars of the change.

(2) For the purposes of subsection (1)—

(a) in relation to a matter particulars of which are included or referred to in a statement given under section 1 otherwise than in instalments, the material date is the date to which the statement relates,

(b) in relation to a matter particulars of which—

(i) are included or referred to in an instalment of a statement given under section 1, or

(ii) are required by section 2(4) to be included in a single document but are not included in an instalment of a statement given under section 1 which does include other particulars to which that provision applies,

the material date is the date to which the instalment relates, and

(c) in relation to any other matter, the material date is the date by which a statement under section 1 is required to be given.

(3) A statement under subsection (1) shall be given at the earliest opportunity and, in any event, not later than—

(a) one month after the change in question, or

(b) where that change results from the employee being required to work outside the United Kingdom for a period of more than one month, the time when he leaves the United Kingdom in order to begin so to work, if that is earlier.

(4) A statement under subsection (1) may refer the employee to the provisions of some other document which is reasonably accessible to the employee for a change in any of the matters specified in sections 1(4)(d)(ii) and (iii) and 3(1)(a) and (c).

(5) A statement under subsection (1) may refer the employee for a change in either of the matters specified in section 1(4)(e) to the law or to the provisions of any collective agreement directly affecting the terms and conditions of the employment which is reasonably accessible to the employee.

(6) Where, after an employer has given to an employee a statement under section 1, either—

(a) the name of the employer (whether an individual or a body corporate or partnership) is changed without any change in the identity of the employer, or

(b) the identity of the employer is changed in circumstances in which the continuity of the employee's period of employment is not broken,

and subsection (7) applies in relation to the change, the person who is the employer immediately after the change is not required to give to the employee a statement under section 1; but the change shall be treated as a change falling within subsection (1) of this section.

(7) This subsection applies in relation to a change if it does not involve any change in any of the matters (other than the names of the parties) particulars of which are required by sections 1 to 3 to be included or referred to in the statement under section 1.

(8) A statement under subsection (1) which informs an employee of a change such as is referred to in subsection (6)(b) shall specify the date on which the employee's period of continuous employment began.

5 Exclusion from rights to statements

(1) Sections 1 to 4 apply to an employee who at any time comes or ceases to come within the exceptions from those sections provided by sections 196 and 199, and under section 209, as if his employment with his employer terminated or began at that time.

(2) The fact that section 1 is directed by subsection (1) to apply to an employee as if his employment began on his ceasing to come within the exceptions referred to in that subsection does not affect the obligation under section 1(3)(b) to specify the date on which his employment actually began.

6 Reasonably accessible document or collective agreement

In sections 2 to 4 references to a document or collective agreement which is reasonably accessible to an employee are references to a document or collective agreement which—

(a) the employee has reasonable opportunities of reading in the course of his employment, or

(b) is made reasonably accessible to the employee in some other way.

7 Power to require particulars of further matters

The Secretary of State may by order provide that section 1 shall have effect as if particulars of such further matters as may be specified in the order were included in the particulars required by that section; and, for that purpose, the order may include such provisions amending that section as appear to the Secretary of State to be expedient.

Right to itemised pay statement

8 Itemised pay statement

(1) An employee has the right to be given by his employer, at or before the time at which any payment of wages or salary is made to him, a written itemised pay statement.

(2) The statement shall contain particulars of—

(a) the gross amount of the wages or salary,

(b) the amounts of any variable, and (subject to section 9) any fixed, deductions from that gross amount and the purposes for which they are made,

(c) the net amount of wages or salary payable, and

(d) where different parts of the net amount are paid in different ways, the amount and method of payment of each part-payment.

9 Standing statement of fixed deductions

(1) A pay statement given in accordance with section 8 need not contain separate particulars of a fixed deduction if—

(a) it contains instead an aggregate amount of fixed deductions, including that deduction, and

(b) the employer has given to the employee, at or before the time at which the pay statement is given, a standing statement of fixed deductions which satisfies subsection (2).

(2) A standing statement of fixed deductions satisfies this subsection if—

(a) it is in writing,

(b) it contains, in relation to each deduction comprised in the aggregate amount of deductions, particulars of—

(i) the amount of the deduction,

(ii) the intervals at which the deduction is to be made, and

(iii) the purpose for which it is made, and

(c) it is (in accordance with subsection (5)) effective at the date on which the pay statement is given.

(3) A standing statement of fixed deductions may be amended, whether by—

(a) addition of a new deduction,

(b) a change in the particulars, or

(c) cancellation of an existing deduction,

by notice in writing, containing particulars of the amendment, given by the employer to the employee.

(4) An employer who has given to an employee a standing statement of fixed deductions shall—

(a) within the period of twelve months beginning with the date on which the first standing statement was given, and

(b) at intervals of not more than twelve months afterwards,

re-issue it in a consolidated form incorporating any amendments notified in accordance with subsection (3).

(5) For the purposes of subsection (2)(c) a standing statement of fixed deductions—

(a) becomes effective on the date on which it is given to the employee, and

(b) ceases to be effective at the end of the period of twelve months beginning with that date or, where it is re-issued in accordance with subsection (4), with the end of the period of twelve months beginning with the date of the last re-issue.

10 Power to amend provisions about pay and standing statements

The Secretary of State may by order—

(a) vary the provisions of sections 8 and 9 as to the particulars which must be included in a pay statement or a standing statement of fixed deductions by adding items to, or removing items from, the particulars listed in those sections or by amending any such particulars, and

(b) vary the provisions of subsections (4) and (5) of section 9 so as to shorten or extend the periods of twelve months referred to in those subsections, or those periods as varied from time to time under this section.

Enforcement

11 References to industrial tribunals

(1) Where an employer does not give an employee a statement as required by section 1, 4 or 8 (either because he gives him no statement or because the statement he gives does not comply with what is required), the employee may require a reference to be made to an industrial tribunal to determine what particulars ought to have been included or referred to in a statement so as to comply with the requirements of the section concerned.

(2) Where—

(a) a statement purporting to be a statement under section 1 or 4, or a pay statement or a standing statement of fixed deductions purporting to comply with section 8 or 9, has been given to an employee, and

(b) a question arises as to the particulars which ought to have been included or referred to in the statement so as to comply with the requirements of this Part,

either the employer or the employee may require the question to be referred to and determined by an industrial tribunal.

(3) For the purposes of this section—

(a) a question as to the particulars which ought to have been included in the note required by section 3 to be included in the statement under section 1 does not include any question whether the employment is, has been or will be contracted-out employment (for the purposes of Part III of the Pension Schemes Act 1993), and

(b) a question as to the particulars which ought to have been included in a pay statement or standing statement of fixed deductions does not include a question solely as to the accuracy of an amount stated in any such particulars.

(4) An industrial tribunal shall not consider a reference under this section in a case where the employment to which the reference relates has ceased unless an application requiring the reference to be made was made—

(a) before the end of the period of three months beginning with the date on which the employment ceased, or

(b) within such further period as the tribunal considers reasonable in a case where it is satisfied that it was not reasonably practicable for the application to be made before the end of that period of three months.

12 Determination of references

(1) Where, on a reference under section 11(1), an industrial tribunal determines particulars as being those which ought to have been included or referred to in a statement given under section 1 or 4, the employer shall be deemed to have given to the employee a statement in which those particulars were included, or referred to, as specified in the decision of the tribunal.

(2) On determining a reference under section 11(2) relating to a statement purporting to be a statement under section 1 or 4, an industrial tribunal may—

(a) confirm the particulars as included or referred to in the statement given by the employer,

(b) amend those particulars, or

(c) substitute other particulars for them,

as the tribunal may determine to be appropriate; and the statement shall be deemed to have been given by the employer to the employee in accordance with the decision of the tribunal.

(3) Where on a reference under section 11 an industrial tribunal finds—

(a) that an employer has failed to give an employee any pay statement in accordance with section 8, or

(b) that a pay statement or standing statement of fixed deductions does not, in relation to a deduction, contain the particulars required to be included in that statement by that section or section 9,

the tribunal shall make a declaration to that effect.

(4) Where on a reference in the case of which subsection (3) applies the tribunal further finds that any unnotified deductions have been made from the pay of the employee during the period of thirteen weeks immediately preceding the date of the application for the reference (whether or not the deductions were made in breach of the contract of employment), the tribunal may order the employer to pay the employee a sum not exceeding the aggregate of the unnotified deductions so made.

(5) For the purposes of subsection (4) a deduction is an unnotified deduction if it is made without the employer giving the employee, in any pay statement or standing statement of fixed deductions, the particulars of the deduction required by section 8 or 9.

PART II

PROTECTION OF WAGES

Deductions by employer

13 Right not to suffer unauthorised deductions

(1) An employer shall not make a deduction from wages of a worker employed by him unless—

(a) the deduction is required or authorised to be made by virtue of a statutory provision or a relevant provision of the worker's contract, or

(b) the worker has previously signified in writing his agreement or consent to the making of the deduction.

(2) In this section "relevant provision", in relation to a worker's contract, means a provision of the contract comprised—

(a) in one or more written terms of the contract of which the employer has given the worker a copy on an occasion prior to the employer making the deduction in question, or

(b) in one or more terms of the contract (whether express or implied and, if express, whether oral or in writing) the existence and effect, or combined effect, of which in relation to the worker the employer has notified to the worker in writing on such an occasion.

(3) Where the total amount of wages paid on any occasion by an employer to a worker employed by him is less than the total amount of the wages properly payable by him

to the worker on that occasion (after deductions), the amount of the deficiency shall be treated for the purposes of this Part as a deduction made by the employer from the worker's wages on that occasion.

(4) Subsection (3) does not apply in so far as the deficiency is attributable to an error of any description on the part of the employer affecting the computation by him of the gross amount of the wages properly payable by him to the worker on that occasion.

(5) For the purposes of this section a relevant provision of a worker's contract having effect by virtue of a variation of the contract does not operate to authorise the making of a deduction on account of any conduct of the worker, or any other event occurring, before the variation took effect.

(6) For the purposes of this section an agreement or consent signified by a worker does not operate to authorise the making of a deduction on account of any conduct of the worker, or any other event occurring, before the agreement or consent was signified.

(7) This section does not affect any other statutory provision by virtue of which a sum payable to a worker by his employer but not constituting "wages" within the meaning of this Part is not to be subject to a deduction at the instance of the employer.

14 Excepted deductions

(1) Section 13 does not apply to a deduction from a worker's wages made by his employer where the purpose of the deduction is the reimbursement of the employer in respect of—

(a) an overpayment of wages, or

(b) an overpayment in respect of expenses incurred by the worker in carrying out his employment,

made (for any reason) by the employer to the worker.

(2) Section 13 does not apply to a deduction from a worker's wages made by his employer in consequence of any disciplinary proceedings if those proceedings were held by virtue of a statutory provision.

(3) Section 13 does not apply to a deduction from a worker's wages made by his employer in pursuance of a requirement imposed on the employer by a statutory provision to deduct and pay over to a public authority amounts determined by that authority as being due to it from the worker if the deduction is made in accordance with the relevant determination of that authority.

(4) Section 13 does not apply to a deduction from a worker's wages made by his employer in pursuance of any arrangements which have been established—

(a) in accordance with a relevant provision of his contract to the inclusion of which in the contract the worker has signified his agreement or consent in writing, or

(b) otherwise with the prior agreement or consent of the worker signified in writing,

and under which the employer is to deduct and pay over to a third person amounts notified to the employer by that person as being due to him from the worker, if the deduction is made in accordance with the relevant notification by that person.

(5) Section 13 does not apply to a deduction from a worker's wages made by his employer where the worker has taken part in a strike or other industrial action and the deduction

is made by the employer on account of the worker's having taken part in that strike or other action.

(6) Section 13 does not apply to a deduction from a worker's wages made by his employer with his prior agreement or consent signified in writing where the purpose of the deduction is the satisfaction (whether wholly or in part) of an order of a court or tribunal requiring the payment of an amount by the worker to the employer.

Payments to employer

15 Right not to have to make payments to employer

(1) An employer shall not receive a payment from a worker employed by him unless—

(a) the payment is required or authorised to be made by virtue of a statutory provision or a relevant provision of the worker's contract, or

(b) the worker has previously signified in writing his agreement or consent to the making of the payment.

(2) In this section "relevant provision", in relation to a worker's contract, means a provision of the contract comprised—

(a) in one or more written terms of the contract of which the employer has given the worker a copy on an occasion prior to the employer receiving the payment in question, or

(b) in one or more terms of the contract (whether express or implied and, if express, whether oral or in writing) the existence and effect, or combined effect, of which in relation to the worker the employer has notified to the worker in writing on such an occasion.

(3) For the purposes of this section a relevant provision of a worker's contract having effect by virtue of a variation of the contract does not operate to authorise the receipt of a payment on account of any conduct of the worker, or any other event occurring, before the variation took effect.

(4) For the purposes of this section an agreement or consent signified by a worker does not operate to authorise the receipt of a payment on account of any conduct of the worker, or any other event occurring, before the agreement or consent was signified.

(5) Any reference in this Part to an employer receiving a payment from a worker employed by him is a reference to his receiving such a payment in his capacity as the worker's employer.

16 Excepted payments

(1) Section 15 does not apply to a payment received from a worker by his employer where the purpose of the payment is the reimbursement of the employer in respect of—

(a) an overpayment of wages, or

(b) an overpayment in respect of expenses incurred by the worker in carrying out his employment,

made (for any reason) by the employer to the worker.

(2) Section 15 does not apply to a payment received from a worker by his employer in consequence of any disciplinary proceedings if those proceedings were held by virtue of a statutory provision.

(3) Section 15 does not apply to a payment received from a worker by his employer where the worker has taken part in a strike or other industrial action and the payment has been required by the employer on account of the worker's having taken part in that strike or other action.

(4) Section 15 does not apply to a payment received from a worker by his employer where the purpose of the payment is the satisfaction (whether wholly or in part) of an order of a court or tribunal requiring the payment of an amount by the worker to the employer.

Cash shortages and stock deficiencies in retail employment

17 Introductory

(1) In the following provisions of this Part—

"cash shortage" means a deficit arising in relation to amounts received in connection with retail transactions, and

"stock deficiency" means a stock deficiency arising in the course of retail transactions.

(2) In the following provisions of this Part "retail employment", in relation to a worker, means employment involving (whether or not on a regular basis)—

(a) the carrying out by the worker of retail transactions directly with members of the public or with fellow workers or other individuals in their personal capacities, or

(b) the collection by the worker of amounts payable in connection with retail transactions carried out by other persons directly with members of the public or with fellow workers or other individuals in their personal capacities.

(3) References in this section to a "retail transaction" are to the sale or supply of goods or the supply of services (including financial services).

(4) References in the following provisions of this Part to a deduction made from wages of a worker in retail employment, or to a payment received from such a worker by his employer, on account of a cash shortage or stock deficiency include references to a deduction or payment so made or received on account of—

(a) any dishonesty or other conduct on the part of the worker which resulted in any such shortage or deficiency, or

(b) any other event in respect of which he (whether or not together with any other workers) has any contractual liability and which so resulted,

in each case whether or not the amount of the deduction or payment is designed to reflect the exact amount of the shortage or deficiency.

(5) References in the following provisions of this Part to the recovery from a worker of an amount in respect of a cash shortage or stock deficiency accordingly include references to the recovery from him of an amount in respect of any such conduct or event as is mentioned in subsection (4)(a) or (b).

(6) In the following provisions of this Part "pay day", in relation to a worker, means a day on which wages are payable to the worker.

18 Limits on amount and time of deductions

(1) Where (in accordance with section 13) the employer of a worker in retail employment makes, on account of one or more cash shortages or stock deficiencies, a deduction or deductions from wages payable to the worker on a pay day, the amount or aggregate amount of the deduction or deductions shall not exceed one-tenth of the gross amount of the wages payable to the worker on that day.

(2) Where the employer of a worker in retail employment makes a deduction from the worker's wages on account of a cash shortage or stock deficiency, the employer shall not be treated as making the deduction in accordance with section 13 unless (in addition to the requirements of that section being satisfied with respect to the deduction)—

- (a) the deduction is made, or
- (b) in the case of a deduction which is one of a series of deductions relating to the shortage or deficiency, the first deduction in the series was made,

not later than the end of the relevant period.

(3) In subsection (2) "the relevant period" means the period of twelve months beginning with the date when the employer established the existence of the shortage or deficiency or (if earlier) the date when he ought reasonably to have done so.

19 Wages determined by reference to shortages etc

(1) This section applies where—

- (a) by virtue of an agreement between a worker in retail employment and his employer, the amount of the worker's wages or any part of them is or may be determined by reference to the incidence of cash shortages or stock deficiencies, and
- (b) the gross amount of the wages payable to the worker on any pay day is, on account of any such shortages or deficiencies, less than the gross amount of the wages that would have been payable to him on that day if there had been no such shortages or deficiencies.

(2) The amount representing the difference between the two amounts referred to in subsection (1)(b) shall be treated for the purposes of this Part as a deduction from the wages payable to the worker on that day made by the employer on account of the cash shortages or stock deficiencies in question.

(3) The second of the amounts referred to in subsection (1)(b) shall be treated for the purposes of this Part (except subsection (1)) as the gross amount of the wages payable to him on that day.

(4) Accordingly—

- (a) section 13, and
- (b) if the requirements of section 13 and subsection (2) of section 18 are satisfied, subsection (1) of section 18,

have effect in relation to the amount referred to in subsection (2) of this section.

20 Limits on method and timing of payments

(1) Where the employer of a worker in retail employment receives from the worker a payment on account of a cash shortage or stock deficiency, the employer shall not be

treated as receiving the payment in accordance with section 15 unless (in addition to the requirements of that section being satisfied with respect to the payment) he has previously—

(a) notified the worker in writing of the worker's total liability to him in respect of that shortage or deficiency, and

(b) required the worker to make the payment by means of a demand for payment made in accordance with the following provisions of this section.

(2) A demand for payment made by the employer of a worker in retail employment in respect of a cash shortage or stock deficiency—

(a) shall be made in writing, and

(b) shall be made on one of the worker's pay days.

(3) A demand for payment in respect of a particular cash shortage or stock deficiency, or (in the case of a series of such demands) the first such demand, shall not be made—

(a) earlier than the first pay day of the worker following the date when he is notified of his total liability in respect of the shortage or deficiency in pursuance of subsection (1)(a) or, where he is so notified on a pay day, earlier than that day, or

(b) later than the end of the period of twelve months beginning with the date when the employer established the existence of the shortage or deficiency or (if earlier) the date when he ought reasonably to have done so.

(4) For the purposes of this Part a demand for payment shall be treated as made by the employer on one of a worker's pay days if it is given to the worker or posted to, or left at, his last known address—

(a) on that pay day, or

(b) in the case of a pay day which is not a working day of the employer's business, on the first such working day following that pay day.

(5) Legal proceedings by the employer of a worker in retail employment for the recovery from the worker of an amount in respect of a cash shortage or stock deficiency shall not be instituted by the employer after the end of the period referred to in subsection (3)(b) unless the employer has within that period made a demand for payment in respect of that amount in accordance with this section.

21 Limit on amount of payments

(1) Where the employer of a worker in retail employment makes on any pay day one or more demands for payment in accordance with section 20, the amount or aggregate amount required to be paid by the worker in pursuance of the demand or demands shall not exceed—

(a) one-tenth of the gross amount of the wages payable to the worker on that day, or

(b) where one or more deductions falling within section 18(1) are made by the employer from those wages, such amount as represents the balance of that one-tenth after subtracting the amount or aggregate amount of the deduction or deductions.

(2) Once an amount has been required to be paid by means of a demand for payment made in accordance with section 20 on any pay day, that amount shall not be taken into account under subsection (1) as it applies to any subsequent pay day, even though the employer is obliged to make further requests for it to be paid.

(3) Where in any legal proceedings the court finds that the employer of a worker in retail employment is (in accordance with section 15 as it applies apart from section 20(1)) entitled to recover an amount from the worker in respect of a cash shortage or stock deficiency, the court shall, in ordering the payment by the worker to the employer of that amount, make such provision as appears to the court to be necessary to ensure that it is paid by the worker at a rate not exceeding that at which it could be recovered from him by the employer in accordance with this section.

22 Final instalments of wages

(1) In this section "final instalment of wages", in relation to a worker, means—

(a) the amount of wages payable to the worker which consists of or includes an amount payable by way of contractual remuneration in respect of the last of the periods for which he is employed under his contract prior to its termination for any reason (but excluding any wages referable to any earlier such period), or

(b) where an amount in lieu of notice is paid to the worker later than the amount referred to in paragraph (a), the amount so paid,

in each case whether the amount in question is paid before or after the termination of the worker's contract.

(2) Section 18(1) does not operate to restrict the amount of any deductions which may (in accordance with section 13(1)) be made by the employer of a worker in retail employment from the worker's final instalment of wages.

(3) Nothing in section 20 or 21 applies to a payment falling within section 20(1) which is made on or after the day on which any such worker's final instalment of wages is paid; but (even if the requirements of section 15 would otherwise be satisfied with respect to it) his employer shall not be treated as receiving any such payment in accordance with that section if the payment was first required to be made after the end of the period referred to in section 20(3)(b).

(4) Section 21(3) does not apply to an amount which is to be paid by a worker on or after the day on which his final instalment of wages is paid.

Enforcement

23 Complaints to industrial tribunals

(1) A worker may present a complaint to an industrial tribunal—

(a) that his employer has made a deduction from his wages in contravention of section 13 (including a deduction made in contravention of that section as it applies by virtue of section 18(2)),

(b) that his employer has received from him a payment in contravention of section 15 (including a payment received in contravention of that section as it applies by virtue of section 20(1)),

(c) that his employer has recovered from his wages by means of one or more deductions falling within section 18(1) an amount or aggregate amount exceeding the limit applying to the deduction or deductions under that provision, or

(d) that his employer has received from him in pursuance of one or more demands for payment made (in accordance with section 20) on a particular pay day, a payment or payments of an amount or aggregate amount exceeding the limit applying to the demand or demands under section 21(1).

(2) Subject to subsection (4), an industrial tribunal shall not consider a complaint under this section unless it is presented before the end of the period of three months beginning with—

(a) in the case of a complaint relating to a deduction by the employer, the date of payment of the wages from which the deduction was made, or

(b) in the case of a complaint relating to a payment received by the employer, the date when the payment was received.

(3) Where a complaint is brought under this section in respect of—

(a) a series of deductions or payments, or

(b) a number of payments falling within subsection (1)(d) and made in pursuance of demands for payment subject to the same limit under section 21(1) but received by the employer on different dates,

the references in subsection (2) to the deduction or payment are to the last deduction or payment in the series or to the last of the payments so received.

(4) Where the industrial tribunal is satisfied that it was not reasonably practicable for a complaint under this section to be presented before the end of the relevant period of three months, the tribunal may consider the complaint if it is presented within such further period as the tribunal considers reasonable.

24 Determination of complaints

Where a tribunal finds a complaint under section 23 well-founded, it shall make a declaration to that effect and shall order the employer—

(a) in the case of a complaint under section 23(1)(a), to pay to the worker the amount of any deduction made in contravention of section 13,

(b) in the case of a complaint under section 23(1)(b), to repay to the worker the amount of any payment received in contravention of section 15,

(c) in the case of a complaint under section 23(1)(c), to pay to the worker any amount recovered from him in excess of the limit mentioned in that provision, and

(d) in the case of a complaint under section 23(1)(d), to repay to the worker any amount received from him in excess of the limit mentioned in that provision.

25 Determinations: supplementary

(1) Where, in the case of any complaint under section 23(1)(a), a tribunal finds that, although neither of the conditions set out in section 13(1)(a) and (b) was satisfied with respect to the whole amount of the deduction, one of those conditions was satisfied with respect to any lesser amount, the amount of the deduction shall for the purposes of section 24(a) be treated as reduced by the amount with respect to which that condition was satisfied.

(2) Where, in the case of any complaint under section 23(1)(b), a tribunal finds that, although neither of the conditions set out in section 15(1)(a) and (b) was satisfied with respect to the whole amount of the payment, one of those conditions was satisfied with respect to any lesser amount, the amount of the payment shall for the purposes of

section 24(b) be treated as reduced by the amount with respect to which that condition was satisfied.

(3) An employer shall not under section 24 be ordered by a tribunal to pay or repay to a worker any amount in respect of a deduction or payment, or in respect of any combination of deductions or payments, in so far as it appears to the tribunal that he has already paid or repaid any such amount to the worker.

(4) Where a tribunal has under section 24 ordered an employer to pay or repay to a worker any amount in respect of a particular deduction or payment falling within section 23(1)(a) to (d), the amount which the employer is entitled to recover (by whatever means) in respect of the matter in relation to which the deduction or payment was originally made or received shall be treated as reduced by that amount.

(5) Where a tribunal has under section 24 ordered an employer to pay or repay to a worker any amount in respect of any combination of deductions or payments falling within section 23(1)(c) or (d), the aggregate amount which the employer is entitled to recover (by whatever means) in respect of the cash shortages or stock deficiencies in relation to which the deductions or payments were originally made or required to be made shall be treated as reduced by that amount.

26 Complaints and other remedies

Section 23 does not affect the jurisdiction of an industrial tribunal to consider a reference under section 11 in relation to any deduction from the wages of a worker; but the aggregate of any amounts ordered by an industrial tribunal to be paid under section 12(4) and under section 24 (whether on the same or different occasions) in respect of a particular deduction shall not exceed the amount of the deduction.

Supplementary

27 Meaning of "wages" etc

(1) In this Part "wages", in relation to a worker, means any sums payable to the worker in connection with his employment, including—

(a) any fee, bonus, commission, holiday pay or other emolument referable to his employment, whether payable under his contract or otherwise,

(b) statutory sick pay under Part XI of the Social Security Contributions and Benefits Act 1992,

(c) statutory maternity pay under Part XII of that Act,

(d) a guarantee payment (under section 28 of this Act),

(e) any payment for time off under Part VI of this Act or section 169 of the Trade Union and Labour Relations (Consolidation) Act 1992 (payment for time off for carrying out trade union duties etc.),

(f) remuneration on suspension on medical grounds under section 64 of this Act and remuneration on suspension on maternity grounds under section 68 of this Act,

(g) any sum payable in pursuance of an order for reinstatement or re-engagement under section 113 of this Act,

(h) any sum payable in pursuance of an order for the continuation of a contract of employment under section 130 of this Act or section 164 of the Trade Union and Labour Relations (Consolidation) Act 1992, and

(j) remuneration under a protective award under section 189 of that Act,

but excluding any payments within subsection (2).

(2) Those payments are—

(a) any payment by way of an advance under an agreement for a loan or by way of an advance of wages (but without prejudice to the application of section 13 to any deduction made from the worker's wages in respect of any such advance),

(b) any payment in respect of expenses incurred by the worker in carrying out his employment,

(c) any payment by way of a pension, allowance or gratuity in connection with the worker's retirement or as compensation for loss of office,

(d) any payment referable to the worker's redundancy, and

(e) any payment to the worker otherwise than in his capacity as a worker.

(3) Where any payment in the nature of a non-contractual bonus is (for any reason) made to a worker by his employer, the amount of the payment shall for the purposes of this Part—

(a) be treated as wages of the worker, and

(b) be treated as payable to him as such on the day on which the payment is made.

(4) In this Part "gross amount", in relation to any wages payable to a worker, means the total amount of those wages before deductions of whatever nature.

(5) For the purposes of this Part any monetary value attaching to any payment or benefit in kind furnished to a worker by his employer shall not be treated as wages of the worker except in the case of any voucher, stamp or similar document which is—

(a) of a fixed value expressed in monetary terms, and

(b) capable of being exchanged (whether on its own or together with other vouchers, stamps or documents, and whether immediately or only after a time) for money, goods or services (or for any combination of two or more of those things).

PART III

GUARANTEE PAYMENTS

28 Right to guarantee payment

(1) Where throughout a day during any part of which an employee would normally be required to work in accordance with his contract of employment the employee is not provided with work by his employer by reason of—

(a) a diminution in the requirements of the employer's business for work of the kind which the employee is employed to do, or

(b) any other occurrence affecting the normal working of the employer's business in relation to work of the kind which the employee is employed to do,

the employee is entitled to be paid by his employer an amount in respect of that day.

(2) In this Act a payment to which an employee is entitled under subsection (1) is referred to as a guarantee payment.

(3) In this Part—

(a) a day falling within subsection (1) is referred to as a "workless day", and
(b) "workless period" has a corresponding meaning.

(4) In this Part "day" means the period of twenty-four hours from midnight to midnight.

(5) Where a period of employment begun on any day extends, or would normally extend, over midnight into the following day—
(a) if the employment before midnight is, or would normally be, of longer duration than that after midnight, the period of employment shall be treated as falling wholly on the first day, and
(b) in any other case, the period of employment shall be treated as falling wholly on the second day.

29 Exclusions from right to guarantee payment

(1) An employee is not entitled to a guarantee payment unless he has been continuously employed for a period of not less than one month ending with the day before that in respect of which the guarantee payment is claimed.

(2) An employee who is employed—
(a) under a contract for a fixed term of three months or less, or
(b) under a contract made in contemplation of the performance of a specific task which is not expected to last for more than three months,

is not entitled to a guarantee payment unless he has been continuously employed for a period of more than three months ending with the day before that in respect of which the guarantee payment is claimed.

(3) An employee is not entitled to a guarantee payment in respect of a workless day if the failure to provide him with work for that day occurs in consequence of a strike, lock-out or other industrial action involving any employee of his employer or of an associated employer.

(4) An employee is not entitled to a guarantee payment in respect of a workless day if—
(a) his employer has offered to provide alternative work for that day which is suitable in all the circumstances (whether or not it is work which the employee is under his contract employed to perform), and
(b) the employee has unreasonably refused that offer.

(5) An employee is not entitled to a guarantee payment if he does not comply with reasonable requirements imposed by his employer with a view to ensuring that his services are available.

30 Calculation of guarantee payment

(1) Subject to section 31, the amount of a guarantee payment payable to an employee in respect of any day is the sum produced by multiplying the number of normal working hours on the day by the guaranteed hourly rate; and, accordingly, no guarantee payment is payable to an employee in whose case there are no normal working hours on the day in question.

(2) The guaranteed hourly rate, in relation to an employee, is the amount of one week's pay divided by the number of normal working hours in a week for that employee when

employed under the contract of employment in force on the day in respect of which the guarantee payment is payable.

(3) But where the number of normal working hours differs from week to week or over a longer period, the amount of one week's pay shall be divided instead by—

(a) the average number of normal working hours calculated by dividing by twelve the total number of the employee's normal working hours during the period of twelve weeks ending with the last complete week before the day in respect of which the guarantee payment is payable, or

(b) where the employee has not been employed for a sufficient period to enable the calculation to be made under paragraph (a), a number which fairly represents the number of normal working hours in a week having regard to such of the considerations specified in subsection (4) as are appropriate in the circumstances.

(4) The considerations referred to in subsection (3)(b) are—

(a) the average number of normal working hours in a week which the employee could expect in accordance with the terms of his contract, and

(b) the average number of normal working hours of other employees engaged in relevant comparable employment with the same employer.

(5) If in any case an employee's contract has been varied, or a new contract has been entered into, in connection with a period of short-time working, subsections (2) and (3) have effect as if for the references to the day in respect of which the guarantee payment is payable there were substituted references to the last day on which the original contract was in force.

31 Limits on amount of and entitlement to guarantee payment

(1) The amount of a guarantee payment payable to an employee in respect of any day shall not exceed £14.50.

(2) An employee is not entitled to guarantee payments in respect of more than the specified number of days in any period of three months.

(3) The specified number of days for the purposes of subsection (2) is the number of days, not exceeding five, on which the employee normally works in a week under the contract of employment in force on the day in respect of which the guarantee payment is claimed.

(4) But where that number of days varies from week to week or over a longer period, the specified number of days is instead—

(a) the average number of such days, not exceeding five, calculated by dividing by twelve the total number of such days during the period of twelve weeks ending with the last complete week before the day in respect of which the guarantee payment is claimed, and rounding up the resulting figure to the next whole number, or

(b) where the employee has not been employed for a sufficient period to enable the calculation to be made under paragraph (a), a number which fairly represents the number of the employee's normal working days in a week, not exceeding five, having regard to such of the considerations specified in subsection (5) as are appropriate in the circumstances.

(5) The considerations referred to in subsection (4)(b) are—

(a) the average number of normal working days in a week which the employee could expect in accordance with the terms of his contract, and

(b) the average number of such days of other employees engaged in relevant comparable employment with the same employer.

(6) If in any case an employee's contract has been varied, or a new contract has been entered into, in connection with a period of short-time working, subsections (3) and (4) have effect as if for the references to the day in respect of which the guarantee payment is claimed there were substituted references to the last day on which the original contract was in force.

(7) The Secretary of State may by order made in accordance with section 208 vary any of the limits specified in this section, and (in particular) vary the length of the period specified in subsection (2), after a review under that section.

32 Contractual remuneration

(1) A right to a guarantee payment does not affect any right of an employee in relation to remuneration under his contract of employment ("contractual remuneration").

(2) Any contractual remuneration paid to an employee in respect of a workless day goes towards discharging any liability of the employer to pay a guarantee payment in respect of that day; and, conversely, any guarantee payment paid in respect of a day goes towards discharging any liability of the employer to pay contractual remuneration in respect of that day.

(3) For the purposes of subsection (2), contractual remuneration shall be treated as paid in respect of a workless day—

(a) where it is expressed to be calculated or payable by reference to that day or any part of that day, to the extent that it is so expressed, and

(b) in any other case, to the extent that it represents guaranteed remuneration, rather than remuneration for work actually done, and is referable to that day when apportioned rateably between that day and any other workless period falling within the period in respect of which the remuneration is paid.

33 Power to modify provisions about guarantee payments

The Secretary of State may by order provide that in relation to any description of employees the provisions of—

(a) sections 28(4) and (5), 30, 31(3) to (5) (as originally enacted or as varied under section 31(7)) and 32, and

(b) so far as they apply for the purposes of those provisions, Chapter II of Part XIV and section 234,

shall have effect subject to such modifications and adaptations as may be prescribed by the order.

34 Complaints to industrial tribunals

(1) An employee may present a complaint to an industrial tribunal that his employer has failed to pay the whole or any part of a guarantee payment to which the employee is entitled.

(2) An industrial tribunal shall not consider a complaint relating to a guarantee payment in respect of any day unless the complaint is presented to the tribunal—

(a) before the end of the period of three months beginning with that day, or

(b) within such further period as the tribunal considers reasonable in a case where it is satisfied that it was not reasonably practicable for the complaint to be presented before the end of that period of three months.

(3) Where an industrial tribunal finds a complaint under this section well-founded, the tribunal shall order the employer to pay to the employee the amount of guarantee payment which it finds is due to him.

35 Exemption orders

(1) Where—

(a) at any time there is in force a collective agreement, or an agricultural wages order, under which employees to whom the agreement or order relates have a right to guaranteed remuneration, and

(b) on the application of all the parties to the agreement, or of the Board making the order, the appropriate Minister (having regard to the provisions of the agreement or order) is satisfied that section 28 should not apply to those employees,

he may make an order under this section excluding those employees from the operation of that section.

(2) In subsection (1) "agricultural wages order" means an order made under—

(a) section 3 of the Agricultural Wages Act 1948, or

(b) section 3 of the Agricultural Wages (Scotland) Act 1949.

(3) In subsection (1) "the appropriate Minister" means—

(a) in relation to a collective agreement or to an order such as is referred to in subsection (2)(b), the Secretary of State, and

(b) in relation to an order such as is referred to in subsection (2)(a), the Minister of Agriculture, Fisheries and Food.

(4) The Secretary of State shall not make an order under this section in respect of an agreement unless—

(a) the agreement provides for procedures to be followed (whether by arbitration or otherwise) in cases where an employee claims that his employer has failed to pay the whole or any part of any guaranteed remuneration to which the employee is entitled under the agreement and those procedures include a right to arbitration or adjudication by an independent referee or body in cases where (by reason of an equality of votes or otherwise) a decision cannot otherwise be reached, or

(b) the agreement indicates that an employee to whom the agreement relates may present a complaint to an industrial tribunal that his employer has failed to pay the whole or any part of any guaranteed remuneration to which the employee is entitled under the agreement.

(5) Where an order under this section is in force in respect of an agreement indicating as described in paragraph (b) of subsection (4) an industrial tribunal shall have jurisdiction over a complaint such as is mentioned in that paragraph as if it were a complaint falling within section 34.

(6) An order varying or revoking an earlier order under this section may be made in pursuance of an application by all or any of the parties to the agreement in question, or the Board which made the order in question, or in the absence of such an application.

PART IV

SUNDAY WORKING FOR SHOP AND BETTING WORKERS

Protected shop workers and betting workers

36 Protected shop workers and betting workers

(1) Subject to subsection (5), a shop worker or betting worker is to be regarded as "protected" for the purposes of any provision of this Act if (and only if) subsection (2) or (3) applies to him.

(2) This subsection applies to a shop worker or betting worker if—

(a) on the day before the relevant commencement date he was employed as a shop worker or a betting worker but not to work only on Sunday,

(b) he has been continuously employed during the period beginning with that day and ending with the day which, in relation to the provision concerned, is the appropriate date, and

(c) throughout that period, or throughout every part of it during which his relations with his employer were governed by a contract of employment, he was a shop worker or a betting worker.

(3) This subsection applies to any shop worker or betting worker whose contract of employment is such that under it he—

(a) is not, and may not be, required to work on Sunday, and

(b) could not be so required even if the provisions of this Part were disregarded.

(4) Where on the day before the relevant commencement date an employee's relations with his employer had ceased to be governed by a contract of employment, he shall be regarded as satisfying subsection (2)(a) if—

(a) that day fell in a week which counts as a period of employment with that employer under section 212(2) or (3) or under regulations under section 219, and

(b) on the last day before the relevant commencement date on which his relations with his employer were governed by a contract of employment, the employee was employed as a shop worker or a betting worker but not to work only on Sunday.

(5) A shop worker is not a protected shop worker, and a betting worker is not a protected betting worker, if—

(a) he has given his employer an opting-in notice on or after the relevant commencement date, and

(b) after giving the notice, he has expressly agreed with his employer to do shop work, or betting work, on Sunday or on a particular Sunday.

(6) In this Act "opting-in notice", in relation to a shop worker or a betting worker, means written notice, signed and dated by the shop worker or betting worker, in which the

shop worker or betting worker expressly states that he wishes to work on Sunday or that he does not object to Sunday working.

(7) In this Act "the relevant commencement date" means—

(a) in relation to a shop worker, 26th August 1994, and

(b) in relation to a betting worker, 3rd January 1995.

37 Contractual requirements relating to Sunday work

(1) Any contract of employment under which a shop worker or betting worker who satisfies section 36(2)(a) was employed on the day before the relevant commencement date is unenforceable to the extent that it—

(a) requires the shop worker to do shop work, or the betting worker to do betting work, on Sunday on or after that date, or

(b) requires the employer to provide the shop worker with shop work, or the betting worker with betting work, on Sunday on or after that date.

(2) Subject to subsection (3), any agreement entered into after the relevant commencement date between a protected shop worker, or a protected betting worker, and his employer is unenforceable to the extent that it—

(a) requires the shop worker to do shop work, or the betting worker to do betting work, on Sunday, or

(b) requires the employer to provide the shop worker with shop work, or the betting worker with betting work, on Sunday.

(3) Where, after giving an opting-in notice, a protected shop worker or a protected betting worker expressly agrees with his employer to do shop work or betting work on Sunday or on a particular Sunday (and so ceases to be protected), his contract of employment shall be taken to be varied to the extent necessary to give effect to the terms of the agreement.

(4) The reference in subsection (2) to a protected shop worker, or a protected betting worker, includes a reference to an employee who although not a protected shop worker, or protected betting worker, at the time when the agreement is entered into is a protected shop worker, or protected betting worker, on the day on which she returns to work in accordance with section 79, or in pursuance of an offer made in the circumstances described in section 96(3), after a period of absence from work occasioned wholly or partly by pregnancy or childbirth.

(5) For the purposes of section 36(2)(b), the appropriate date—

(a) in relation to subsections (2) and (3) of this section, is the day on which the agreement is entered into, and

(b) in relation to subsection (4) of this section, is the day on which the employee returns to work.

38 Contracts with guaranteed hours

(1) This section applies where—

(a) under the contract of employment under which a shop worker or betting worker who satisfies section 36(2)(a) was employed on the day before the relevant commencement date, the employer is, or may be, required to provide him with shop work, or betting work, for a specified number of hours each week,

(b) under the contract the shop worker or betting worker was, or might have been, required to work on Sunday before that date, and

(c) the shop worker has done shop work, or the betting worker betting work, on Sunday in that employment (whether or not before that day) but has, on or after that date, ceased to do so.

(2) So long as the shop worker remains a protected shop worker, or the betting worker remains a protected betting worker, the contract shall not be regarded as requiring the employer to provide him with shop work, or betting work, on weekdays in excess of the hours normally worked by the shop worker or betting worker on weekdays before he ceased to do shop work, or betting work, on Sunday.

(3) For the purposes of section 36(2)(b), the appropriate date in relation to this section is any time in relation to which the contract is to be enforced.

39 Reduction of pay etc

(1) This section applies where—

(a) under the contract of employment under which a shop worker or betting worker who satisfies section 36(2)(a) was employed on the day before the relevant commencement date, the shop worker or betting worker was, or might have been, required to work on Sunday before the relevant commencement date,

(b) the shop worker has done shop work, or the betting worker has done betting work, on Sunday in that employment (whether or not before that date) but has, on or after that date, ceased to do so, and

(c) it is not apparent from the contract what part of the remuneration payable, or of any other benefit accruing, to the shop worker or betting worker was intended to be attributable to shop work, or betting work, on Sunday.

(2) So long as the shop worker remains a protected shop worker, or the betting worker remains a protected betting worker, the contract shall be regarded as enabling the employer to reduce the amount of remuneration paid, or the extent of the other benefit provided, to the shop worker or betting worker in respect of any period by the relevant proportion.

(3) In subsection (2) "the relevant proportion" means the proportion which the hours of shop work, or betting work, which (apart from this Part) the shop worker, or betting worker, could have been required to do on Sunday in the period ("the contractual Sunday hours") bears to the aggregate of those hours and the hours of work actually done by the shop worker, or betting worker, in the period.

(4) Where, under the contract of employment, the hours of work actually done on weekdays in any period would be taken into account in determining the contractual Sunday hours, they shall be taken into account in determining the contractual Sunday hours for the purposes of subsection (3).

(5) For the purposes of section 36(2)(b), the appropriate date in relation to this section is the end of the period in respect of which the remuneration is paid or the benefit accrues.

Opting-out of Sunday work

40 Notice of objection to Sunday working

(1) A shop worker or betting worker to whom this section applies may at any time give his employer written notice, signed and dated by the shop worker or betting worker, to the effect that he objects to Sunday working.

(2) In this Act "opting-out notice" means a notice given under subsection (1) by a shop worker or betting worker to whom this section applies.

(3) This section applies to any shop worker or betting worker who under his contract of employment—

- (a) is or may be required to work on Sunday (whether or not as a result of previously giving an opting-in notice), but
- (b) is not employed to work only on Sunday.

41 Opted-out shop workers and betting workers

(1) Subject to subsection (2), a shop worker or betting worker is to be regarded as "opted-out" for the purposes of any provision of this Act if (and only if)—

- (a) he has given his employer an opting-out notice,
- (b) he has been continuously employed during the period beginning with the day on which the notice was given and ending with the day which, in relation to the provision concerned, is the appropriate date, and
- (c) throughout that period, or throughout every part of it during which his relations with his employer were governed by a contract of employment, he was a shop worker or a betting worker.

(2) A shop worker is not an opted-out shop worker, and a betting worker is not an opted-out betting worker, if—

- (a) after giving the opting-out notice concerned, he has given his employer an opting-in notice, and
- (b) after giving the opting-in notice, he has expressly agreed with his employer to do shop work, or betting work, on Sunday or on a particular Sunday.

(3) In this Act "notice period", in relation to an opted-out shop worker or an opted-out betting worker, means, subject to section 42(2), the period of three months beginning with the day on which the opting-out notice concerned was given.

42 Explanatory statement

(1) Where a person becomes a shop worker or betting worker to whom section 40 applies, his employer shall, before the end of the period of two months beginning with the day on which that person becomes such a worker, give him a written statement in the prescribed form.

(2) If—

- (a) an employer fails to comply with subsection (1) in relation to any shop worker or betting worker, and
- (b) the shop worker or betting worker, on giving the employer an opting-out notice, becomes an opted-out shop worker or an opted-out betting worker,

section 41(3) has effect in relation to the shop worker or betting worker with the substitution for "three months" of "one month".

(3) An employer shall not be regarded as failing to comply with subsection (1) in any case where, before the end of the period referred to in that subsection, the shop worker or betting worker has given him an opting-out notice.

(4) Subject to subsection (6), the prescribed form in the case of a shop worker is as follows—

"SATUTORY RIGHTS IN RELATION TO SUNDAY SHOP WORK

You have become employed as a shop worker and are or can be required under your contract of employment to do the Sunday work your contract provides for.

However, if you wish, you can give a notice, as described in the next paragraph, to your employer and you will then have the right not to work in or about a shop on any Sunday on which the shop is open once three months have passed from the date on which you gave the notice.

Your notice must—

be in writing;

be signed and dated by you;

say that you object to Sunday working.

For three months after you give the notice, your employer can still require you to do all the Sunday work your contract provides for. After the three month period has ended, you have the right to complain to an industrial tribunal if, because of your refusal to work on Sundays on which the shop is open, your employer—

dismisses you, or

does something else detrimental to you, for example, failing to promote you.

Once you have the rights described, you can surrender them only by giving your employer a further notice, signed and dated by you, saying that you wish to work on Sunday or that you do not object to Sunday working and then agreeing with your employer to work on Sundays or on a particular Sunday."

(5) Subject to subsection (6), the prescribed form in the case of a betting worker is as follows—

"STATUTORY RIGHTS IN RELATION TO SUNDAY BETTING WORK

You have become employed under a contract of employment under which you are or can be required to do Sunday betting work, that is to say, work—

at a track on a Sunday on which your employer is taking bets at the track, or

in a licensed betting office on a Sunday on which it is open for business.

However, if you wish, you can give a notice, as described in the next paragraph, to your employer and you will then have the right not to do Sunday betting work once three months have passed from the date on which you gave the notice.

Your notice must—

be in writing;

be signed and dated by you;

say that you object to doing Sunday betting work.

For three months after you give the notice, your employer can still require you to do all the Sunday betting work your contract provides for. After the three month period has ended, you have the right to complain to an industrial tribunal if, because of your refusal to do Sunday betting work, your employer—

dismisses you, or

does something else detrimental to you, for example, failing to promote you.

Once you have the rights described, you can surrender them only by giving your employer a further notice, signed and dated by you, saying that you wish to do Sunday betting work or that you do not object to doing Sunday betting work and then agreeing with your employer to do such work on Sundays or on a particular Sunday."

(6) The Secretary of State may by order amend the prescribed forms set out in subsections (4) and (5).

43 Contractual requirements relating to Sunday work

(1) Where a shop worker or betting worker gives his employer an opting-out notice, the contract of employment under which he was employed immediately before he gave that notice becomes unenforceable to the extent that it—

(a) requires the shop worker to do shop work, or the betting worker to do betting work, on Sunday after the end of the notice period, or

(b) requires the employer to provide the shop worker with shop work, or the betting worker with betting work, on Sunday after the end of that period.

(2) Subject to subsection (3), any agreement entered into between an opted-out shop worker, or an opted-out betting worker, and his employer is unenforceable to the extent that it—

(a) requires the shop worker to do shop work, or the betting worker to do betting work, on Sunday after the end of the notice period, or

(b) requires the employer to provide the shop worker with shop work, or the betting worker with betting work, on Sunday after the end of that period.

(3) Where, after giving an opting-in notice, an opted-out shop worker or an opted-out betting worker expressly agrees with his employer to do shop work or betting work on Sunday or on a particular Sunday (and so ceases to be opted-out), his contract of employment shall be taken to be varied to the extent necessary to give effect to the terms of the agreement.

(4) The reference in subsection (2) to an opted-out shop worker, or an opted-out betting worker, includes a reference to an employee who although not an opted-out shop worker, or an opted-out betting worker, at the time when the agreement is entered into—

(a) had given her employer an opting-out notice before that time, and

(b) is an opted-out shop worker, or an opted-out betting worker, on the day on which she returns to work in accordance with section 79, or in pursuance of an offer made in the circumstances described in section 96(3), after a period of absence from work occasioned wholly or partly by pregnancy or childbirth.

(5) For the purposes of section 41(1)(b), the appropriate date—

(a) in relation to subsections (2) and (3) of this section, is the day on which the agreement is entered into, and

(b) in relation to subsection (4) of this section, is the day on which the employee returns to work.

PART V

PROTECTION FROM SUFFERING DETRIMENT IN EMPLOYMENT

Rights not to suffer detriment

44 Health and safety cases

(1) An employee has the right not to be subjected to any detriment by any act, or any deliberate failure to act, by his employer done on the ground that—

(a) having been designated by the employer to carry out activities in connection with preventing or reducing risks to health and safety at work, the employee carried out (or proposed to carry out) any such activities,

(b) being a representative of workers on matters of health and safety at work or member of a safety committee—

(i) in accordance with arrangements established under or by virtue of any enactment, or

(ii) by reason of being acknowledged as such by the employer,

the employee performed (or proposed to perform) any functions as such a representative or a member of such a committee,

(c) being an employee at a place where—

(i) there was no such representative or safety committee, or

(ii) there was such a representative or safety committee but it was not reasonably practicable for the employee to raise the matter by those means,

he brought to his employer's attention, by reasonable means, circumstances connected with his work which he reasonably believed were harmful or potentially harmful to health or safety,

(d) in circumstances of danger which the employee reasonably believed to be serious and imminent and which he could not reasonably have been expected to avert, he left (or proposed to leave) or (while the danger persisted) refused to return to his place of work or any dangerous part of his place of work, or

(e) in circumstances of danger which the employee reasonably believed to be serious and imminent, he took (or proposed to take) appropriate steps to protect himself or other persons from the danger.

(2) For the purposes of subsection (1)(e) whether steps which an employee took (or proposed to take) were appropriate is to be judged by reference to all the circumstances including, in particular, his knowledge and the facilities and advice available to him at the time.

(3) An employee is not to be regarded as having been subjected to any detriment on the ground specified in subsection (1)(e) if the employer shows that it was (or would have

been) so negligent for the employee to take the steps which he took (or proposed to take) that a reasonable employer might have treated him as the employer did.

(4) Except where an employee is dismissed in circumstances in which, by virtue of section 197, Part X does not apply to the dismissal, this section does not apply where the detriment in question amounts to dismissal (within the meaning of that Part).

45 Sunday working for shop and betting workers

(1) An employee who is—

(a) a protected shop worker or an opted-out shop worker, or

(b) a protected betting worker or an opted-out betting worker,

has the right not to be subjected to any detriment by any act, or any deliberate failure to act, by his employer done on the ground that the employee refused (or proposed to refuse) to do shop work, or betting work, on Sunday or on a particular Sunday.

(2) Subsection (1) does not apply to anything done in relation to an opted-out shop worker or an opted-out betting worker on the ground that he refused (or proposed to refuse) to do shop work, or betting work, on any Sunday or Sundays falling before the end of the notice period.

(3) An employee who is a shop worker or a betting worker has the right not to be subjected to any detriment by any act, or any deliberate failure to act, by his employer done on the ground that the employee gave (or proposed to give) an opting-out notice to his employer.

(4) Subsections (1) and (3) do not apply where the detriment in question amounts to dismissal (within the meaning of Part X).

(5) For the purposes of this section a shop worker or betting worker who does not work on Sunday or on a particular Sunday is not to be regarded as having been subjected to any detriment by—

(a) a failure to pay remuneration in respect of shop work, or betting work, on a Sunday which he has not done,

(b) a failure to provide him with any other benefit, where that failure results from the application (in relation to a Sunday on which the employee has not done shop work, or betting work) of a contractual term under which the extent of that benefit varies according to the number of hours worked by the employee or the remuneration of the employee, or

(c) a failure to provide him with any work, remuneration or other benefit which by virtue of section 38 or 39 the employer is not obliged to provide.

(6) Where an employer offers to pay a sum specified in the offer to any one or more employees—

(a) who are protected shop workers or opted-out shop workers or protected betting workers or opted-out betting workers, or

(b) who under their contracts of employment are not obliged to do shop work, or betting work, on Sunday,

if they agree to do shop work, or betting work, on Sunday or on a particular Sunday subsections (7) and (8) apply.

(7) An employee to whom the offer is not made is not to be regarded for the purposes of this section as having been subjected to any detriment by any failure to make the offer to him or to pay him the sum specified in the offer.

(8) An employee who does not accept the offer is not to be regarded for the purposes of this section as having been subjected to any detriment by any failure to pay him the sum specified in the offer.

(9) For the purposes of section 36(2)(b) or 41(1)(b), the appropriate date in relation to this section is the date of the act or failure to act.

(10) For the purposes of subsection (9)—

(a) where an act extends over a period, the "date of the act" means the first day of that period, and

(b) a deliberate failure to act shall be treated as done when it was decided on;

and, in the absence of evidence establishing the contrary, an employer shall be taken to decide on a failure to act when he does an act inconsistent with doing the failed act or, if he has done no such inconsistent act, when the period expires within which he might reasonably have been expected to do the failed act if it was to be done.

46 Trustees of occupational pension schemes

(1) An employee has the right not to be subjected to any detriment by any act, or any deliberate failure to act, by his employer done on the ground that, being a trustee of a relevant occupational pension scheme which relates to his employment, the employee performed (or proposed to perform) any functions as such a trustee.

(2) Except where an employee is dismissed in circumstances in which, by virtue of section 197, Part X does not apply to the dismissal, this section does not apply where the detriment in question amounts to dismissal (within the meaning of that Part).

(3) In this section "relevant occupational pension scheme" means an occupational pension scheme (as defined in section 1 of the Pension Schemes Act 1993) established under a trust.

47 Employee representatives

(1) An employee has the right not to be subjected to any detriment by any act, or any deliberate failure to act, by his employer done on the ground that, being—

(a) an employee representative for the purposes of Chapter II of Part IV of the Trade Union and Labour Relations (Consolidation) Act 1992 (redundancies) or Regulations 10 and 11 of the Transfer of Undertakings (Protection of Employment) Regulations 1981, or

(b) a candidate in an election in which any person elected will, on being elected, be such an employee representative,

he performed (or proposed to perform) any functions or activities as such an employee representative or candidate.

(2) Except where an employee is dismissed in circumstances in which, by virtue of section 197, Part X does not apply to the dismissal, this section does not apply where the detriment in question amounts to a dismissal (within the meaning of that Part).

Enforcement

48 Complaints to industrial tribunals

(1) An employee may present a complaint to an industrial tribunal that he has been subjected to a detriment in contravention of section 44, 45, 46 or 47.

(2) On such a complaint it is for the employer to show the ground on which any act, or deliberate failure to act, was done.

(3) An industrial tribunal shall not consider a complaint under this section unless it is presented—

(a) before the end of the period of three months beginning with the date of the act or failure to act to which the complaint relates or, where that act or failure is part of a series of similar acts or failures, the last of them, or

(b) within such further period as the tribunal considers reasonable in a case where it is satisfied that it was not reasonably practicable for the complaint to be presented before the end of that period of three months.

(4) For the purposes of subsection (3)—

(a) where an act extends over a period, the "date of the act" means the last day of that period, and

(b) a deliberate failure to act shall be treated as done when it was decided on;

and, in the absence of evidence establishing the contrary, an employer shall be taken to decide on a failure to act when he does an act inconsistent with doing the failed act or, if he has done no such inconsistent act, when the period expires within which he might reasonably have been expected to do the failed act if it was to be done.

49 Remedies

(1) Where an industrial tribunal finds a complaint under section 48 well-founded, the tribunal—

(a) shall make a declaration to that effect, and

(b) may make an award of compensation to be paid by the employer to the complainant in respect of the act or failure to act to which the complaint relates.

(2) The amount of the compensation awarded shall be such as the tribunal considers just and equitable in all the circumstances having regard to—

(a) the infringement to which the complaint relates, and

(b) any loss which is attributable to the act, or failure to act, which infringed the complainant's right.

(3) The loss shall be taken to include—

(a) any expenses reasonably incurred by the complainant in consequence of the act, or failure to act, to which the complaint relates, and

(b) loss of any benefit which he might reasonably be expected to have had but for that act or failure to act.

(4) In ascertaining the loss the tribunal shall apply the same rule concerning the duty of a person to mitigate his loss as applies to damages recoverable under the common law of England and Wales or (as the case may be) Scotland.

(5) Where the tribunal finds that the act, or failure to act, to which the complaint relates was to any extent caused or contributed to by action of the complainant, it shall reduce the amount of the compensation by such proportion as it considers just and equitable having regard to that finding.

PART VI

TIME OFF WORK

Public duties

50 Right to time off for public duties

(1) An employer shall permit an employee of his who is a justice of the peace to take time off during the employee's working hours for the purpose of performing any of the duties of his office.

(2) An employer shall permit an employee of his who is a member of—

(a) a local authority,

(b) a statutory tribunal,

(c) a police authority,

(d) a board of prison visitors or a prison visiting committee,

(e) a relevant health body,

(f) a relevant education body, or

(g) the Environment Agency or the Scottish Environment Protection Agency,

to take time off during the employee's working hours for the purposes specified in subsection (3).

(3) The purposes referred to in subsection (2) are—

(a) attendance at a meeting of the body or any of its committees or sub-committees, and

(b) the doing of any other thing approved by the body, or anything of a class so approved, for the purpose of the discharge of the functions of the body or of any of its committees or sub-committees.

(4) The amount of time off which an employee is to be permitted to take under this section, and the occasions on which and any conditions subject to which time off may be so taken, are those that are reasonable in all the circumstances having regard, in particular, to—

(a) how much time off is required for the performance of the duties of the office or as a member of the body in question, and how much time off is required for the performance of the particular duty,

(b) how much time off the employee has already been permitted under this section or sections 168 and 170 of the Trade Union and Labour Relations (Consolidation) Act 1992 (time off for trade union duties and activities), and

(c) the circumstances of the employer's business and the effect of the employee's absence on the running of that business.

(5) In subsection (2)(a) "a local authority" means—

(a) a local authority within the meaning of the Local Government Act 1972,
(b) a council constituted under section 2 of the Local Government etc. (Scotland) Act 1994,
(c) the Common Council of the City of London,
(d) a National Park authority, or
(e) the Broads Authority.

(6) The reference in subsection (2) to a member of a police authority is to a person appointed as such a member under Schedule 2 to the Police Act 1996.

(7) In subsection (2)(d)—
(a) "a board of prison visitors" means a board of visitors appointed under section 6(2) of the Prison Act 1952, and
(b) "a prison visiting committee" means a visiting committee appointed under section 19(3) of the Prisons (Scotland) Act 1989 or constituted by virtue of rules made under section 39 (as read with section 8(1)) of that Act.

(8) In subsection (2)(e) "a relevant health body" means—
(a) a National Health Service trust established under Part I of the National Health Service and Community Care Act 1990 or the National Health Service (Scotland) Act 1978,
(b) a Health Authority established under section 8 of the National Health Service Act 1977 or a Special Health Authority established under section 11 of that Act, or
(c) a Health Board constituted under section 2 of the National Health Service (Scotland) Act 1978.

(9) In subsection (2)(f) "a relevant education body" means—
(a) a managing or governing body of an educational establishment maintained by a local education authority,
(b) a governing body of a grant-maintained school, further education corporation or higher education corporation,
(c) a school council appointed under section 125(1) of the Local Government (Scotland) Act 1973,
(d) a school board within the meaning of section 1(1) of the School Boards (Scotland) Act 1988,
(e) a board of management of a self-governing school within the meaning of section 135(1) of the Education (Scotland) Act 1980,
(f) a board of management of a college of further education within the meaning of section 36(1) of the Further and Higher Education (Scotland) Act 1992,
(g) a governing body of a central institution within the meaning of section 135(1) of the Education (Scotland) Act 1980, or
(h) a governing body of a designated institution within the meaning of Part II of the Further and Higher Education (Scotland) Act 1992.

(10) The Secretary of State may by order—
(a) modify the provisions of subsections (1) and (2) and (5) to (9) by adding any office or body, removing any office or body or altering the description of any office or body, or
(b) modify the provisions of subsection (3).

(11) For the purposes of this section the working hours of an employee shall be taken to be any time when, in accordance with his contract of employment, the employee is required to be at work.

51 Complaints to industrial tribunals

(1) An employee may present a complaint to an industrial tribunal that his employer has failed to permit him to take time off as required by section 50.

(2) An industrial tribunal shall not consider a complaint under this section that an employer has failed to permit an employee to take time off unless it is presented—

(a) before the end of the period of three months beginning with the date on which the failure occurred, or

(b) within such further period as the tribunal considers reasonable in a case where it is satisfied that it was not reasonably practicable for the complaint to be presented before the end of that period of three months.

(3) Where an industrial tribunal finds a complaint under this section well-founded, the tribunal—

(a) shall make a declaration to that effect, and

(b) may make an award of compensation to be paid by the employer to the employee.

(4) The amount of the compensation shall be such as the tribunal considers just and equitable in all the circumstances having regard to—

(a) the employer's default in failing to permit time off to be taken by the employee, and

(b) any loss sustained by the employee which is attributable to the matters to which the complaint relates.

Looking for work and making arrangements for training

52 Right to time off to look for work or arrange training

(1) An employee who is given notice of dismissal by reason of redundancy is entitled to be permitted by his employer to take reasonable time off during the employee's working hours before the end of his notice in order to—

(a) look for new employment, or

(b) make arrangements for training for future employment.

(2) An employee is not entitled to take time off under this section unless, on whichever is the later of—

(a) the date on which the notice is due to expire, and

(b) the date on which it would expire were it the notice required to be given by section 86(1),

he will have been (or would have been) continuously employed for a period of two years or more.

(3) For the purposes of this section the working hours of an employee shall be taken to be any time when, in accordance with his contract of employment, the employee is required to be at work.

53 Right to remuneration for time off under section 52

(1) An employee who is permitted to take time off under section 52 is entitled to be paid remuneration by his employer for the period of absence at the appropriate hourly rate.

(2) The appropriate hourly rate, in relation to an employee, is the amount of one week's pay divided by the number of normal working hours in a week for that employee when employed under the contract of employment in force on the day when the notice of dismissal was given.

(3) But where the number of normal working hours differs from week to week or over a longer period, the amount of one week's pay shall be divided instead by the average number of normal working hours calculated by dividing by twelve the total number of the employee's normal working hours during the period of twelve weeks ending with the last complete week before the day on which the notice was given.

(4) If an employer unreasonably refuses to permit an employee to take time off from work as required by section 52, the employee is entitled to be paid an amount equal to the remuneration to which he would have been entitled under subsection (1) if he had been permitted to take the time off.

(5) The amount of an employer's liability to pay remuneration under subsection (1) shall not exceed, in respect of the notice period of any employee, forty per cent. of a week's pay of that employee.

(6) A right to any amount under subsection (1) or (4) does not affect any right of an employee in relation to remuneration under his contract of employment ("contractual remuneration").

(7) Any contractual remuneration paid to an employee in respect of a period of time off under section 52 goes towards discharging any liability of the employer to pay remuneration under subsection (1) in respect of that period; and, conversely, any payment of remuneration under subsection (1) in respect of a period goes towards discharging any liability of the employer to pay contractual remuneration in respect of that period.

54 Complaints to industrial tribunals

(1) An employee may present a complaint to an industrial tribunal that his employer—

(a) has unreasonably refused to permit him to take time off as required by section 52, or

(b) has failed to pay the whole or any part of any amount to which the employee is entitled under section 53(1) or (4).

(2) An industrial tribunal shall not consider a complaint under this section unless it is presented—

(a) before the end of the period of three months beginning with the date on which it is alleged that the time off should have been permitted, or

(b) within such further period as the tribunal considers reasonable in a case where it is satisfied that it was not reasonably practicable for the complaint to be presented before the end of that period of three months.

(3) Where an industrial tribunal finds a complaint under this section well-founded, the tribunal shall—

(a) make a declaration to that effect, and

(b) order the employer to pay to the employee the amount which it finds due to him.

(4) The amount which may be ordered by a tribunal to be paid by an employer under subsection (3) (or, where the employer is liable to pay remuneration under section 53, the aggregate of that amount and the amount of that liability) shall not exceed, in respect of the notice period of any employee, forty per cent. of a week's pay of that employee.

Ante-natal care

55 Right to time off for ante-natal care

(1) An employee who—

(a) is pregnant, and

(b) has, on the advice of a registered medical practitioner, registered midwife or registered health visitor, made an appointment to attend at any place for the purpose of receiving ante-natal care,

is entitled to be permitted by her employer to take time off during the employee's working hours in order to enable her to keep the appointment.

(2) An employee is not entitled to take time off under this section to keep an appointment unless, if her employer requests her to do so, she produces for his inspection—

(a) a certificate from a registered medical practitioner, registered midwife or registered health visitor stating that the employee is pregnant, and

(b) an appointment card or some other document showing that the appointment has been made.

(3) Subsection (2) does not apply where the employee's appointment is the first appointment during her pregnancy for which she seeks permission to take time off in accordance with subsection (1).

(4) For the purposes of this section the working hours of an employee shall be taken to be any time when, in accordance with her contract of employment, the employee is required to be at work.

56 Right to remuneration for time off under section 55

(1) An employee who is permitted to take time off under section 55 is entitled to be paid remuneration by her employer for the period of absence at the appropriate hourly rate.

(2) The appropriate hourly rate, in relation to an employee, is the amount of one week's pay divided by the number of normal working hours in a week for that employee when employed under the contract of employment in force on the day when the time off is taken.

(3) But where the number of normal working hours differs from week to week or over a longer period, the amount of one week's pay shall be divided instead by—

(a) the average number of normal working hours calculated by dividing by twelve the total number of the employee's normal working hours during the period of twelve weeks ending with the last complete week before the day on which the time off is taken, or

(b) where the employee has not been employed for a sufficient period to enable the calculation to be made under paragraph (a), a number which fairly represents the number of normal working hours in a week having regard to such of the considerations specified in subsection (4) as are appropriate in the circumstances.

(4) The considerations referred to in subsection (3)(b) are—

(a) the average number of normal working hours in a week which the employee could expect in accordance with the terms of her contract, and

(b) the average number of normal working hours of other employees engaged in relevant comparable employment with the same employer.

(5) A right to any amount under subsection (1) does not affect any right of an employee in relation to remuneration under her contract of employment ("contractual remuneration").

(6) Any contractual remuneration paid to an employee in respect of a period of time off under section 55 goes towards discharging any liability of the employer to pay remuneration under subsection (1) in respect of that period; and, conversely, any payment of remuneration under subsection (1) in respect of a period goes towards discharging any liability of the employer to pay contractual remuneration in respect of that period.

57 Complaints to industrial tribunals

(1) An employee may present a complaint to an industrial tribunal that her employer—

(a) has unreasonably refused to permit her to take time off as required by section 55, or

(b) has failed to pay the whole or any part of any amount to which the employee is entitled under section 56.

(2) An industrial tribunal shall not consider a complaint under this section unless it is presented—

(a) before the end of the period of three months beginning with the date of the appointment concerned, or

(b) within such further period as the tribunal considers reasonable in a case where it is satisfied that it was not reasonably practicable for the complaint to be presented before the end of that period of three months.

(3) Where an industrial tribunal finds a complaint under this section well-founded, the tribunal shall make a declaration to that effect.

(4) If the complaint is that the employer has unreasonably refused to permit the employee to take time off, the tribunal shall also order the employer to pay to the employee an amount equal to the remuneration to which she would have been entitled under section 56 if the employer had not refused.

(5) If the complaint is that the employer has failed to pay the employee the whole or part of any amount to which she is entitled under section 56, the tribunal shall also order the employer to pay to the employee the amount which it finds due to her.

Occupational pension scheme trustees

58 Right to time off for pension scheme trustees

(1) The employer in relation to a relevant occupational pension scheme shall permit an employee of his who is a trustee of the scheme to take time off during the employee's working hours for the purpose of—

(a) performing any of his duties as such a trustee, or

(b) undergoing training relevant to the performance of those duties.

(2) The amount of time off which an employee is to be permitted to take under this section and the purposes for which, the occasions on which and any conditions subject to which time off may be so taken are those that are reasonable in all the circumstances having regard, in particular, to—

(a) how much time off is required for the performance of the duties of a trustee of the scheme and the undergoing of relevant training, and how much time off is required for performing the particular duty or for undergoing the particular training, and

(b) the circumstances of the employer's business and the effect of the employee's absence on the running of that business.

(3) In this section—

(a) "relevant occupational pension scheme" means an occupational pension scheme (as defined in section 1 of the Pension Schemes Act 1993) established under a trust, and

(b) references to the employer, in relation to such a scheme, are to an employer of persons in the description or category of employment to which the scheme relates.

(4) For the purposes of this section the working hours of an employee shall be taken to be any time when, in accordance with his contract of employment, the employee is required to be at work.

59 Right to payment for time off under section 58

(1) An employer who permits an employee to take time off under section 58 shall pay him for the time taken off pursuant to the permission.

(2) Where the employee's remuneration for the work he would ordinarily have been doing during that time does not vary with the amount of work done, he must be paid as if he had worked at that work for the whole of that time.

(3) Where the employee's remuneration for the work he would ordinarily have been doing during that time varies with the amount of work done, he must be paid an amount calculated by reference to the average hourly earnings for that work.

(4) The average hourly earnings mentioned in subsection (3) are—

(a) those of the employee concerned, or

(b) if no fair estimate can be made of those earnings, the average hourly earnings for work of that description of persons in comparable employment with the same employer or, if there are no such persons, a figure of average hourly earnings which is reasonable in the circumstances.

(5) A right to be paid an amount under subsection (1) does not affect any right of an employee in relation to remuneration under his contract of employment ("contractual remuneration").

(6) Any contractual remuneration paid to an employee in respect of a period of time off under section 58 goes towards discharging any liability of the employer under subsection (1) in respect of that period; and, conversely, any payment under subsection (1) in respect of a period goes towards discharging any liability of the employer to pay contractual remuneration in respect of that period.

60 Complaints to industrial tribunals

(1) An employee may present a complaint to an industrial tribunal that his employer—

(a) has failed to permit him to take time off as required by section 58, or

(b) has failed to pay him in accordance with section 59.

(2) An industrial tribunal shall not consider a complaint under this section unless it is presented—

(a) before the end of the period of three months beginning with the date when the failure occurred, or

(b) within such further period as the tribunal considers reasonable in a case where it is satisfied that it was not reasonably practicable for the complaint to be presented before the end of that period of three months.

(3) Where an industrial tribunal finds a complaint under subsection (1)(a) well-founded, the tribunal—

(a) shall make a declaration to that effect, and

(b) may make an award of compensation to be paid by the employer to the employee.

(4) The amount of the compensation shall be such as the tribunal considers just and equitable in all the circumstances having regard to—

(a) the employer's default in failing to permit time off to be taken by the employee, and

(b) any loss sustained by the employee which is attributable to the matters complained of.

(5) Where on a complaint under subsection (1)(b) an industrial tribunal finds that an employer has failed to pay an employee in accordance with section 59, it shall order the employer to pay the amount which it finds to be due.

Employee representatives

61 Right to time off for employee representatives

(1) An employee who is—

(a) an employee representative for the purposes of Chapter II of Part IV of the Trade Union and Labour Relations (Consolidation) Act 1992 (redundancies) or Regulations 10 and 11 of the Transfer of Undertakings (Protection of Employment) Regulations 1981, or

(b) a candidate in an election in which any person elected will, on being elected, be such an employee representative,

is entitled to be permitted by his employer to take reasonable time off during the employee's working hours in order to perform his functions as such an employee representative or candidate.

(2) For the purposes of this section the working hours of an employee shall be taken to be any time when, in accordance with his contract of employment, the employee is required to be at work.

62 Right to remuneration for time off under section 61

(1) An employee who is permitted to take time off under section 61 is entitled to be paid remuneration by his employer for the time taken off at the appropriate hourly rate.

(2) The appropriate hourly rate, in relation to an employee, is the amount of one week's pay divided by the number of normal working hours in a week for that employee when employed under the contract of employment in force on the day when the time off is taken.

(3) But where the number of normal working hours differs from week to week or over a longer period, the amount of one week's pay shall be divided instead by—

(a) the average number of normal working hours calculated by dividing by twelve the total number of the employee's normal working hours during the period of twelve weeks ending with the last complete week before the day on which the time off is taken, or

(b) where the employee has not been employed for a sufficient period to enable the calculation to be made under paragraph (a), a number which fairly represents the number of normal working hours in a week having regard to such of the considerations specified in subsection (4) as are appropriate in the circumstances.

(4) The considerations referred to in subsection (3)(b) are—

(a) the average number of normal working hours in a week which the employee could expect in accordance with the terms of his contract, and

(b) the average number of normal working hours of other employees engaged in relevant comparable employment with the same employer.

(5) A right to any amount under subsection (1) does not affect any right of an employee in relation to remuneration under his contract of employment ("contractual remuneration").

(6) Any contractual remuneration paid to an employee in respect of a period of time off under section 61 goes towards discharging any liability of the employer to pay remuneration under subsection (1) in respect of that period; and, conversely, any payment of remuneration under subsection (1) in respect of a period goes towards discharging any liability of the employer to pay contractual remuneration in respect of that period.

63 Complaints to industrial tribunals

(1) An employee may present a complaint to an industrial tribunal that his employer—

(a) has unreasonably refused to permit him to take time off as required by section 61, or

(b) has failed to pay the whole or any part of any amount to which the employee is entitled under section 62.

(2) An industrial tribunal shall not consider a complaint under this section unless it is presented—

(a) before the end of the period of three months beginning with the day on which the time off was taken or on which it is alleged the time off should have been permitted, or

(b) within such further period as the tribunal considers reasonable in a case where it is satisfied that it was not reasonably practicable for the complaint to be presented before the end of that period of three months.

(3) Where an industrial tribunal finds a complaint under this section well-founded, the tribunal shall make a declaration to that effect.

(4) If the complaint is that the employer has unreasonably refused to permit the employee to take time off, the tribunal shall also order the employer to pay to the employee an amount equal to the remuneration to which he would have been entitled under section 62 if the employer had not refused.

(5) If the complaint is that the employer has failed to pay the employee the whole or part of any amount to which he is entitled under section 62, the tribunal shall also order the employer to pay to the employee the amount which it finds due to him.

PART VII

SUSPENSION FROM WORK

Suspension on medical grounds

64 Right to remuneration on suspension on medical grounds

(1) An employee who is suspended from work by his employer on medical grounds is entitled to be paid by his employer remuneration while he is so suspended for a period not exceeding twenty-six weeks.

(2) For the purposes of this Part an employee is suspended from work on medical grounds if he is suspended from work in consequence of—

(a) a requirement imposed by or under a provision of an enactment or of an instrument made under an enactment, or

(b) a recommendation in a provision of a code of practice issued or approved under section 16 of the Health and Safety at Work etc. Act 1974,

and the provision is for the time being specified in subsection (3).

(3) The provisions referred to in subsection (2) are—

Regulation 16 of the Control of Lead at Work Regulations 1980,

Regulation 16 of the Ionising Radiations Regulations 1985, and

Regulation 11 of the Control of Substances Hazardous to Health Regulations 1988.

(4) The Secretary of State may by order add provisions to or remove provisions from the list of provisions specified in subsection (3).

(5) For the purposes of this Part an employee shall be regarded as suspended from work on medical grounds only if and for so long as he—

(a) continues to be employed by his employer, but

(b) is not provided with work or does not perform the work he normally performed before the suspension.

65 Exclusions from right to remuneration

(1) An employee is not entitled to remuneration under section 64 unless he has been continuously employed for a period of not less than one month ending with the day before that on which the suspension begins.

(2) An employee who is employed—

(a) under a contract for a fixed term of three months or less, or

(b) under a contract made in contemplation of the performance of a specific task which is not expected to last for more than three months,

is not entitled to remuneration under section 64 unless he has been continuously employed for a period of more than three months ending with the day before that on which the suspension begins.

(3) An employee is not entitled to remuneration under section 64 in respect of any period during which he is incapable of work by reason of disease or bodily or mental disablement.

(4) An employee is not entitled to remuneration under section 64 in respect of any period if—

(a) his employer has offered to provide him with suitable alternative work during the period (whether or not it is work which the employee is under his contract, or was under the contract in force before the suspension, employed to perform) and the employee has unreasonably refused to perform that work, or

(b) he does not comply with reasonable requirements imposed by his employer with a view to ensuring that his services are available.

Suspension on maternity grounds

66 Meaning of suspension on maternity grounds

(1) For the purposes of this Part an employee is suspended from work on maternity grounds if, in consequence of any relevant requirement or relevant recommendation, she is suspended from work by her employer on the ground that she is pregnant, has recently given birth or is breastfeeding a child.

(2) In subsection (1)—

"relevant requirement" means a requirement imposed by or under a specified provision of an enactment or of an instrument made under an enactment, and "relevant recommendation" means a recommendation in a specified provision of a code of practice issued or approved under section 16 of the Health and Safety at Work etc. Act 1974;

and in this subsection "specified provision" means a provision for the time being specified in an order made by the Secretary of State under this subsection.

(3) For the purposes of this Part an employee shall be regarded as suspended from work on maternity grounds only if and for so long as she—

(a) continues to be employed by her employer, but

(b) is not provided with work or (disregarding alternative work for the purposes of section 67) does not perform the work she normally performed before the suspension.

67 Right to offer of alternative work

(1) Where an employer has available suitable alternative work for an employee, the employee has a right to be offered to be provided with the alternative work before being suspended from work on maternity grounds.

(2) For alternative work to be suitable for an employee for the purposes of this section—

(a) the work must be of a kind which is both suitable in relation to her and appropriate for her to do in the circumstances, and

(b) the terms and conditions applicable to her for performing the work, if they differ from the corresponding terms and conditions applicable to her for performing the work she normally performs under her contract of employment, must not be substantially less favourable to her than those corresponding terms and conditions.

68 Right to remuneration

(1) An employee who is suspended from work on maternity grounds is entitled to be paid remuneration by her employer while she is so suspended.

(2) An employee is not entitled to remuneration under this section in respect of any period if—

(a) her employer has offered to provide her during the period with work which is suitable alternative work for her for the purposes of section 67, and

(b) the employee has unreasonably refused to perform that work.

General

69 Calculation of remuneration

(1) The amount of remuneration payable by an employer to an employee under section 64 or 68 is a week's pay in respect of each week of the period of suspension; and if in any week remuneration is payable in respect of only part of that week the amount of a week's pay shall be reduced proportionately.

(2) A right to remuneration under section 64 or 68 does not affect any right of an employee in relation to remuneration under the employee's contract of employment ("contractual remuneration").

(3) Any contractual remuneration paid by an employer to an employee in respect of any period goes towards discharging the employer's liability under section 64 or 68 in respect of that period; and, conversely, any payment of remuneration in discharge of an employer's liability under section 64 or 68 in respect of any period goes towards discharging any obligation of the employer to pay contractual remuneration in respect of that period.

70 Complaints to industrial tribunals

(1) An employee may present a complaint to an industrial tribunal that his or her employer has failed to pay the whole or any part of remuneration to which the employee is entitled under section 64 or 68.

(2) An industrial tribunal shall not consider a complaint under subsection (1) relating to remuneration in respect of any day unless it is presented—

(a) before the end of the period of three months beginning with that day, or

(b) within such further period as the tribunal considers reasonable in a case where it is satisfied that it was not reasonably practicable for the complaint to be presented within that period of three months.

(3) Where an industrial tribunal finds a complaint under subsection (1) well-founded, the tribunal shall order the employer to pay the employee the amount of remuneration which it finds is due to him or her.

(4) An employee may present a complaint to an industrial tribunal that in contravention of section 67 her employer has failed to offer to provide her with work.

(5) An industrial tribunal shall not consider a complaint under subsection (4) unless it is presented—

(a) before the end of the period of three months beginning with the first day of the suspension, or

(b) within such further period as the tribunal considers reasonable in a case where it is satisfied that it was not reasonably practicable for the complaint to be presented within that period of three months.

(6) Where an industrial tribunal finds a complaint under subsection (4) well-founded, the tribunal may make an award of compensation to be paid by the employer to the employee.

(7) The amount of the compensation shall be such as the tribunal considers just and equitable in all the circumstances having regard to—

(a) the infringement of the employee's right under section 67 by the failure on the part of the employer to which the complaint relates, and

(b) any loss sustained by the employee which is attributable to that failure.

PART VIII

MATERNITY RIGHTS

General right to maternity leave

71 General right to maternity leave

(1) An employee who is absent from work at any time during her maternity leave period is (subject to sections 74 and 75) entitled to the benefit of the terms and conditions of employment which would have been applicable to her if she had not been absent (and had not been pregnant or given birth to a child).

(2) Subsection (1) does not confer any entitlement to remuneration.

72 Commencement of maternity leave period

(1) Subject to subsection (2), an employee's maternity leave period commences with the earlier of—

(a) the date which, in accordance with section 74(1) to (3), she notifies to her employer as the date on which she intends her period of absence from work in exercise of the right conferred by section 71 to commence, and

(b) the first day after the beginning of the sixth week before the expected week of childbirth on which she is absent from work wholly or partly because of pregnancy.

(2) Where the employee's maternity leave period has not commenced by virtue of subsection (1) when childbirth occurs, her maternity leave period commences with the day on which childbirth occurs.

(3) The Secretary of State may by order vary subsections (1) and (2).

73 Duration of maternity leave period

(1) Subject to subsections (2) and (3), an employee's maternity leave period continues for the period of fourteen weeks from its commencement or until the birth of the child, if later.

(2) Subject to subsection (3), where any requirement imposed by or under any relevant statutory provision prohibits the employee from working for any period after the end of the period mentioned in subsection (1) by reason of her having recently given birth, her maternity leave period continues until the end of that later period.

(3) Where the employee is dismissed after the commencement of her maternity leave period but before the time when (apart from this subsection) that period would end, the period ends at the time of the dismissal.

(4) In subsection (2) "relevant statutory provision" means a provision of—

(a) an enactment, or

(b) an instrument made under an enactment,

other than a provision for the time being specified in an order made under section 66(2).

(5) The Secretary of State may by order vary subsections (1) to (4).

74 Requirement to notify commencement of leave

(1) Subject to subsections (4) and (5), an employee does not have the right conferred by section 71 unless she notifies her employer of the date on which she intends her period of absence from work in exercise of the right to commence.

(2) No date occurring before the beginning of the eleventh week before the expected week of childbirth may be notified under subsection (1).

(3) Notification under subsection (1) shall be given by an employee—

(a) not less than twenty-one days before the date on which she intends her period of absence from work in exercise of the right conferred by section 71 to commence, or

(b) if that is not reasonably practicable, as soon as is reasonably practicable.

(4) Where an employee's maternity leave period commences with the first day after the beginning of the sixth week before the expected week of childbirth on which she is absent from work wholly or partly because of pregnancy—

(a) subsection (1) does not require her to notify her employer of the date specified in that subsection, but

(b) (whether or not she has notified him of that date) she does not have the right conferred by section 71 unless she notifies him as soon as is reasonably practicable that she is absent from work wholly or partly because of pregnancy.

(5) Where an employee's maternity leave period commences with the day on which childbirth occurs—

(a) subsection (1) does not require her to notify her employer of the date specified in that subsection, but

(b) (whether or not she has notified him of that date) she does not have the right conferred by section 71 unless she notifies him as soon as is reasonably practicable after the birth that she has given birth.

(6) Any notification required by this section shall, if the employer so requests, be given in writing.

75 Requirement to notify pregnancy etc

(1) An employee does not have the right conferred by section 71 unless at least twenty-one days before her maternity leave period commences or, if that is not reasonably practicable, as soon as is reasonably practicable, she informs her employer in writing of—

(a) her pregnancy, and

(b) the expected week of childbirth,

or, if childbirth has occurred, of the date on which it occurred.

(2) An employee does not have the right conferred by section 71 unless, if requested to do so by her employer, she produces for his inspection a certificate from—

(a) a registered medical practitioner, or

(b) a registered midwife,

stating the expected week of childbirth.

76 Requirement to notify return during maternity leave period

(1) An employee who intends to return to work earlier than the end of her maternity leave period shall give to her employer not less than seven days' notice of the date on which she intends to return.

(2) If an employee attempts to return to work earlier than the end of her maternity leave period without complying with subsection (1), her employer shall be entitled to postpone her return to a date such as will secure, subject to subsection (3), that he has seven days' notice of her return.

(3) An employer is not entitled under subsection (2) to postpone an employee's return to work to a date after the end of her maternity leave period.

(4) If an employee whose return to work has been postponed under subsection (2) has been notified that she is not to return to work before the date to which her return was postponed, the employer is under no contractual obligation to pay her remuneration until the date to which her return was postponed if she returns to work before that date.

77 Redundancy during maternity leave period

(1) This section applies where during an employee's maternity leave period it is not practicable by reason of redundancy for the employer to continue to employ her under her existing contract of employment.

(2) Where there is a suitable available vacancy, the employee is entitled to be offered (before the ending of her employment under her existing contract) alternative employment with her employer or his successor, or an associated employer, under a new contract of employment which complies with subsection (3) (and takes effect immediately on the ending of her employment under the previous contract).

(3) The new contract of employment must be such that—

(a) the work to be done under it is of a kind which is both suitable in relation to the employee and appropriate for her to do in the circumstances, and

(b) its provisions as to the capacity and place in which she is to be employed, and as to the other terms and conditions of her employment, are not substantially less favourable to her than if she had continued to be employed under the previous contract.

78 Contractual rights to maternity leave

(1) An employee who has both the right to maternity leave under section 71 and another right to maternity leave (under a contract of employment or otherwise) may not exercise the two rights separately but may, in taking maternity leave, take advantage of whichever right is, in any particular respect, the more favourable.

(2) The provisions of sections 72 to 77 apply, subject to any modifications necessary to give effect to any more favourable contractual terms, to the exercise of the composite right described in subsection (1) as they apply to the exercise of the right under section 71.

Right to return to work

79 Right to return to work

(1) An employee who—

(a) has the right conferred by section 71, and

(b) has, at the beginning of the eleventh week before the expected week of childbirth, been continuously employed for a period of not less than two years,

also has the right to return to work at any time during the period beginning at the end of her maternity leave period and ending twenty-nine weeks after the beginning of the week in which childbirth occurs.

(2) An employee's right to return to work under this section is the right to return to work with the person who was her employer before the end of her maternity leave period, or (where appropriate) his successor, in the job in which she was then employed—

(a) on terms and conditions as to remuneration not less favourable than those which would have been applicable to her had she not been absent from work at any time since the commencement of her maternity leave period,

(b) with her seniority, pension rights and similar rights as they would have been if the period or periods of her employment prior to the end of her maternity leave period were continuous with her employment following her return to work (but subject to the requirements of paragraph 5 of Schedule 5 to the Social Security Act 1989 (credit for the period of absence in certain cases)), and

(c) otherwise on terms and conditions not less favourable than those which would have been applicable to her had she not been absent from work after the end of her maternity leave period.

(3) The Secretary of State may by order vary the period of two years specified in subsection (1) or that period as varied by an order under this subsection.

80 Requirement to notify return

(1) An employee does not have the right conferred by section 79 unless she includes with the information required by section 75(1) the information that she intends to exercise the right.

(2) Where, not earlier than twenty-one days before the end of her maternity leave period, an employee is requested in accordance with subsection (3) by her employer, or a successor of his, to give him written confirmation that she intends to exercise the right conferred by section 79, the employee is not entitled to that right unless she gives the requested confirmation—

(a) within fourteen days of receiving the request, or

(b) if that is not reasonably practicable, as soon as is reasonably practicable.

(3) A request under subsection (2) shall be—

(a) made in writing, and

(b) accompanied by a written statement of the effect of that subsection.

81 Redundancy before return

(1) This section applies where an employee has the right conferred by section 79 but it is not practicable by reason of redundancy for the employer to permit her to return in accordance with that right.

(2) Where there is a suitable available vacancy, the employee is entitled to be offered alternative employment with her employer or his successor, or an associated employer, under a new contract of employment which complies with subsection (3).

(3) The new contract of employment must be such that—

(a) the work to be done under it is of a kind which is both suitable in relation to the employee and appropriate for her to do in the circumstances, and

(b) its provisions as to the capacity and place in which she is to be employed, and as to the other terms and conditions of her employment, are not substantially less favourable to her than if she had returned to work pursuant to the right conferred by section 79.

82 Exercise of right to return

(1) An employee shall exercise the right conferred by section 79 by giving written notice to the employer (who may be her employer before the end of her maternity leave period or a successor of his) at least twenty-one days before the day on which she proposes to return of her proposal to return on that day (the "notified day of return").

(2) An employer may postpone an employee's return to work until a date not more than four weeks after the notified day of return if he notifies her before that day that for specified reasons he is postponing her return until that date; and, accordingly, she will be entitled to return to work with him on that date.

(3) An employee to whom subsection (4) applies may—

(a) postpone her return to work until a date not more than four weeks after the notified day of return (even if that date falls after the end of the period of twenty-nine weeks beginning with the week in which childbirth occurred), and

(b) where no day of return has been notified to the employer, extend the time during which she may exercise her right to return in accordance with subsection (1), so that she returns to work not more than four weeks after the end of that period of twenty-nine weeks.

(4) This subsection applies to an employee if she gives to her employer, before the notified day of return (or the end of the period of twenty-nine weeks), a certificate from a registered medical practitioner stating that by reason of disease or bodily or mental disablement she will be incapable of work on the notified day of return (or at the end of that period).

(5) Where an employee has once exercised a right of postponement or extension under subsection (3), she is not entitled again to exercise a right of postponement or extension under that subsection in connection with the same return to work.

(6) If an employee has notified a day of return but there is an interruption of work (whether due to industrial action or some other reason) which renders it unreasonable to expect the employee to return to work on the notified day of return, she may instead return to work when work resumes after the interruption or as soon as reasonably practicable afterwards.

(7) Where in the case of an employee who has not already notified a day of return—

(a) there is an interruption of work (whether due to industrial action or some other reason) which renders it unreasonable to expect the employee to return to work before the end of the period of twenty-nine weeks beginning with the week in which childbirth occurred, or which appears likely to have that effect, and

(b) in consequence, the employee does not notify a day of return,

the employee may exercise her right to return in accordance with subsection (1) so that she returns to work at any time before the end of the period of twenty-eight days after the end of the interruption even though that means that she returns to work outside the period of twenty-nine weeks.

(8) Where an employee has exercised the right under subsection (3)(b) to extend the period during which she may exercise her right to return, subsection (7) applies as if for the reference to the end of the period of twenty-nine weeks there were substituted a reference to the end of the further period of four weeks after the end of that period.

(9) Where in the case of an interruption of work an employee has refrained from notifying the day of return in the circumstances described in subsection (7), subsection (3)(b) applies as if for the reference to the end of the period of twenty-nine weeks there were substituted a reference to the end of the period of twenty-eight days after the end of the interruption of work.

83 Notified day of return

(1) Subject to subsection (2), in this Act "notified day of return" shall be construed in accordance with section 82(1).

(2) Where—

(a) an employee's return is postponed under subsection (2) or (3)(a) of section 82, or

(b) the employee returns to work on a day later than the notified day of return in the circumstances described in subsection (6) of that section,

then, subject to subsection (5) of that section, references in subsections (2), (3)(a) and (6) of that section and the following provisions of this Act to the notified day of return shall be construed as references to the day to which the return is postponed or that later day.

84 Employee dismissed at or after end of maternity leave period

(1) This section applies where an employee has the right to return to work conferred by section 79 and either—

(a) her maternity leave period ends by reason of dismissal, or

(b) she is dismissed after the end of her maternity leave period, otherwise than in the course of attempting to return to work in accordance with her contract in circumstances in which section 85 applies.

(2) Where this section applies, the right conferred by section 79 is exercisable only on the employee repaying any compensation for unfair dismissal, or redundancy payment, paid in respect of the dismissal if the employer requests repayment.

85 Contractual rights to return

(1) An employee who has both the right to return to work conferred by section 79 and another right to return to work after absence because of pregnancy or childbirth (under a contract of employment or otherwise) may not exercise the two rights separately but may, in returning to work, take advantage of whichever right is, in any particular respect, the more favourable.

(2) Sections 79 and 81 to 84, and the provisions of the following Parts of this Act relating to the right conferred by section 79 (other than section 137(2)), apply, subject to any modifications necessary to give effect to any more favourable contractual terms, to the exercise of the composite right described in subsection (1) as they apply to the exercise of the right conferred by section 79.

PART IX

TERMINATION OF EMPLOYMENT

Minimum period of notice

86 Rights of employer and employee to minimum notice

(1) The notice required to be given by an employer to terminate the contract of employment of a person who has been continuously employed for one month or more—

(a) is not less than one week's notice if his period of continuous employment is less than two years,

(b) is not less than one week's notice for each year of continuous employment if his period of continuous employment is two years or more but less than twelve years, and

(c) is not less than twelve weeks' notice if his period of continuous employment is twelve years or more.

(2) The notice required to be given by an employee who has been continuously employed for one month or more to terminate his contract of employment is not less than one week.

(3) Any provision for shorter notice in any contract of employment with a person who has been continuously employed for one month or more has effect subject to subsections (1) and (2); but this section does not prevent either party from waiving his right to notice on any occasion or from accepting a payment in lieu of notice.

(4) Any contract of employment of a person who has been continuously employed for three months or more which is a contract for a term certain of one month or less shall have effect as if it were for an indefinite period; and, accordingly, subsections (1) and (2) apply to the contract.

(5) Subsections (1) and (2) do not apply to a contract made in contemplation of the performance of a specific task which is not expected to last for more than three months unless the employee has been continuously employed for a period of more than three months.

(6) This section does not affect any right of either party to a contract of employment to treat the contract as terminable without notice by reason of the conduct of the other party.

87 Rights of employee in period of notice

(1) If an employer gives notice to terminate the contract of employment of a person who has been continuously employed for one month or more, the provisions of sections 88 to 91 have effect as respects the liability of the employer for the period of notice required by section 86(1).

(2) If an employee who has been continuously employed for one month or more gives notice to terminate his contract of employment, the provisions of sections 88 to 91 have effect as respects the liability of the employer for the period of notice required by section 86(2).

(3) In sections 88 to 91 "period of notice" means—

- (a) where notice is given by an employer, the period of notice required by section 86(1), and
- (b) where notice is given by an employee, the period of notice required by section 86(2).

(4) This section does not apply in relation to a notice given by the employer or the employee if the notice to be given by the employer to terminate the contract must be at least one week more than the notice required by section 86(1).

88 Employments with normal working hours

(1) If an employee has normal working hours under the contract of employment in force during the period of notice and during any part of those normal working hours—

- (a) the employee is ready and willing to work but no work is provided for him by his employer,
- (b) the employee is incapable of work because of sickness or injury,
- (c) the employee is absent from work wholly or partly because of pregnancy or childbirth, or
- (d) the employee is absent from work in accordance with the terms of his employment relating to holidays,

the employer is liable to pay the employee for the part of normal working hours covered by any of paragraphs (a), (b), (c) and (d) a sum not less than the amount of remuneration for that part of normal working hours calculated at the average hourly rate of remuneration produced by dividing a week's pay by the number of normal working hours.

(2) Any payments made to the employee by his employer in respect of the relevant part of the period of notice (whether by way of sick pay, statutory sick pay, maternity pay, statutory maternity pay, holiday pay or otherwise) go towards meeting the employer's liability under this section.

(3) Where notice was given by the employee, the employer's liability under this section does not arise unless and until the employee leaves the service of the employer in pursuance of the notice.

89 Employments without normal working hours

(1) If an employee does not have normal working hours under the contract of employment in force in the period of notice, the employer is liable to pay the employee for each week of the period of notice a sum not less than a week's pay.

(2) The employer's liability under this section is conditional on the employee being ready and willing to do work of a reasonable nature and amount to earn a week's pay.

(3) Subsection (2) does not apply—

(a) in respect of any period during which the employee is incapable of work because of sickness or injury,

(b) in respect of any period during which the employee is absent from work wholly or partly because of pregnancy or childbirth, or

(c) in respect of any period during which the employee is absent from work in accordance with the terms of his employment relating to holidays.

(4) Any payment made to an employee by his employer in respect of a period within subsection (3) (whether by way of sick pay, statutory sick pay, maternity pay, statutory maternity pay, holiday pay or otherwise) shall be taken into account for the purposes of this section as if it were remuneration paid by the employer in respect of that period.

(5) Where notice was given by the employee, the employer's liability under this section does not arise unless and until the employee leaves the service of the employer in pursuance of the notice.

90 Short-term incapacity benefit and industrial injury benefit

(1) This section has effect where the arrangements in force relating to the employment are such that—

(a) payments by way of sick pay are made by the employer to employees to whom the arrangements apply, in cases where any such employees are incapable of work because of sickness or injury, and

(b) in calculating any payment so made to any such employee an amount representing, or treated as representing, short-term incapacity benefit or industrial injury benefit is taken into account, whether by way of deduction or by way of calculating the payment as a supplement to that amount.

(2) If—

(a) during any part of the period of notice the employee is incapable of work because of sickness or injury,

(b) one or more payments by way of sick pay are made to him by the employer in respect of that part of the period of notice, and

(c) in calculating any such payment such an amount as is referred to in paragraph (b) of subsection (1) is taken into account as mentioned in that paragraph,

for the purposes of section 88 or 89 the amount so taken into account shall be treated as having been paid by the employer to the employee by way of sick pay in respect of that part of that period, and shall go towards meeting the liability of the employer under that section accordingly.

91 Supplementary

(1) An employer is not liable under section 88 or 89 to make any payment in respect of a period during which an employee is absent from work with the leave of the employer granted at the request of the employee, including any period of time off taken in accordance with—

(a) Part VI of this Act, or

(b) section 168 or 170 of the Trade Union and Labour Relations (Consolidation) Act 1992 (trade union duties and activities).

(2) No payment is due under section 88 or 89 in consequence of a notice to terminate a contract given by an employee if, after the notice is given and on or before the termination of the contract, the employee takes part in a strike of employees of the employer.

(3) If, during the period of notice, the employer breaks the contract of employment, payments received under section 88 or 89 in respect of the part of the period after the breach go towards mitigating the damages recoverable by the employee for loss of earnings in that part of the period of notice.

(4) If, during the period of notice, the employee breaks the contract and the employer rightfully treats the breach as terminating the contract, no payment is due to the employee under section 88 or 89 in respect of the part of the period falling after the termination of the contract.

(5) If an employer fails to give the notice required by section 86, the rights conferred by sections 87 to 90 and this section shall be taken into account in assessing his liability for breach of the contract.

(6) Sections 86 to 90 and this section apply in relation to a contract all or any of the terms of which are terms which take effect by virtue of any provision contained in or having effect under an Act (whether public or local) as in relation to any other contract; and the reference in this subsection to an Act includes, subject to any express provision to the contrary, an Act passed after this Act.

Written statement of reasons for dismissal

92 Right to written statement of reasons for dismissal

(1) An employee is entitled to be provided by his employer with a written statement giving particulars of the reasons for the employee's dismissal—

(a) if the employee is given by the employer notice of termination of his contract of employment,

(b) if the employee's contract of employment is terminated by the employer without notice, or

(c) if the employee is employed under a contract for a fixed term and that term expires without being renewed under the same contract.

(2) Subject to subsection (4), an employee is entitled to a written statement under this section only if he makes a request for one; and a statement shall be provided within fourteen days of such a request.

(3) Subject to subsection (4), an employee is not entitled to a written statement under this section unless on the effective date of termination he has been, or will have been, continuously employed for a period of not less than two years ending with that date.

(4) An employee is entitled to a written statement under this section without having to request it and irrespective of whether she has been continuously employed for any period if she is dismissed—

(a) at any time while she is pregnant, or

(b) after childbirth in circumstances in which her maternity leave period ends by reason of the dismissal.

(5) A written statement under this section is admissible in evidence in any proceedings.

(6) Subject to subsection (7), in this section "the effective date of termination"—

(a) in relation to an employee whose contract of employment is terminated by notice, means the date on which the notice expires,

(b) in relation to an employee whose contract of employment is terminated without notice, means the date on which the termination takes effect, and

(c) in relation to an employee who is employed under a contract for a fixed term which expires without being renewed under the same contract, means the date on which the term expires.

(7) Where—

(a) the contract of employment is terminated by the employer, and

(b) the notice required by section 86 to be given by an employer would, if duly given on the material date, expire on a date later than the effective date of termination (as defined by subsection (6)),

the later date is the effective date of termination.

(8) In subsection (7)(b) "the material date" means—

(a) the date when notice of termination was given by the employer, or

(b) where no notice was given, the date when the contract of employment was terminated by the employer.

93 Complaints to industrial tribunal

(1) A complaint may be presented to an industrial tribunal by an employee on the ground that—

(a) the employer unreasonably failed to provide a written statement under section 92, or

(b) the particulars of reasons given in purported compliance with that section are inadequate or untrue.

(2) Where an industrial tribunal finds a complaint under this section well-founded, the tribunal—

(a) may make a declaration as to what it finds the employer's reasons were for dismissing the employee, and

(b) shall make an award that the employer pay to the employee a sum equal to the amount of two weeks' pay.

(3) An industrial tribunal shall not consider a complaint under this section relating to the reasons for a dismissal unless it is presented to the tribunal at such a time that

the tribunal would, in accordance with section 111, consider a complaint of unfair dismissal in respect of that dismissal presented at the same time.

PART X

UNFAIR DISMISSAL

CHAPTER I

RIGHT NOT TO BE UNFAIRLY DISMISSED

The right

94 The right

(1) An employee has the right not to be unfairly dismissed by his employer.

(2) Subsection (1) has effect subject to the following provisions of this Part (in particular sections 108 to 110) and to the provisions of the Trade Union and Labour Relations (Consolidation) Act 1992 (in particular sections 237 to 239).

Dismissal

95 Circumstances in which an employee is dismissed

(1) For the purposes of this Part an employee is dismissed by his employer if (and, subject to subsection (2) and section 96, only if)—

(a) the contract under which he is employed is terminated by the employer (whether with or without notice),

(b) he is employed under a contract for a fixed term and that term expires without being renewed under the same contract, or

(c) the employee terminates the contract under which he is employed (with or without notice) in circumstances in which he is entitled to terminate it without notice by reason of the employer's conduct.

(2) An employee shall be taken to be dismissed by his employer for the purposes of this Part if—

(a) the employer gives notice to the employee to terminate his contract of employment, and

(b) at a time within the period of that notice the employee gives notice to the employer to terminate the contract of employment on a date earlier than the date on which the employer's notice is due to expire;

and the reason for the dismissal is to be taken to be the reason for which the employer's notice is given.

96 Failure to permit return after childbirth treated as dismissal

(1) Where an employee who—

(a) has the right conferred by section 79, and

(b) has exercised it in accordance with section 82,

is not permitted to return to work, she shall (subject to the following provisions of this section) be taken for the purposes of this Part to be dismissed for the reason for which she was not permitted to return with effect from the notified day of return (being deemed to have been continuously employed until that day).

(2) Subsection (1) does not apply in relation to an employee if—

(a) immediately before the end of her maternity leave period (or, if it ends by reason of dismissal, immediately before the dismissal) the number of employees employed by her employer, added to the number employed by any associated employer of his, did not exceed five, and

(b) it is not reasonably practicable for the employer (who may be the same employer or a successor of his) to permit her to return to work under section 79 or for him or an associated employer to offer her employment under a contract of employment satisfying the conditions specified in subsection (4).

(3) Subsection (1) does not apply in relation to an employee if—

(a) it is not reasonably practicable for a reason other than redundancy for the employer (who may be the same employer or a successor of his) to permit her to return to work under section 79,

(b) he or an associated employer offers her employment under a contract of employment satisfying the conditions specified in subsection (4), and

(c) she accepts or unreasonably refuses that offer.

(4) The conditions referred to in subsections (2) and (3) are—

(a) that the work to be done under the contract is of a kind which is both suitable in relation to the employee and appropriate for her to do in the circumstances, and

(b) that the provisions of the contract as to the capacity and place in which she is to be employed, and as to the other terms and conditions of her employment, are not substantially less favourable to her than if she had returned to work under section 79.

(5) Where on a complaint of unfair dismissal any question arises as to whether the operation of subsection (1) is excluded by the provisions of subsection (2) or (3), it is for the employer to show that the provisions in question were satisfied in relation to the complainant.

(6) Where subsection (1) applies to an employee who was employed as a shop worker, or a betting worker, under her contract of employment on the last day of her maternity leave period, she shall be treated for the purposes of this Act as if she had been employed as a shop worker, or a betting worker, on the day with effect from which she is treated as dismissed.

97 Effective date of termination

(1) Subject to the following provisions of this section, in this Part "the effective date of termination"—

(a) in relation to an employee whose contract of employment is terminated by notice, whether given by his employer or by the employee, means the date on which the notice expires,

(b) in relation to an employee whose contract of employment is terminated without notice, means the date on which the termination takes effect, and

(c) in relation to an employee who is employed under a contract for a fixed term which expires without being renewed under the same contract, means the date on which the term expires.

(2) Where—

(a) the contract of employment is terminated by the employer, and

(b) the notice required by section 86 to be given by an employer would, if duly given on the material date, expire on a date later than the effective date of termination (as defined by subsection (1)),

for the purposes of sections 108(1), 119(1) and 227(3) the later date is the effective date of termination.

(3) In subsection (2)(b) "the material date" means—

(a) the date when notice of termination was given by the employer, or

(b) where no notice was given, the date when the contract of employment was terminated by the employer.

(4) Where—

(a) the contract of employment is terminated by the employee,

(b) the material date does not fall during a period of notice given by the employer to terminate that contract, and

(c) had the contract been terminated not by the employee but by notice given on the material date by the employer, that notice would have been required by section 86 to expire on a date later than the effective date of termination (as defined by subsection (1)),

for the purposes of sections 108(1), 119(1) and 227(3) the later date is the effective date of termination.

(5) In subsection (4) "the material date" means—

(a) the date when notice of termination was given by the employee, or

(b) where no notice was given, the date when the contract of employment was terminated by the employee.

(6) Where an employee is taken to be dismissed for the purposes of this Part by virtue of section 96, references in this Part to the effective date of termination are to the notified date of return.

Fairness

98 General

(1) In determining for the purposes of this Part whether the dismissal of an employee is fair or unfair, it is for the employer to show—

(a) the reason (or, if more than one, the principal reason) for the dismissal, and

(b) that it is either a reason falling within subsection (2) or some other substantial reason of a kind such as to justify the dismissal of an employee holding the position which the employee held.

(2) A reason falls within this subsection if it—

(a) relates to the capability or qualifications of the employee for performing work of the kind which he was employed by the employer to do,

(b) relates to the conduct of the employee,

(c) is that the employee was redundant, or

(d) is that the employee could not continue to work in the position which he held without contravention (either on his part or on that of his employer) of a duty or restriction imposed by or under an enactment.

(3) In subsection (2)(a)—

(a) "capability", in relation to an employee, means his capability assessed by reference to skill, aptitude, health or any other physical or mental quality, and

(b) "qualifications", in relation to an employee, means any degree, diploma or other academic, technical or professional qualification relevant to the position which he held.

(4) Where the employer has fulfilled the requirements of subsection (1), the determination of the question whether the dismissal is fair or unfair (having regard to the reason shown by the employer)—

(a) depends on whether in the circumstances (including the size and administrative resources of the employer's undertaking) the employer acted reasonably or unreasonably in treating it as a sufficient reason for dismissing the employee, and

(b) shall be determined in accordance with equity and the substantial merits of the case.

(5) Where the employee is taken to be dismissed for the purposes of this Part by virtue of section 96, subsection (4)(a) applies as if for the words "acted reasonably" onwards there were substituted the words "would have been acting reasonably or unreasonably in treating it as a sufficient reason for dismissing the employee if she had not been absent from work, and".

(6) Subsections (4) and (5) are subject to—

(a) sections 99 to 107 of this Act, and

(b) sections 152, 153 and 238 of the Trade Union and Labour Relations (Consolidation) Act 1992 (dismissal on ground of trade union membership or activities or in connection with industrial action).

99 Pregnancy and childbirth

(1) An employee who is dismissed shall be regarded for the purposes of this Part as unfairly dismissed if—

(a) the reason (or, if more than one, the principal reason) for the dismissal is that she is pregnant or any other reason connected with her pregnancy,

(b) her maternity leave period is ended by the dismissal and the reason (or, if more than one, the principal reason) for the dismissal is that she has given birth to a child or any other reason connected with her having given birth to a child,

(c) her contract of employment is terminated after the end of her maternity leave period and the reason (or, if more than one, the principal reason) for the dismissal is that she took, or availed herself of the benefits of, maternity leave,

(d) the reason (or, if more than one, the principal reason) for the dismissal is a relevant requirement, or a relevant recommendation, as defined by section 66(2), or

(e) her maternity leave period is ended by the dismissal, the reason (or, if more than one, the principal reason) for the dismissal is that she is redundant and section 77 has not been complied with.

(2) For the purposes of subsection (1)(c)—

(a) a woman takes maternity leave if she is absent from work during her maternity leave period, and

(b) a woman avails herself of the benefits of maternity leave if, during her maternity leave period, she avails herself of the benefit of any of the terms and conditions of her employment preserved by section 71 during that period.

(3) An employee who is dismissed shall also be regarded for the purposes of this Part as unfairly dismissed if—

(a) before the end of her maternity leave period she gave to her employer a certificate from a registered medical practitioner stating that by reason of disease or bodily or mental disablement she would be incapable of work after the end of that period,

(b) her contract of employment was terminated within the period of four weeks beginning immediately after the end of her maternity leave period in circumstances in which she continued to be incapable of work and the certificate remained current, and

(c) the reason (or, if more than one, the principal reason) for the dismissal is that she has given birth to a child or any other reason connected with her having given birth to a child.

(4) Where—

(a) an employee has the right conferred by section 79,

(b) it is not practicable by reason of redundancy for the employer to permit her to return in accordance with that right, and

(c) no offer is made of such alternative employment as is referred to in section 81,

the dismissal of the employee which is treated as taking place by virtue of section 96 is to be regarded for the purposes of this Part as unfair.

100 Health and safety cases

(1) An employee who is dismissed shall be regarded for the purposes of this Part as unfairly dismissed if the reason (or, if more than one, the principal reason) for the dismissal is that—

(a) having been designated by the employer to carry out activities in connection with preventing or reducing risks to health and safety at work, the employee carried out (or proposed to carry out) any such activities,

(b) being a representative of workers on matters of health and safety at work or member of a safety committee—

(i) in accordance with arrangements established under or by virtue of any enactment, or

(ii) by reason of being acknowledged as such by the employer,

the employee performed (or proposed to perform) any functions as such a representative or a member of such a committee,

(c) being an employee at a place where—

(i) there was no such representative or safety committee, or

(ii) there was such a representative or safety committee but it was not reasonably practicable for the employee to raise the matter by those means,

he brought to his employer's attention, by reasonable means, circumstances connected with his work which he reasonably believed were harmful or potentially harmful to health or safety,

(d) in circumstances of danger which the employee reasonably believed to be serious and imminent and which he could not reasonably have been expected to avert, he left (or proposed to leave) or (while the danger persisted) refused to return to his place of work or any dangerous part of his place of work, or

(e) in circumstances of danger which the employee reasonably believed to be serious and imminent, he took (or proposed to take) appropriate steps to protect himself or other persons from the danger.

(2) For the purposes of subsection (1)(e) whether steps which an employee took (or proposed to take) were appropriate is to be judged by reference to all the circumstances including, in particular, his knowledge and the facilities and advice available to him at the time.

(3) Where the reason (or, if more than one, the principal reason) for the dismissal of an employee is that specified in subsection (1)(e), he shall not be regarded as unfairly dismissed if the employer shows that it was (or would have been) so negligent for the employee to take the steps which he took (or proposed to take) that a reasonable employer might have dismissed him for taking (or proposing to take) them.

101 Shop workers and betting workers who refuse Sunday work

(1) Where an employee who is—

(a) a protected shop worker or an opted-out shop worker, or

(b) a protected betting worker or an opted-out betting worker,

is dismissed, he shall be regarded for the purposes of this Part as unfairly dismissed if the reason (or, if more than one, the principal reason) for the dismissal is that he refused (or proposed to refuse) to do shop work, or betting work, on Sunday or on a particular Sunday.

(2) Subsection (1) does not apply in relation to an opted-out shop worker or an opted-out betting worker where the reason (or principal reason) for the dismissal is that he refused (or proposed to refuse) to do shop work, or betting work, on any Sunday or Sundays falling before the end of the notice period.

(3) A shop worker or betting worker who is dismissed shall be regarded for the purposes of this Part as unfairly dismissed if the reason (or, if more than one, the principal reason) for the dismissal is that the shop worker or betting worker gave (or proposed to give) an opting-out notice to the employer.

(4) For the purposes of section 36(2)(b) or 41(1)(b), the appropriate date in relation to this section is the effective date of termination.

102 Trustees of occupational pension schemes

(1) An employee who is dismissed shall be regarded for the purposes of this Part as unfairly dismissed if the reason (or, if more than one, the principal reason) for the dismissal is that, being a trustee of a relevant occupational pension scheme which

relates to his employment, the employee performed (or proposed to perform) any functions as such a trustee.

(2) In this section "relevant occupational pension scheme" means an occupational pension scheme (as defined in section 1 of the Pension Schemes Act 1993) established under a trust.

103 Employee representatives

An employee who is dismissed shall be regarded for the purposes of this Part as unfairly dismissed if the reason (or, if more than one, the principal reason) for the dismissal is that the employee, being—

(a) an employee representative for the purposes of Chapter II of Part IV of the Trade Union and Labour Relations (Consolidation) Act 1992 (redundancies) or Regulations 10 and 11 of the Transfer of Undertakings (Protection of Employment) Regulations 1981, or

(b) a candidate in an election in which any person elected will, on being elected, be such an employee representative,

performed (or proposed to perform) any functions or activities as such an employee representative or candidate.

104 Assertion of statutory right

(1) An employee who is dismissed shall be regarded for the purposes of this Part as unfairly dismissed if the reason (or, if more than one, the principal reason) for the dismissal is that the employee—

(a) brought proceedings against the employer to enforce a right of his which is a relevant statutory right, or

(b) alleged that the employer had infringed a right of his which is a relevant statutory right.

(2) It is immaterial for the purposes of subsection (1)—

(a) whether or not the employee has the right, or

(b) whether or not the right has been infringed;

but, for that subsection to apply, the claim to the right and that it has been infringed must be made in good faith.

(3) It is sufficient for subsection (1) to apply that the employee, without specifying the right, made it reasonably clear to the employer what the right claimed to have been infringed was.

(4) The following are relevant statutory rights for the purposes of this section—

(a) any right conferred by this Act for which the remedy for its infringement is by way of a complaint or reference to an industrial tribunal,

(b) the right conferred by section 86 of this Act, and

(c) the rights conferred by sections 68, 86, 146, 168, 169 and 170 of the Trade Union and Labour Relations (Consolidation) Act 1992 (deductions from pay, union activities and time off).

105 Redundancy

(1) An employee who is dismissed shall be regarded for the purposes of this Part as unfairly dismissed if—

(a) the reason (or, if more than one, the principal reason) for the dismissal is that the employee was redundant,

(b) it is shown that the circumstances constituting the redundancy applied equally to one or more other employees in the same undertaking who held positions similar to that held by the employee and who have not been dismissed by the employer, and

(c) it is shown that any of subsections (2) to (7) applies.

(2) This subsection applies if the reason (or, if more than one, the principal reason) for which the employee was selected for dismissal was that specified in any of paragraphs (a) to (d) of subsection (1) of section 99 (read with subsection (2) of that section) or subsection (3) of that section (and any requirements of the paragraph, or subsection, not relating to the reason are satisfied).

(3) This subsection applies if the reason (or, if more than one, the principal reason) for which the employee was selected for dismissal was one of those specified in subsection (1) of section 100 (read with subsections (2) and (3) of that section).

(4) This subsection applies if either—

(a) the employee was a protected shop worker or an opted-out shop worker, or a protected betting worker or an opted-out betting worker, and the reason (or, if more than one, the principal reason) for which the employee was selected for dismissal was that specified in subsection (1) of section 101 (read with subsection (2) of that section), or

(b) the employee was a shop worker or a betting worker and the reason (or, if more than one, the principal reason) for which the employee was selected for dismissal was that specified in subsection (3) of that section.

(5) This subsection applies if the reason (or, if more than one, the principal reason) for which the employee was selected for dismissal was that specified in section 102(1).

(6) This subsection applies if the reason (or, if more than one, the principal reason) for which the employee was selected for dismissal was that specified in section 103.

(7) This subsection applies if the reason (or, if more than one, the principal reason) for which the employee was selected for dismissal was one of those specified in subsection (1) of section 104 (read with subsections (2) and (3) of that section).

(8) For the purposes of section 36(2)(b) or 41(1)(b), the appropriate date in relation to this section is the effective date of termination.

(9) In this Part "redundancy case" means a case where paragraphs (a) and (b) of subsection (1) of this section are satisfied.

106 Replacements

(1) Where this section applies to an employee he shall be regarded for the purposes of section 98(1)(b) as having been dismissed for a substantial reason of a kind such as to justify the dismissal of an employee holding the position which the employee held.

(2) This section applies to an employee where—

(a) on engaging him the employer informs him in writing that his employment will be terminated on the resumption of work by another employee who is, or will be, absent wholly or partly because of pregnancy or childbirth, and

(b) the employer dismisses him in order to make it possible to give work to the other employee.

(3) This section also applies to an employee where—

(a) on engaging him the employer informs him in writing that his employment will be terminated on the end of a suspension of another employee from work on medical grounds or maternity grounds (within the meaning of Part VII), and

(b) the employer dismisses him in order to make it possible to allow the resumption of work by the other employee.

(4) Subsection (1) does not affect the operation of section 98(4) in a case to which this section applies.

107 Pressure on employer to dismiss unfairly

(1) This section applies where there falls to be determined for the purposes of this Part a question—

(a) as to the reason, or principal reason, for which an employee was dismissed,

(b) whether the reason or principal reason for which an employee was dismissed was a reason fulfilling the requirement of section 98(1)(b), or

(c) whether an employer acted reasonably in treating the reason or principal reason for which an employee was dismissed as a sufficient reason for dismissing him.

(2) In determining the question no account shall be taken of any pressure which by calling, organising, procuring or financing a strike or other industrial action, or threatening to do so, was exercised on the employer to dismiss the employee; and the question shall be determined as if no such pressure had been exercised.

Exclusion of right

108 Qualifying period of employment

(1) Section 94 does not apply to the dismissal of an employee unless he has been continuously employed for a period of not less than two years ending with the effective date of termination.

(2) If an employee is dismissed by reason of any such requirement or recommendation as is referred to in section 64(2), subsection (1) has effect in relation to that dismissal as if for the words "two years" there were substituted the words "one month".

(3) Subsection (1) does not apply if—

(a) section 84 or 96(1) applies,

(b) subsection (1) of section 99 (read with subsection (2) of that section) or subsection (3) of that section applies,

(c) subsection (1) of section 100 (read with subsections (2) and (3) of that section) applies,

(d) subsection (1) of section 101 (read with subsection (2) of that section) or subsection (3) of that section applies,
(e) section 102 applies,
(f) section 103 applies,
(g) subsection (1) of section 104 (read with subsections (2) and (3) of that section) applies, or
(h) section 105 applies.

109 Upper age limit

(1) Section 94 does not apply to the dismissal of an employee if on or before the effective date of termination he has attained—
(a) in a case where—
(i) in the undertaking in which the employee was employed there was a normal retiring age for an employee holding the position held by the employee, and
(ii) the age was the same whether the employee holding that position was a man or a woman,
that normal retiring age, and
(b) in any other case, the age of sixty-five.

(2) Subsection (1) does not apply if—
(a) section 84 or 96(1) applies,
(b) subsection (1) of section 99 (read with subsection (2) of that section) or subsection (3) of that section applies,
(c) subsection (1) of section 100 (read with subsections (2) and (3) of that section) applies,
(d) subsection (1) of section 101 (read with subsection (2) of that section) or subsection (3) of that section applies,
(e) section 102 applies,
(f) section 103 applies,
(g) subsection (1) of section 104 (read with subsections (2) and (3) of that section) applies, or
(h) section 105 applies.

110 Dismissal procedures agreements

(1) Where a dismissal procedures agreement is designated by an order under subsection (3) which is for the time being in force—
(a) the provisions of that agreement relating to dismissal shall have effect in substitution for any rights under section 94, and
(b) accordingly, section 94 does not apply to the dismissal of an employee from any employment if it is employment to which, and he is an employee to whom, those provisions of the agreement apply.

(2) Subsection (1) does not apply if—
(a) section 84 or 96(1) applies,
(b) subsection (1) of section 99 (read with subsection (2) of that section) or subsection (3) of that section applies,

(c) subsection (1) of section 101 (read with subsection (2) of that section) or subsection (3) of that section applies,

(d) subsection (1) of section 104 (read with subsections (2) and (3) of that section) applies, or

(e) section 105(1) and (4) applies.

(3) An order designating a dismissal procedures agreement may be made by the Secretary of State, on an application being made to him jointly by all the parties to the agreement, if he is satisfied that—

(a) every trade union which is a party to the agreement is an independent trade union,

(b) the agreement provides for procedures to be followed in cases where an employee claims that he has been, or is in the course of being, unfairly dismissed,

(c) those procedures are available without discrimination to all employees falling within any description to which the agreement applies,

(d) the remedies provided by the agreement in respect of unfair dismissal are on the whole as beneficial as (but not necessarily identical with) those provided in respect of unfair dismissal by this Part,

(e) the procedures provided by the agreement include a right to arbitration or adjudication by an independent referee, or by a tribunal or other independent body, in cases where (by reason of an equality of votes or for any other reason) a decision cannot otherwise be reached, and

(f) the provisions of the agreement are such that it can be determined with reasonable certainty whether or not a particular employee is one to whom the agreement applies.

(4) If at any time when an order under subsection (3) is in force in relation to a dismissal procedures agreement the Secretary of State is satisfied, whether on an application made to him by any of the parties to the agreement or otherwise, either—

(a) that it is the desire of all the parties to the agreement that the order should be revoked, or

(b) that the agreement no longer satisfies all the conditions specified in subsection (3),

the Secretary of State shall revoke the order by an order under this subsection.

(5) The transitional provisions which may be made in an order under subsection (4) include, in particular, provisions directing—

(a) that an employee—

(i) shall not be excluded from his right under section 94 where the effective date of termination falls within a transitional period which ends with the date on which the order takes effect and which is specified in the order, and

(ii) shall have an extended time for presenting a complaint under section 111 in respect of a dismissal where the effective date of termination falls within that period, and

(b) that, where the effective date of termination falls within such a transitional period, an industrial tribunal shall, in determining any complaint of unfair dismissal presented by an employee to whom the dismissal procedures agreement applies, have regard to such considerations as are specified in the order (in addition to those specified in this Part and section 10(4) and (5) of the Industrial Tribunals Act 1996).

CHAPTER II

REMEDIES FOR UNFAIR DISMISSAL

Introductory

111 Complaints to industrial tribunal

(1) A complaint may be presented to an industrial tribunal against an employer by any person that he was unfairly dismissed by the employer.

(2) Subject to subsection (3), an industrial tribunal shall not consider a complaint under this section unless it is presented to the tribunal—

- (a) before the end of the period of three months beginning with the effective date of termination, or
- (b) within such further period as the tribunal considers reasonable in a case where it is satisfied that it was not reasonably practicable for the complaint to be presented before the end of that period of three months.

(3) Where a dismissal is with notice, an industrial tribunal shall consider a complaint under this section if it is presented after the notice is given but before the effective date of termination.

(4) In relation to a complaint which is presented as mentioned in subsection (3), the provisions of this Act, so far as they relate to unfair dismissal, have effect as if—

- (a) references to a complaint by a person that he was unfairly dismissed by his employer included references to a complaint by a person that his employer has given him notice in such circumstances that he will be unfairly dismissed when the notice expires,
- (b) references to reinstatement included references to the withdrawal of the notice by the employer,
- (c) references to the effective date of termination included references to the date which would be the effective date of termination on the expiry of the notice, and
- (d) references to an employee ceasing to be employed included references to an employee having been given notice of dismissal.

112 The remedies: orders and compensation

(1) This section applies where, on a complaint under section 111, an industrial tribunal finds that the grounds of the complaint are well-founded.

(2) The tribunal shall—

- (a) explain to the complainant what orders may be made under section 113 and in what circumstances they may be made, and
- (b) ask him whether he wishes the tribunal to make such an order.

(3) If the complainant expresses such a wish, the tribunal may make an order under section 113.

(4) If no order is made under section 113, the tribunal shall make an award of compensation for unfair dismissal (calculated in accordance with sections 118 to 127) to be paid by the employer to the employee.

Orders for reinstatement or re-engagement

113 The orders

An order under this section may be—

(a) an order for reinstatement (in accordance with section 114), or

(b) an order for re-engagement (in accordance with section 115),

as the tribunal may decide.

114 Order for reinstatement

(1) An order for reinstatement is an order that the employer shall treat the complainant in all respects as if he had not been dismissed.

(2) On making an order for reinstatement the tribunal shall specify—

(a) any amount payable by the employer in respect of any benefit which the complainant might reasonably be expected to have had but for the dismissal (including arrears of pay) for the period between the date of termination of employment and the date of reinstatement,

(b) any rights and privileges (including seniority and pension rights) which must be restored to the employee, and

(c) the date by which the order must be complied with.

(3) If the complainant would have benefited from an improvement in his terms and conditions of employment had he not been dismissed, an order for reinstatement shall require him to be treated as if he had benefited from that improvement from the date on which he would have done so but for being dismissed.

(4) In calculating for the purposes of subsection (2)(a) any amount payable by the employer, the tribunal shall take into account, so as to reduce the employer's liability, any sums received by the complainant in respect of the period between the date of termination of employment and the date of reinstatement by way of—

(a) wages in lieu of notice or ex gratia payments paid by the employer, or

(b) remuneration paid in respect of employment with another employer,

and such other benefits as the tribunal thinks appropriate in the circumstances.

(5) Where a dismissal is treated as taking place by virtue of section 96, references in this section to the date of termination of employment are to the notified date of return.

115 Order for re-engagement

(1) An order for re-engagement is an order, on such terms as the tribunal may decide, that the complainant be engaged by the employer, or by a successor of the employer

or by an associated employer, in employment comparable to that from which he was dismissed or other suitable employment.

(2) On making an order for re-engagement the tribunal shall specify the terms on which re-engagement is to take place, including—

(a) the identity of the employer,

(b) the nature of the employment,

(c) the remuneration for the employment,

(d) any amount payable by the employer in respect of any benefit which the complainant might reasonably be expected to have had but for the dismissal (including arrears of pay) for the period between the date of termination of employment and the date of re-engagement,

(e) any rights and privileges (including seniority and pension rights) which must be restored to the employee, and

(f) the date by which the order must be complied with.

(3) In calculating for the purposes of subsection (2)(d) any amount payable by the employer, the tribunal shall take into account, so as to reduce the employer's liability, any sums received by the complainant in respect of the period between the date of termination of employment and the date of re-engagement by way of—

(a) wages in lieu of notice or ex gratia payments paid by the employer, or

(b) remuneration paid in respect of employment with another employer,

and such other benefits as the tribunal thinks appropriate in the circumstances.

(4) Where a dismissal is treated as taking place by virtue of section 96, references in this section to the date of termination of employment are to the notified date of return.

116 Choice of order and its terms

(1) In exercising its discretion under section 113 the tribunal shall first consider whether to make an order for reinstatement and in so doing shall take into account—

(a) whether the complainant wishes to be reinstated,

(b) whether it is practicable for the employer to comply with an order for reinstatement, and

(c) where the complainant caused or contributed to some extent to the dismissal, whether it would be just to order his reinstatement.

(2) If the tribunal decides not to make an order for reinstatement it shall then consider whether to make an order for re-engagement and, if so, on what terms.

(3) In so doing the tribunal shall take into account—

(a) any wish expressed by the complainant as to the nature of the order to be made,

(b) whether it is practicable for the employer (or a successor or an associated employer) to comply with an order for re-engagement, and

(c) where the complainant caused or contributed to some extent to the dismissal, whether it would be just to order his re-engagement and (if so) on what terms.

(4) Except in a case where the tribunal takes into account contributory fault under subsection (3)(c) it shall, if it orders re-engagement, do so on terms which are, so far as is reasonably practicable, as favourable as an order for reinstatement.

(5) Where in any case an employer has engaged a permanent replacement for a dismissed employee, the tribunal shall not take that fact into account in determining, for the purposes of subsection (1)(b) or (3)(b), whether it is practicable to comply with an order for reinstatement or re-engagement.

(6) Subsection (5) does not apply where the employer shows—

(a) that it was not practicable for him to arrange for the dismissed employee's work to be done without engaging a permanent replacement, or

(b) that—

(i) he engaged the replacement after the lapse of a reasonable period, without having heard from the dismissed employee that he wished to be reinstated or re-engaged, and

(ii) when the employer engaged the replacement it was no longer reasonable for him to arrange for the dismissed employee's work to be done except by a permanent replacement.

117 Enforcement of order and compensation

(1) An industrial tribunal shall make an award of compensation, to be paid by the employer to the employee, if—

(a) an order under section 113 is made and the complainant is reinstated or re-engaged, but

(b) the terms of the order are not fully complied with.

(2) Subject to section 124, the amount of the compensation shall be such as the tribunal thinks fit having regard to the loss sustained by the complainant in consequence of the failure to comply fully with the terms of the order.

(3) Subject to subsections (1) and (2), if an order under section 113 is made but the complainant is not reinstated or re-engaged in accordance with the order, the tribunal shall make—

(a) an award of compensation for unfair dismissal (calculated in accordance with sections 118 to 127), and

(b) except where this paragraph does not apply, an additional award of compensation of the appropriate amount,

to be paid by the employer to the employee.

(4) Subsection (3)(b) does not apply where—

(a) the employer satisfies the tribunal that it was not practicable to comply with the order, or

(b) the reason (or, if more than one, the principal reason)—

(i) in a redundancy case, for selecting the employee for dismissal, or

(ii) otherwise, for the dismissal,

is one of those specified in section 100(1)(a) and (b), 102(1) or 103.

(5) In subsection (3)(b) "the appropriate amount" means—

(a) where the dismissal is of a description referred to in subsection (6), not less than twenty-six nor more than fifty-two weeks' pay, and

(b) in any other case, not less than thirteen nor more than twenty-six weeks' pay.

(6) The descriptions of dismissal in respect of which an employer may incur a higher additional award in accordance with subsection (5)(a) are—

(a) a dismissal which is an act of discrimination within the meaning of the Sex Discrimination Act 1975 which is unlawful by virtue of that Act, and

(b) a dismissal which is an act of discrimination within the meaning of the Race Relations Act 1976 which is unlawful by virtue of that Act.

(7) Where in any case an employer has engaged a permanent replacement for a dismissed employee, the tribunal shall not take that fact into account in determining for the purposes of subsection (4)(a) whether it was practicable to comply with the order for reinstatement or re-engagement unless the employer shows that it was not practicable for him to arrange for the dismissed employee's work to be done without engaging a permanent replacement.

(8) Where in any case an industrial tribunal finds that the complainant has unreasonably prevented an order under section 113 from being complied with, in making an award of compensation for unfair dismissal (in accordance with sections 118 to 127) it shall take that conduct into account as a failure on the part of the complainant to mitigate his loss.

Compensation

118 General

(1) Where a tribunal makes an award of compensation for unfair dismissal under section 112(4) or 117(3)(a) the award shall consist of—

(a) a basic award (calculated in accordance with sections 119 to 122 and 126), and

(b) a compensatory award (calculated in accordance with sections 123, 124, 126 and 127).

(2) Where this subsection applies, the award shall also include a special award calculated in accordance with section 125 unless—

(a) the complainant does not request the tribunal to make an order under section 113, or

(b) the case falls within section 121.

(3) Subsection (2) applies where the reason (or, if more than one, the principal reason)—

(a) in a redundancy case, for selecting the employee for dismissal, or

(b) otherwise, for the dismissal,

is one of those specified in section 100(1)(a) and (b), 102(1) or 103.

119 Basic award

(1) Subject to the provisions of this section, sections 120 to 122 and section 126, the amount of the basic award shall be calculated by—

(a) determining the period, ending with the effective date of termination, during which the employee has been continuously employed,

(b) reckoning backwards from the end of that period the number of years of employment falling within that period, and

(c) allowing the appropriate amount for each of those years of employment.

(2) In subsection (1)(c) "the appropriate amount" means—

(a) one and a half weeks' pay for a year of employment in which the employee was not below the age of forty-one,

(b) one week's pay for a year of employment (not within paragraph (a)) in which he was not below the age of twenty-two, and

(c) half a week's pay for a year of employment not within paragraph (a) or (b).

(3) Where twenty years of employment have been reckoned under subsection (1), no account shall be taken under that subsection of any year of employment earlier than those twenty years.

(4) Where the effective date of termination is after the sixty-fourth anniversary of the day of the employee's birth, the amount arrived at under subsections (1) to (3) shall be reduced by the appropriate fraction.

(5) In subsection (4) "the appropriate fraction" means the fraction of which—

(a) the numerator is the number of whole months reckoned from the sixty-fourth anniversary of the day of the employee's birth in the period beginning with that anniversary and ending with the effective date of termination, and

(b) the denominator is twelve.

(6) Subsections (4) and (5) do not apply to a case within section 96(1).

120 Basic award: minimum in certain cases

(1) The amount of the basic award (before any reduction under section 122) shall not be less than £2,770 where the reason (or, if more than one, the principal reason)—

(a) in a redundancy case, for selecting the employee for dismissal, or

(b) otherwise, for the dismissal,

is one of those specified in section 100(1)(a) and (b), 102(1) or 103.

(2) The Secretary of State may by order increase the sum specified in subsection (1).

121 Basic award of two weeks' pay in certain cases

The amount of the basic award shall be two weeks' pay where the tribunal finds that the reason (or, where there is more than one, the principal reason) for the dismissal of the employee is that he was redundant and the employee—

(a) by virtue of section 138 is not regarded as dismissed for the purposes of Part XI, or

(b) by virtue of section 141 is not, or (if he were otherwise entitled) would not be, entitled to a redundancy payment.

122 Basic award: reductions

(1) Where the tribunal finds that the complainant has unreasonably refused an offer by the employer which (if accepted) would have the effect of reinstating the complainant in his employment in all respects as if he had not been dismissed, the tribunal shall reduce or further reduce the amount of the basic award to such extent as it considers just and equitable having regard to that finding.

(2) Where the tribunal considers that any conduct of the complainant before the dismissal (or, where the dismissal was with notice, before the notice was given) was such that it would be just and equitable to reduce or further reduce the amount of the basic award to any extent, the tribunal shall reduce or further reduce that amount accordingly.

(3) Subsection (2) does not apply in a redundancy case unless the reason for selecting the employee for dismissal was one of those specified in section 100(1)(a) and (b), 102(1) or 103; and in such a case subsection (2) applies only to so much of the basic award as is payable because of section 120.

(4) The amount of the basic award shall be reduced or further reduced by the amount of—

(a) any redundancy payment awarded by the tribunal under Part XI in respect of the same dismissal, or

(b) any payment made by the employer to the employee on the ground that the dismissal was by reason of redundancy (whether in pursuance of Part XI or otherwise).

123 Compensatory award

(1) Subject to the provisions of this section and sections 124 and 126, the amount of the compensatory award shall be such amount as the tribunal considers just and equitable in all the circumstances having regard to the loss sustained by the complainant in consequence of the dismissal in so far as that loss is attributable to action taken by the employer.

(2) The loss referred to in subsection (1) shall be taken to include—

(a) any expenses reasonably incurred by the complainant in consequence of the dismissal, and

(b) subject to subsection (3), loss of any benefit which he might reasonably be expected to have had but for the dismissal.

(3) The loss referred to in subsection (1) shall be taken to include in respect of any loss of—

(a) any entitlement or potential entitlement to a payment on account of dismissal by reason of redundancy (whether in pursuance of Part XI or otherwise), or

(b) any expectation of such a payment,

only the loss referable to the amount (if any) by which the amount of that payment would have exceeded the amount of a basic award (apart from any reduction under section 122) in respect of the same dismissal.

(4) In ascertaining the loss referred to in subsection (1) the tribunal shall apply the same rule concerning the duty of a person to mitigate his loss as applies to damages recoverable under the common law of England and Wales or (as the case may be) Scotland.

(5) In determining, for the purposes of subsection (1), how far any loss sustained by the complainant was attributable to action taken by the employer, no account shall be taken of any pressure which by—

(a) calling, organising, procuring or financing a strike or other industrial action, or

(b) threatening to do so,

was exercised on the employer to dismiss the employee; and that question shall be determined as if no such pressure had been exercised.

(6) Where the tribunal finds that the dismissal was to any extent caused or contributed to by any action of the complainant, it shall reduce the amount of the compensatory award by such proportion as it considers just and equitable having regard to that finding.

(7) If the amount of any payment made by the employer to the employee on the ground that the dismissal was by reason of redundancy (whether in pursuance of Part XI or otherwise) exceeds the amount of the basic award which would be payable but for section 122(4), that excess goes to reduce the amount of the compensatory award.

124 Limit of compensatory award etc

(1) The amount of—

(a) any compensation awarded to a person under section 117(1) and (2), or

(b) a compensatory award to a person calculated in accordance with section 123,

shall not exceed £11,300.

(2) The Secretary of State may by order increase the sum specified in subsection (1).

(3) In the case of compensation awarded to a person under section 117(1) and (2), the limit imposed by this section may be exceeded to the extent necessary to enable the award fully to reflect the amount specified as payable under section 114(2)(a) or section 115(2)(d).

(4) Where—

(a) a compensatory award is an award under paragraph (a) of subsection (3) of section 117, and

(b) an additional award falls to be made under paragraph (b) of that subsection,

the limit imposed by this section on the compensatory award may be exceeded to the extent necessary to enable the aggregate of the compensatory and additional awards fully to reflect the amount specified as payable under section 114(2)(a) or section 115(2)(d).

(5) The limit imposed by this section applies to the amount which the industrial tribunal would, apart from this section, award in respect of the subject matter of the complaint after taking into account—

(a) any payment made by the respondent to the complainant in respect of that matter, and

(b) any reduction in the amount of the award required by any enactment or rule of law.

125 Special award

(1) Subject to the following provisions, the amount of the special award shall be—

(a) one week's pay multiplied by 104, or

(b) £13,775,

whichever is the greater, but shall not exceed £27,500.

(2) Where the award of compensation is made under section 117(3)(a) then, unless the employer satisfies the tribunal that it was not practicable to comply with the order under section 113, the amount of the special award shall be increased to—

(a) one week's pay multiplied by 156, or

(b) £20,600,

whichever is the greater (but subject to the following provisions).

(3) In a case where the amount of the basic award is reduced under section 119(4), the amount of the special award shall be reduced by the same fraction.

(4) Where the tribunal considers that any conduct of the complainant before the dismissal (or, where the dismissal was with notice, before the notice was given) was such that it would be just and equitable to reduce or further reduce the amount of the special award to any extent, the tribunal shall reduce or further reduce that amount accordingly.

(5) Where the tribunal finds that the complainant has unreasonably—

(a) prevented an order under section 113 from being complied with, or

(b) refused an offer by the employer (made otherwise than in compliance with such an order) which, if accepted, would have the effect of reinstating the complainant in his employment in all respects as if he had not been dismissed,

the tribunal shall reduce or further reduce the amount of the special award to such extent as it considers just and equitable having regard to that finding.

(6) Where the employer has engaged a permanent replacement for the complainant, the tribunal shall not take that fact into account in determining for the purposes of subsection (2) whether it was practicable to comply with an order under section 113 unless the employer shows that it was not practicable for him to arrange for the complainant's work to be done without engaging a permanent replacement.

(7) The Secretary of State may by order increase any of the sums specified in subsections (1) and (2).

126 Acts which are both unfair dismissal and discrimination

(1) This section applies where compensation falls to be awarded in respect of any act both under—

(a) the provisions of this Act relating to unfair dismissal, and

(b) either or both of the Sex Discrimination Act 1975 and the Race Relations Act 1976.

(2) An industrial tribunal shall not award compensation under any one of those two or three Acts in respect of any loss or other matter which is or has been taken into account under the other, or any of the others, by the tribunal (or another industrial tribunal) in awarding compensation on the same or another complaint in respect of that act.

127 Dismissal of woman at or after end of maternity leave period

Where section 84 applies in relation to an employee, compensation in any unfair dismissal proceedings shall be assessed without regard to the right conferred on the employee by section 79.

Interim relief

128 Interim relief pending determination of complaint

(1) An employee who presents a complaint to an industrial tribunal—

(a) that he has been unfairly dismissed by his employer, and

(b) that the reason (or, if more than one, the principal reason) for the dismissal is one of those specified in section 100(1)(a) and (b), 102(1) or 103,

may apply to the tribunal for interim relief.

(2) The tribunal shall not entertain an application for interim relief unless it is presented to the tribunal before the end of the period of seven days immediately following the effective date of termination (whether before, on or after that date).

(3) The tribunal shall determine the application for interim relief as soon as practicable after receiving the application.

(4) The tribunal shall give to the employer not later than seven days before the date of the hearing a copy of the application together with notice of the date, time and place of the hearing.

(5) The tribunal shall not exercise any power it has of postponing the hearing of an application for interim relief except where it is satisfied that special circumstances exist which justify it in doing so.

129 Procedure on hearing of application and making of order

(1) This section applies where, on hearing an employee's application for interim relief, it appears to the tribunal that it is likely that on determining the complaint to which the application relates the tribunal will find that the reason (or, if more than one, the principal reason) for his dismissal is one of those specified in section 100(1)(a) and (b), 102(1) or 103.

(2) The tribunal shall announce its findings and explain to both parties (if present)—

(a) what powers the tribunal may exercise on the application, and

(b) in what circumstances it will exercise them.

(3) The tribunal shall ask the employer (if present) whether he is willing, pending the determination or settlement of the complaint—

(a) to reinstate the employee (that is, to treat him in all respects as if he had not been dismissed), or

(b) if not, to re-engage him in another job on terms and conditions not less favourable than those which would have been applicable to him if he had not been dismissed.

(4) For the purposes of subsection (3)(b) "terms and conditions not less favourable than those which would have been applicable to him if he had not been dismissed" means, as regards seniority, pension rights and other similar rights, that the period prior to the dismissal should be regarded as continuous with his employment following the dismissal.

(5) If the employer states that he is willing to reinstate the employee, the tribunal shall make an order to that effect.

(6) If the employer—

(a) states that he is willing to re-engage the employee in another job, and

(b) specifies the terms and conditions on which he is willing to do so,

the tribunal shall ask the employee whether he is willing to accept the job on those terms and conditions.

(7) If the employee is willing to accept the job on those terms and conditions, the tribunal shall make an order to that effect.

(8) If the employee is not willing to accept the job on those terms and conditions—

(a) where the tribunal is of the opinion that the refusal is reasonable, the tribunal shall make an order for the continuation of his contract of employment, and

(b) otherwise, the tribunal shall make no order.

(9) If on the hearing of an application for interim relief the employer—

(a) fails to attend before the tribunal, or

(b) states that he is unwilling either to reinstate or re-engage the employee as mentioned in subsection (3),

the tribunal shall make an order for the continuation of the employee's contract of employment.

130 Order for continuation of contract of employment

(1) An order under section 129 for the continuation of a contract of employment is an order that the contract of employment continue in force—

(a) for the purposes of pay or any other benefit derived from the employment, seniority, pension rights and other similar matters, and

(b) for the purposes of determining for any purpose the period for which the employee has been continuously employed,

from the date of its termination (whether before or after the making of the order) until the determination or settlement of the complaint.

(2) Where the tribunal makes such an order it shall specify in the order the amount which is to be paid by the employer to the employee by way of pay in respect of each normal pay period, or part of any such period, falling between the date of dismissal and the determination or settlement of the complaint.

(3) Subject to the following provisions, the amount so specified shall be that which the employee could reasonably have been expected to earn during that period, or part, and shall be paid—

(a) in the case of a payment for any such period falling wholly or partly after the making of the order, on the normal pay day for that period, and

(b) in the case of a payment for any past period, within such time as may be specified in the order.

(4) If an amount is payable in respect only of part of a normal pay period, the amount shall be calculated by reference to the whole period and reduced proportionately.

(5) Any payment made to an employee by an employer under his contract of employment, or by way of damages for breach of that contract, in respect of a normal pay period, or part of any such period, goes towards discharging the employer's liability in respect of that period under subsection (2); and, conversely, any payment under that subsection in respect of a period goes towards discharging any liability of the employer under, or in respect of breach of, the contract of employment in respect of that period.

(6) If an employee, on or after being dismissed by his employer, receives a lump sum which, or part of which, is in lieu of wages but is not referable to any normal pay

period, the tribunal shall take the payment into account in determining the amount of pay to be payable in pursuance of any such order.

(7) For the purposes of this section, the amount which an employee could reasonably have been expected to earn, his normal pay period and the normal pay day for each such period shall be determined as if he had not been dismissed.

131 Application for variation or revocation of order

(1) At any time between—

(a) the making of an order under section 129, and

(b) the determination or settlement of the complaint,

the employer or the employee may apply to an industrial tribunal for the revocation or variation of the order on the ground of a relevant change of circumstances since the making of the order.

(2) Sections 128 and 129 apply in relation to such an application as in relation to an original application for interim relief except that, in the case of an application by the employer, section 128(4) has effect with the substitution of a reference to the employee for the reference to the employer.

132 Consequence of failure to comply with order

(1) If, on the application of an employee, an industrial tribunal is satisfied that the employer has not complied with the terms of an order for the reinstatement or re-engagement of the employee under section 129(5) or (7), the tribunal shall—

(a) make an order for the continuation of the employee's contract of employment, and

(b) order the employer to pay compensation to the employee.

(2) Compensation under subsection (1)(b) shall be of such amount as the tribunal considers just and equitable in all the circumstances having regard—

(a) to the infringement of the employee's right to be reinstated or re-engaged in pursuance of the order, and

(b) to any loss suffered by the employee in consequence of the non-compliance.

(3) Section 130 applies to an order under subsection (1)(a) as in relation to an order under section 129.

(4) If on the application of an employee an industrial tribunal is satisfied that the employer has not complied with the terms of an order for the continuation of a contract of employment subsection (5) or (6) applies.

(5) Where the non-compliance consists of a failure to pay an amount by way of pay specified in the order—

(a) the tribunal shall determine the amount owed by the employer on the date of the determination, and

(b) if on that date the tribunal also determines the employee's complaint that he has been unfairly dismissed, it shall specify that amount separately from any other sum awarded to the employee.

(6) In any other case, the tribunal shall order the employer to pay the employee such compensation as the tribunal considers just and equitable in all the circumstances

having regard to any loss suffered by the employee in consequence of the non-compliance.

CHAPTER III

SUPPLEMENTARY

133 Death of employer or employee

(1) Where—

(a) an employer has given notice to an employee to terminate his contract of employment, and

(b) before that termination the employee or the employer dies,

this Part applies as if the contract had been duly terminated by the employer by notice expiring on the date of the death.

(2) Where—

(a) an employee's contract of employment has been terminated,

(b) by virtue of subsection (2) or (4) of section 97 a date later than the effective date of termination as defined in subsection (1) of that section is to be treated for certain purposes as the effective date of termination, and

(c) the employer or the employee dies before that date,

subsection (2) or (4) of section 97 applies as if the notice referred to in that subsection as required by section 86 expired on the date of the death.

(3) Where an employee has died, sections 113 to 116 do not apply; and, accordingly, if the industrial tribunal finds that the grounds of the complaint are well-founded, the case shall be treated as falling within section 112(4) as a case in which no order is made under section 113.

(4) Subsection (3) does not prejudice an order for reinstatement or re-engagement made before the employee's death.

(5) Where an order for reinstatement or re-engagement has been made and the employee dies before the order is complied with—

(a) if the employer has before the death refused to reinstate or re-engage the employee in accordance with the order, subsections (3) to (6) of section 117 apply, and an award shall be made under subsection (3)(b) of that section, unless the employer satisfies the tribunal that it was not practicable at the time of the refusal to comply with the order, and

(b) if there has been no such refusal, subsections (1) and (2) of that section apply if the employer fails to comply with any ancillary terms of the order which remain capable of fulfilment after the employee's death as they would apply to such a failure to comply fully with the terms of an order where the employee had been reinstated or re-engaged.

134 Teachers in aided schools

(1) Where a teacher in an aided school is dismissed by the governors of the school in pursuance of a requirement of the local education authority under paragraph (a) of the

proviso to section 24(2) of the Education Act 1944, this Part has effect in relation to the dismissal as if—

(a) the local education authority had at all material times been the teacher's employer,

(b) the local education authority had dismissed him, and

(c) the reason or principal reason for which they did so had been the reason or principal reason for which they required his dismissal.

(2) For the purposes of a complaint under section 111 as it has effect by virtue of subsection (1)—

(a) section 117(4)(a) applies as if for the words "not practicable to comply" there were substituted the words "not practicable for the local education authority to permit compliance", and

(b) section 123(5) applies as if the references in it to the employer were to the local education authority.

PART XI

REDUNDANCY PAYMENTS ETC.

CHAPTER I

RIGHT TO REDUNDANCY PAYMENT

135 The right

(1) An employer shall pay a redundancy payment to any employee of his if the employee—

(a) is dismissed by the employer by reason of redundancy, or

(b) is eligible for a redundancy payment by reason of being laid off or kept on short-time.

(2) Subsection (1) has effect subject to the following provisions of this Part (including, in particular, sections 140 to 144, 149 to 152, 155 to 161 and 164).

CHAPTER II

RIGHT ON DISMISSAL BY REASON OF REDUNDANCY

Dismissal by reason of redundancy

136 Circumstances in which an employee is dismissed

(1) Subject to the provisions of this section and sections 137 and 138, for the purposes of this Part an employee is dismissed by his employer if (and only if)—

(a) the contract under which he is employed by the employer is terminated by the employer (whether with or without notice),

(b) he is employed under a contract for a fixed term and that term expires without being renewed under the same contract, or

(c) the employee terminates the contract under which he is employed (with or without notice) in circumstances in which he is entitled to terminate it without notice by reason of the employer's conduct.

(2) Subsection (1)(c) does not apply if the employee terminates the contract without notice in circumstances in which he is entitled to do so by reason of a lock-out by the employer.

(3) An employee shall be taken to be dismissed by his employer for the purposes of this Part if—

(a) the employer gives notice to the employee to terminate his contract of employment, and

(b) at a time within the obligatory period of notice the employee gives notice in writing to the employer to terminate the contract of employment on a date earlier than the date on which the employer's notice is due to expire.

(4) In this Part the "obligatory period of notice", in relation to notice given by an employer to terminate an employee's contract of employment, means—

(a) the actual period of the notice in a case where the period beginning at the time when the notice is given and ending at the time when it expires is equal to the minimum period which (by virtue of any enactment or otherwise) is required to be given by the employer to terminate the contract of employment, and

(b) the period which—

(i) is equal to the minimum period referred to in paragraph (a), and

(ii) ends at the time when the notice expires,

in any other case.

(5) Where in accordance with any enactment or rule of law—

(a) an act on the part of an employer, or

(b) an event affecting an employer (including, in the case of an individual, his death),

operates to terminate a contract under which an employee is employed by him, the act or event shall be taken for the purposes of this Part to be a termination of the contract by the employer.

137 Failure to permit return after childbirth treated as dismissal

(1) Subject to subsection (2) and section 138, where an employee who—

(a) has the right conferred by section 79, and

(b) has exercised it in accordance with section 82,

is not permitted to return to work, she shall be taken for the purposes of this Part to be dismissed for the reason for which she was not permitted to return with effect from the notified day of return (being deemed to have been continuously employed until that day).

(2) Where in proceedings arising out of a failure to permit an employee to return to work pursuant to the right conferred by section 79 the employer shows—

(a) that the reason for the failure is that the employee is redundant, and

(b) that the employee was, or (had she continued to be employed by him) would have been, dismissed by reason of redundancy on a day falling after the commencement of her maternity leave period and before the notified day of return,

for the purposes of this Part the employee shall not be taken to be dismissed with effect from the notified day of return but shall be taken to be dismissed by reason of redundancy with effect from that earlier day (being deemed to have been continuously employed until that earlier day).

138 No dismissal in cases of renewal of contract or re-engagement

(1) Where—

(a) an employee's contract of employment is renewed, or he is re-engaged under a new contract of employment in pursuance of an offer (whether in writing or not) made before the end of his employment under the previous contract, and

(b) the renewal or re-engagement takes effect either immediately on, or after an interval of not more than four weeks after, the end of that employment,

the employee shall not be regarded for the purposes of this Part as dismissed by his employer by reason of the ending of his employment under the previous contract.

(2) Subsection (1) does not apply if—

(a) the provisions of the contract as renewed, or of the new contract, as to—

(i) the capacity and place in which the employee is employed, and

(ii) the other terms and conditions of his employment,

differ (wholly or in part) from the corresponding provisions of the previous contract, and

(b) during the period specified in subsection (3)—

(i) the employee (for whatever reason) terminates the renewed or new contract, or gives notice to terminate it and it is in consequence terminated, or

(ii) the employer, for a reason connected with or arising out of any difference between the renewed or new contract and the previous contract, terminates the renewed or new contract, or gives notice to terminate it and it is in consequence terminated.

(3) The period referred to in subsection (2)(b) is the period—

(a) beginning at the end of the employee's employment under the previous contract, and

(b) ending with—

(i) the period of four weeks beginning with the date on which the employee starts work under the renewed or new contract, or

(ii) such longer period as may be agreed in accordance with subsection (6) for the purpose of retraining the employee for employment under that contract;

and is in this Part referred to as the "trial period".

(4) Where subsection (2) applies, for the purposes of this Part—

(a) the employee shall be regarded as dismissed on the date on which his employment under the previous contract (or, if there has been more than one trial period, the original contract) ended, and

(b) the reason for the dismissal shall be taken to be the reason for which the employee was then dismissed, or would have been dismissed had the offer (or original offer) of renewed or new employment not been made, or the reason which resulted in that offer being made.

(5) Subsection (2) does not apply if the employee's contract of employment is again renewed, or he is again re-engaged under a new contract of employment, in circumstances such that subsection (1) again applies.

(6) For the purposes of subsection (3)(b)(ii) a period of retraining is agreed in accordance with this subsection only if the agreement—

(a) is made between the employer and the employee or his representative before the employee starts work under the contract as renewed, or the new contract,

(b) is in writing,

(c) specifies the date on which the period of retraining ends, and

(d) specifies the terms and conditions of employment which will apply in the employee's case after the end of that period.

139 Redundancy

(1) For the purposes of this Act an employee who is dismissed shall be taken to be dismissed by reason of redundancy if the dismissal is wholly or mainly attributable to—

(a) the fact that his employer has ceased or intends to cease—

(i) to carry on the business for the purposes of which the employee was employed by him, or

(ii) to carry on that business in the place where the employee was so employed, or

(b) the fact that the requirements of that business—

(i) for employees to carry out work of a particular kind, or

(ii) for employees to carry out work of a particular kind in the place where the employee was employed by the employer,

have ceased or diminished or are expected to cease or diminish.

(2) For the purposes of subsection (1) the business of the employer together with the business or businesses of his associated employers shall be treated as one (unless either of the conditions specified in paragraphs (a) and (b) of that subsection would be satisfied without so treating them).

(3) For the purposes of subsection (1) the activities carried on by a local education authority with respect to the schools maintained by it, and the activities carried on by the governors of those schools, shall be treated as one business (unless either of the conditions specified in paragraphs (a) and (b) of that subsection would be satisfied without so treating them).

(4) Where—

(a) the contract under which a person is employed is treated by section 136(5) as terminated by his employer by reason of an act or event, and

(b) the employee's contract is not renewed and he is not re-engaged under a new contract of employment,

he shall be taken for the purposes of this Act to be dismissed by reason of redundancy if the circumstances in which his contract is not renewed, and he is not re-engaged, are wholly or mainly attributable to either of the facts stated in paragraphs (a) and (b) of subsection (1).

(5) In its application to a case within subsection (4), paragraph (a)(i) of subsection (1) has effect as if the reference in that subsection to the employer included a reference to any person to whom, in consequence of the act or event, power to dispose of the business has passed.

(6) In subsection (1) "cease" and "diminish" mean cease and diminish either permanently or temporarily and for whatever reason.

Exclusions

140 Summary dismissal

(1) Subject to subsections (2) and (3), an employee is not entitled to a redundancy payment by reason of dismissal where his employer, being entitled to terminate his contract of employment without notice by reason of the employee's conduct, terminates it either—

(a) without notice,

(b) by giving shorter notice than that which, in the absence of conduct entitling the employer to terminate the contract without notice, the employer would be required to give to terminate the contract, or

(c) by giving notice which includes, or is accompanied by, a statement in writing that the employer would, by reason of the employee's conduct, be entitled to terminate the contract without notice.

(2) Where an employee who—

(a) has been given notice by his employer to terminate his contract of employment, or

(b) has given notice to his employer under section 148(1) indicating his intention to claim a redundancy payment in respect of lay-off or short-time,

takes part in a strike at any relevant time in circumstances which entitle the employer to treat the contract of employment as terminable without notice, subsection (1) does not apply if the employer terminates the contract by reason of his taking part in the strike.

(3) Where the contract of employment of an employee who—

(a) has been given notice by his employer to terminate his contract of employment, or

(b) has given notice to his employer under section 148(1) indicating his intention to claim a redundancy payment in respect of lay-off or short-time,

is terminated as mentioned in subsection (1) at any relevant time otherwise than by reason of his taking part in a strike, an industrial tribunal may determine that the employer is liable to make an appropriate payment to the employee if on a reference to the tribunal it appears to the tribunal, in the circumstances of the case, to be just and equitable that the employee should receive it.

(4) In subsection (3) "appropriate payment" means—

(a) the whole of the redundancy payment to which the employee would have been entitled apart from subsection (1), or

(b) such part of that redundancy payment as the tribunal thinks fit.

(5) In this section "relevant time"—

(a) in the case of an employee who has been given notice by his employer to terminate his contract of employment, means any time within the obligatory period of notice, and

(b) in the case of an employee who has given notice to his employer under section 148(1), means any time after the service of the notice.

141 Renewal of contract or re-engagement

(1) This section applies where an offer (whether in writing or not) is made to an employee before the end of his employment—

(a) to renew his contract of employment, or

(b) to re-engage him under a new contract of employment,

with renewal or re-engagement to take effect either immediately on, or after an interval of not more than four weeks after, the end of his employment.

(2) Where subsection (3) is satisfied, the employee is not entitled to a redundancy payment if he unreasonably refuses the offer.

(3) This subsection is satisfied where—

(a) the provisions of the contract as renewed, or of the new contract, as to—

(i) the capacity and place in which the employee would be employed, and

(ii) the other terms and conditions of his employment,

would not differ from the corresponding provisions of the previous contract, or

(b) those provisions of the contract as renewed, or of the new contract, would differ from the corresponding provisions of the previous contract but the offer constitutes an offer of suitable employment in relation to the employee.

(4) The employee is not entitled to a redundancy payment if—

(a) his contract of employment is renewed, or he is re-engaged under a new contract of employment, in pursuance of the offer,

(b) the provisions of the contract as renewed or new contract as to the capacity or place in which he is employed or the other terms and conditions of his employment differ (wholly or in part) from the corresponding provisions of the previous contract,

(c) the employment is suitable in relation to him, and

(d) during the trial period he unreasonably terminates the contract, or unreasonably gives notice to terminate it and it is in consequence terminated.

142 Employee anticipating expiry of employer's notice

(1) Subject to subsection (3), an employee is not entitled to a redundancy payment where—

(a) he is taken to be dismissed by virtue of section 136(3) by reason of giving to his employer notice terminating his contract of employment on a date earlier than the date on which notice by the employer terminating the contract is due to expire,

(b) before the employee's notice is due to expire, the employer gives him a notice such as is specified in subsection (2), and

(c) the employee does not comply with the requirements of that notice.

(2) The employer's notice referred to in subsection (1)(b) is a notice in writing—

(a) requiring the employee to withdraw his notice terminating the contract of employment and to continue in employment until the date on which the employer's notice terminating the contract expires, and

(b) stating that, unless he does so, the employer will contest any liability to pay to him a redundancy payment in respect of the termination of his contract of employment.

(3) An industrial tribunal may determine that the employer is liable to make an appropriate payment to the employee if on a reference to the tribunal it appears to the tribunal, having regard to—

(a) the reasons for which the employee seeks to leave the employment, and

(b) the reasons for which the employer requires him to continue in it,

to be just and equitable that the employee should receive the payment.

(4) In subsection (3) "appropriate payment" means—

(a) the whole of the redundancy payment to which the employee would have been entitled apart from subsection (1), or

(b) such part of that redundancy payment as the tribunal thinks fit.

143 Strike during currency of employer's notice

(1) This section applies where—

(a) an employer has given notice to an employee to terminate his contract of employment ("notice of termination"),

(b) after the notice is given the employee begins to take part in a strike of employees of the employer, and

(c) the employer serves on the employee a notice of extension.

(2) A notice of extension is a notice in writing which—

(a) requests the employee to agree to extend the contract of employment beyond the time of expiry by a period comprising as many available days as the number of working days lost by striking ("the proposed period of extension"),

(b) indicates the reasons for which the employer makes that request, and

(c) states that the employer will contest any liability to pay the employee a redundancy payment in respect of the dismissal effected by the notice of termination unless either—

(i) the employee complies with the request, or

(ii) the employer is satisfied that, in consequence of sickness or injury or otherwise, the employee is unable to comply with it or that (even though he is able to comply with it) it is reasonable in the circumstances for him not to do so.

(3) Subject to subsections (4) and (5), if the employee does not comply with the request contained in the notice of extension, he is not entitled to a redundancy payment by reason of the dismissal effected by the notice of termination.

(4) Subsection (3) does not apply if the employer agrees to pay a redundancy payment to the employee in respect of the dismissal effected by the notice of termination even though he has not complied with the request contained in the notice of extension.

(5) An industrial tribunal may determine that the employer is liable to make an appropriate payment to the employee if on a reference to the tribunal it appears to the tribunal that—

(a) the employee has not complied with the request contained in the notice of extension and the employer has not agreed to pay a redundancy payment in respect of the dismissal effected by the notice of termination, but

(b) either the employee was unable to comply with the request or it was reasonable in the circumstances for him not to comply with it.

(6) In subsection (5) "appropriate payment" means—

(a) the whole of the redundancy payment to which the employee would have been entitled apart from subsection (3), or

(b) such part of that redundancy payment as the tribunal thinks fit.

(7) If the employee—

(a) complies with the request contained in the notice of extension, or

(b) does not comply with it but attends at his proper or usual place of work and is ready and willing to work on one or more (but not all) of the available days within the proposed period of extension,

the notice of termination has effect, and shall be deemed at all material times to have had effect, as if the period specified in it had been appropriately extended; and sections 87 to 91 accordingly apply as if the period of notice required by section 86 were extended to a corresponding extent.

(8) In subsection (7) "appropriately extended" means—

(a) in a case within paragraph (a) of that subsection, extended beyond the time of expiry by an additional period equal to the proposed period of extension, and

(b) in a case within paragraph (b) of that subsection, extended beyond the time of expiry up to the end of the day (or last of the days) on which he attends at his proper or usual place of work and is ready and willing to work.

144 Provisions supplementary to section 143

(1) For the purposes of section 143 an employee complies with the request contained in a notice of extension if, but only if, on each available day within the proposed period of extension, he—

(a) attends at his proper or usual place of work, and

(b) is ready and willing to work,

whether or not he has signified his agreement to the request in any other way.

(2) The reference in section 143(2) to the number of working days lost by striking is a reference to the number of working days in the period—

(a) beginning with the date of service of the notice of termination, and

(b) ending with the time of expiry,

which are days on which the employee in question takes part in a strike of employees of his employer.

(3) In section 143 and this section—

"available day", in relation to an employee, means a working day beginning at or after the time of expiry which is a day on which he is not taking part in a strike of employees of the employer, "available day within the proposed period of extension" means an available day which begins before the end of the proposed period of extension,

"time of expiry", in relation to a notice of termination, means the time at which the notice would expire apart from section 143, and

"working day", in relation to an employee, means a day on which, in accordance with his contract of employment, he is normally required to work.

(4) Neither the service of a notice of extension nor any extension by virtue of section 143(7) of the period specified in a notice of termination affects—

(a) any right either of the employer or of the employee to terminate the contract of employment (whether before, at or after the time of expiry) by a further notice or without notice, or

(b) the operation of this Part in relation to any such termination of the contract of employment.

Supplementary

145 The relevant date

(1) For the purposes of the provisions of this Act relating to redundancy payments "the relevant date" in relation to the dismissal of an employee has the meaning given by this section.

(2) Subject to the following provisions of this section, "the relevant date"—

(a) in relation to an employee whose contract of employment is terminated by notice, whether given by his employer or by the employee, means the date on which the notice expires,

(b) in relation to an employee whose contract of employment is terminated without notice, means the date on which the termination takes effect, and

(c) in relation to an employee who is employed under a contract for a fixed term which expires without being renewed under the same contract, means the date on which the term expires.

(3) Where the employee is taken to be dismissed by virtue of section 136(3) the "relevant date" means the date on which the employee's notice to terminate his contract of employment expires.

(4) Where the employee is regarded by virtue of section 138(4) as having been dismissed on the date on which his employment under an earlier contract ended, "the relevant date" means—

(a) for the purposes of section 164(1), the date which is the relevant date as defined by subsection (2) in relation to the renewed or new contract or, where there has been more than one trial period, the last such contract, and

(b) for the purposes of any other provision, the date which is the relevant date as defined by subsection (2) in relation to the previous contract or, where there has been more than one such trial period, the original contract.

(5) Where—

(a) the contract of employment is terminated by the employer, and

(b) the notice required by section 86 to be given by an employer would, if duly given on the material date, expire on a date later than the relevant date (as defined by the previous provisions of this section), for the purposes of sections 155, 162(1) and 227(3) the later date is the relevant date.

(6) In subsection (5)(b) "the material date" means—

(a) the date when notice of termination was given by the employer, or

(b) where no notice was given, the date when the contract of employment was terminated by the employer.

(7) Where an employee is taken to be dismissed for the purposes of this Part by virtue of section 137(1), references in this Part to the relevant date are (unless the context otherwise requires) to the notified date of return.

146 Provisions supplementing sections 138 and 141

(1) In sections 138 and 141—

(a) references to re-engagement are to re-engagement by the employer or an associated employer, and

(b) references to an offer are to an offer made by the employer or an associated employer.

(2) For the purposes of the application of section 138(1) or 141(1) to a contract under which the employment ends on a Friday, Saturday or Sunday—

(a) the renewal or re-engagement shall be treated as taking effect immediately on the ending of the employment under the previous contract if it takes effect on or before the next Monday after that Friday, Saturday or Sunday, and

(b) the interval of four weeks to which those provisions refer shall be calculated as if the employment had ended on that next Monday.

(3) Where section 138 or 141 applies in a case within section 137(1)—

(a) references to a renewal or re-engagement taking effect immediately on, or after an interval of not more than four weeks after, the end of the employment are to a renewal or re-engagement taking effect on, or after an interval of not more than four weeks after, the notified day of return, and

(b) references to provisions of the previous contract are to the provisions of the contract under which the employee worked immediately before the beginning of her maternity leave period.

CHAPTER III

RIGHT BY REASON OF LAY-OFF OR SHORT-TIME

Lay-off and short-time

147 Meaning of "lay-off" and "short-time"

(1) For the purposes of this Part an employee shall be taken to be laid off for a week if—

(a) he is employed under a contract on terms and conditions such that his remuneration under the contract depends on his being provided by the employer with work of the kind which he is employed to do, but

(b) he is not entitled to any remuneration under the contract in respect of the week because the employer does not provide such work for him.

(2) For the purposes of this Part an employee shall be taken to be kept on short-time for a week if by reason of a diminution in the work provided for the employee by his employer (being work of a kind which under his contract the employee is employed to do) the employee's remuneration for the week is less than half a week's pay.

148 Eligibility by reason of lay-off or short-time

(1) Subject to the following provisions of this Part, for the purposes of this Part an employee is eligible for a redundancy payment by reason of being laid off or kept on short-time if—

(a) he gives notice in writing to his employer indicating (in whatever terms) his intention to claim a redundancy payment in respect of lay-off or short-time (referred to in this Part as "notice of intention to claim"), and

(b) before the service of the notice he has been laid off or kept on short-time in circumstances in which subsection (2) applies.

(2) This subsection applies if the employee has been laid off or kept on short-time—

(a) for four or more consecutive weeks of which the last before the service of the notice ended on, or not more than four weeks before, the date of service of the notice, or

(b) for a series of six or more weeks (of which not more than three were consecutive) within a period of thirteen weeks, where the last week of the series before the service of the notice ended on, or not more than four weeks before, the date of service of the notice.

Exclusions

149 Counter-notices

Where an employee gives to his employer notice of intention to claim but—

(a) the employer gives to the employee, within seven days after the service of that notice, notice in writing (referred to in this Part as a "counter-notice") that he will contest any liability to pay to the employee a redundancy payment in pursuance of the employee's notice, and

(b) the employer does not withdraw the counter-notice by a subsequent notice in writing,

the employee is not entitled to a redundancy payment in pursuance of his notice of intention to claim except in accordance with a decision of an industrial tribunal.

150 Resignation

(1) An employee is not entitled to a redundancy payment by reason of being laid off or kept on short-time unless he terminates his contract of employment by giving such period of notice as is required for the purposes of this section before the end of the relevant period.

(2) The period of notice required for the purposes of this section—

(a) where the employee is required by his contract of employment to give more than one week's notice to terminate the contract, is the minimum period which he is required to give, and

(b) otherwise, is one week.

(3) In subsection (1) "the relevant period"—

(a) if the employer does not give a counter-notice within seven days after the service of the notice of intention to claim, is three weeks after the end of those seven days,

(b) if the employer gives a counter-notice within that period of seven days but withdraws it by a subsequent notice in writing, is three weeks after the service of the notice of withdrawal, and

(c) if—

(i) the employer gives a counter-notice within that period of seven days, and does not so withdraw it, and

(ii) a question as to the right of the employee to a redundancy payment in pursuance of the notice of intention to claim is referred to an industrial tribunal,

is three weeks after the tribunal has notified to the employee its decision on that reference.

(4) For the purposes of subsection (3)(c) no account shall be taken of—

(a) any appeal against the decision of the tribunal, or

(b) any proceedings or decision in consequence of any such appeal.

151 Dismissal

(1) An employee is not entitled to a redundancy payment by reason of being laid off or kept on short-time if he is dismissed by his employer.

(2) Subsection (1) does not prejudice any right of the employee to a redundancy payment in respect of the dismissal.

152 Likelihood of full employment

(1) An employee is not entitled to a redundancy payment in pursuance of a notice of intention to claim if—

(a) on the date of service of the notice it was reasonably to be expected that the employee (if he continued to be employed by the same employer) would, not later than four weeks after that date, enter on a period of employment of not less than thirteen weeks during which he would not be laid off or kept on short-time for any week, and

(b) the employer gives a counter-notice to the employee within seven days after the service of the notice of intention to claim.

(2) Subsection (1) does not apply where the employee—

(a) continues or has continued, during the next four weeks after the date of service of the notice of intention to claim, to be employed by the same employer, and

(b) is or has been laid off or kept on short-time for each of those weeks.

Supplementary

153 The relevant date

For the purposes of the provisions of this Act relating to redundancy payments "the relevant date" in relation to a notice of intention to claim or a right to a redundancy payment in pursuance of such a notice—

(a) in a case falling within paragraph (a) of subsection (2) of section 148, means the date on which the last of the four or more consecutive weeks before the service of the notice came to an end, and

(b) in a case falling within paragraph (b) of that subsection, means the date on which the last of the series of six or more weeks before the service of the notice came to an end.

154 Provisions supplementing sections 148 and 152

For the purposes of sections 148(2) and 152(2)—

(a) it is immaterial whether a series of weeks consists wholly of weeks for which the employee is laid off or wholly of weeks for which he is kept on short-time or partly of the one and partly of the other, and

(b) no account shall be taken of any week for which an employee is laid off or kept on short-time where the lay-off or short-time is wholly or mainly attributable to a strike or a lock-out (whether or not in the trade or industry in which the employee is employed and whether in Great Britain or elsewhere).

CHAPTER IV

GENERAL EXCLUSIONS FROM RIGHT

155 Qualifying period of employment

An employee does not have any right to a redundancy payment unless he has been continuously employed for a period of not less than two years ending with the relevant date.

156 Upper age limit

(1) An employee does not have any right to a redundancy payment if before the relevant date he has attained—

(a) in a case where—

(i) in the business for the purposes of which the employee was employed there was a normal retiring age of less than sixty-five for an employee holding the position held by the employee, and

(ii) the age was the same whether the employee holding that position was a man or woman,

that normal retiring age, and

(b) in any other case, the age of sixty-five.

(2) Subsection (1) does not apply to a case within section 137(1).

157 Exemption orders

(1) Where an order under this section is in force in respect of an agreement covered by this section, an employee who, immediately before the relevant date, is an employee to whom the agreement applies does not have any right to a redundancy payment.

(2) An agreement is covered by this section if it is an agreement between—

(a) one or more employers or organisations of employers, and

(b) one or more trade unions representing employees,

under which employees to whom the agreement applies have a right in certain circumstances to payments on the termination of their contracts of employment.

(3) Where, on the application of all the parties to an agreement covered by this section, the Secretary of State is satisfied, having regard to the provisions of the agreement, that the employees to whom the agreement applies should not have any right to a redundancy payment, he may make an order under this section in respect of the agreement.

(4) The Secretary of State shall not make an order under this section in respect of an agreement unless the agreement indicates (in whatever terms) the willingness of the parties to it to submit to an industrial tribunal any question arising under the agreement as to—

(a) the right of an employee to a payment on the termination of his employment, or

(b) the amount of such a payment.

(5) An order revoking an earlier order under this section may be made in pursuance of an application by all or any of the parties to the agreement in question or in the absence of such an application.

(6) Subsection (1) does not apply to a case within section 137(1).

158 Pension rights

(1) The Secretary of State shall by regulations make provision for excluding the right to a redundancy payment, or reducing the amount of any redundancy payment, in such cases to which subsection (2) applies as are prescribed by the regulations.

(2) This subsection applies to cases in which an employee has (whether by virtue of any statutory provision or otherwise) a right or claim (whether or not legally enforceable) to a periodical payment or lump sum by way of pension, gratuity or superannuation allowance which—

(a) is to be paid by reference to his employment by a particular employer, and

(b) is to be paid, or to begin to be paid, at the time when he leaves the employment or within such period after he leaves the employment as may be prescribed by the regulations.

(3) The regulations shall secure that the right to a redundancy payment shall not be excluded, and that the amount of a redundancy payment shall not be reduced, by reason of any right or claim to a periodical payment or lump sum, in so far as the payment or lump sum—

(a) represents compensation for loss of employment or for loss or diminution of emoluments or of pension rights, and

(b) is payable under a statutory provision (whether passed or made before or after the passing of this Act).

(4) In relation to any case where (in accordance with any provision of this Part) an industrial tribunal determines that an employer is liable to pay part (but not the whole) of a redundancy payment the references in this section to a redundancy payment, or to the amount of a redundancy payment, are to the part of the redundancy payment, or to the amount of the part.

159 Public offices etc

A person does not have any right to a redundancy payment in respect of any employment which—

(a) is employment in a public office within the meaning of section 39 of the Superannuation Act 1965, or

(b) is for the purposes of pensions and other superannuation benefits treated (whether by virtue of that Act or otherwise) as service in the civil service of the State.

160 Overseas government employment

(1) A person does not have any right to a redundancy payment in respect of employment in any capacity under the Government of an overseas territory.

(2) The reference in subsection (1) to the Government of an overseas territory includes a reference to—

(a) a Government constituted for two or more overseas territories, and

(b) any authority established for the purpose of providing or administering services which are common to, or relate to matters of common interest to, two or more overseas territories.

(3) In this section references to an overseas territory are to any territory or country outside the United Kingdom.

161 Domestic servants

(1) A person does not have any right to a redundancy payment in respect of employment as a domestic servant in a private household where the employer is the parent (or step-parent), grandparent, child (or step-child), grandchild or brother or sister (or half-brother or half-sister) of the employee.

(2) Subject to that, the provisions of this Part apply to an employee who is employed as a domestic servant in a private household as if—

(a) the household were a business, and

(b) the maintenance of the household were the carrying on of that business by the employer.

CHAPTER V

OTHER PROVISIONS ABOUT REDUNDANCY PAYMENTS

162 Amount of a redundancy payment

(1) The amount of a redundancy payment shall be calculated by—

(a) determining the period, ending with the relevant date, during which the employee has been continuously employed,

(b) reckoning backwards from the end of that period the number of years of employment falling within that period, and

(c) allowing the appropriate amount for each of those years of employment.

(2) In subsection (1)(c) "the appropriate amount" means—

(a) one and a half weeks' pay for a year of employment in which the employee was not below the age of forty-one,

(b) one week's pay for a year of employment (not within paragraph (a)) in which he was not below the age of twenty-two, and

(c) half a week's pay for each year of employment not within paragraph (a) or (b).

(3) Where twenty years of employment have been reckoned under subsection (1), no account shall be taken under that subsection of any year of employment earlier than those twenty years.

(4) Where the relevant date is after the sixty-fourth anniversary of the day of the employee's birth, the amount arrived at under subsections (1) to (3) shall be reduced by the appropriate fraction.

(5) In subsection (4) "the appropriate fraction" means the fraction of which—

(a) the numerator is the number of whole months reckoned from the sixty-fourth anniversary of the day of the employee's birth in the period beginning with that anniversary and ending with the relevant date, and

(b) the denominator is twelve.

(6) Subsections (1) to (5) apply for the purposes of any provision of this Part by virtue of which an industrial tribunal may determine that an employer is liable to pay to an employee—

(a) the whole of the redundancy payment to which the employee would have had a right apart from some other provision, or

(b) such part of the redundancy payment to which the employee would have had a right apart from some other provision as the tribunal thinks fit,

as if any reference to the amount of a redundancy payment were to the amount of the redundancy payment to which the employee would have been entitled apart from that other provision.

(7) Subsections (4) and (5) do not apply to a case within section 137(1).

(8) This section has effect subject to any regulations under section 158 by virtue of which the amount of a redundancy payment, or part of a redundancy payment, may be reduced.

163 References to industrial tribunals

(1) Any question arising under this Part as to—

(a) the right of an employee to a redundancy payment, or

(b) the amount of a redundancy payment,

shall be referred to and determined by an industrial tribunal.

(2) For the purposes of any such reference, an employee who has been dismissed by his employer shall, unless the contrary is proved, be presumed to have been so dismissed by reason of redundancy.

(3) Any question whether an employee will become entitled to a redundancy payment if he is not dismissed by his employer and he terminates his contract of employment as mentioned in section 150(1) shall for the purposes of this Part be taken to be a question as to the right of the employee to a redundancy payment.

(4) Where an order under section 157 is in force in respect of an agreement, this section has effect in relation to any question arising under the agreement as to the right of an employee to a payment on the termination of his employment, or as to the amount of such a payment, as if the payment were a redundancy payment and the question arose under this Part.

164 Claims for redundancy payment

(1) An employee does not have any right to a redundancy payment unless, before the end of the period of six months beginning with the relevant date—

(a) the payment has been agreed and paid,

(b) the employee has made a claim for the payment by notice in writing given to the employer,

(c) a question as to the employee's right to, or the amount of, the payment has been referred to an industrial tribunal, or

(d) a complaint relating to his dismissal has been presented by the employee under section 111.

(2) An employee is not deprived of his right to a redundancy payment by subsection (1) if, during the period of six months immediately following the period mentioned in that subsection, the employee—

(a) makes a claim for the payment by notice in writing given to the employer,

(b) refers to an industrial tribunal a question as to his right to, or the amount of, the payment, or

(c) presents a complaint relating to his dismissal under section 111,

and it appears to the tribunal to be just and equitable that the employee should receive a redundancy payment.

(3) In determining under subsection (2) whether it is just and equitable that an employee should receive a redundancy payment an industrial tribunal shall have regard to—

(a) the reason shown by the employee for his failure to take any such step as is referred to in subsection (2) within the period mentioned in subsection (1), and

(b) all the other relevant circumstances.

165 Written particulars of redundancy payment

(1) On making any redundancy payment, otherwise than in pursuance of a decision of a tribunal which specifies the amount of the payment to be made, the employer shall give to the employee a written statement indicating how the amount of the payment has been calculated.

(2) An employer who without reasonable excuse fails to comply with subsection (1) is guilty of an offence and liable on summary conviction to a fine not exceeding level 1 on the standard scale.

(3) If an employer fails to comply with the requirements of subsection (1), the employee may by notice in writing to the employer require him to give to the employee a written statement complying with those requirements within such period (not being less than one week beginning with the day on which the notice is given) as may be specified in the notice.

(4) An employer who without reasonable excuse fails to comply with a notice under subsection (3) is guilty of an offence and liable on summary conviction to a fine not exceeding level 3 on the standard scale.

CHAPTER VI

PAYMENTS BY SECRETARY OF STATE

166 Applications for payments

(1) Where an employee claims that his employer is liable to pay to him an employer's payment and either—

(a) that the employee has taken all reasonable steps, other than legal proceedings, to recover the payment from the employer and the employer has refused or failed to pay it, or has paid part of it and has refused or failed to pay the balance, or

(b) that the employer is insolvent and the whole or part of the payment remains unpaid,

the employee may apply to the Secretary of State for a payment under this section.

(2) In this Part "employer's payment", in relation to an employee, means—

(a) a redundancy payment which his employer is liable to pay to him under this Part, or

(b) a payment which his employer is, under an agreement in respect of which an order is in force under section 157, liable to make to him on the termination of his contract of employment.

(3) In relation to any case where (in accordance with any provision of this Part) an industrial tribunal determines that an employer is liable to pay part (but not the whole) of a redundancy payment the reference in subsection (2)(a) to a redundancy payment is to the part of the redundancy payment.

(4) In subsection (1)(a) "legal proceedings"—

(a) does not include any proceedings before an industrial tribunal, but

(b) includes any proceedings to enforce a decision or award of an industrial tribunal.

(5) An employer is insolvent for the purposes of subsection (1)(b)—

(a) where the employer is an individual, if (but only if) subsection (6) is satisfied, and

(b) where the employer is a company, if (but only if) subsection (7) is satisfied.

(6) This subsection is satisfied in the case of an employer who is an individual—

(a) in England and Wales if—

(i) he has been adjudged bankrupt or has made a composition or arrangement with his creditors, or

(ii) he has died and his estate falls to be administered in accordance with an order under section 421 of the Insolvency Act 1986, and

(b) in Scotland if—

(i) sequestration of his estate has been awarded or he has executed a trust deed for his creditors or has entered into a composition contract, or

(ii) he has died and a judicial factor appointed under section 11A of the Judicial Factors (Scotland) Act 1889 is required by that section to divide his insolvent estate among his creditors.

(7) This subsection is satisfied in the case of an employer which is a company—

(a) if a winding up order or an administration order has been made, or a resolution for voluntary winding up has been passed, with respect to the company,

(b) if a receiver or (in England and Wales only) a manager of the company's undertaking has been duly appointed, or (in England and Wales only) possession has been taken, by or on behalf of the holders of any debentures secured by a floating charge, of any property of the company comprised in or subject to the charge, or

(c) if a voluntary arrangement proposed in the case of the company for the purposes of Part I of the Insolvency Act 1986 has been approved under that Part of that Act.

167 Making of payments

(1) Where, on an application under section 166 by an employee in relation to an employer's payment, the Secretary of State is satisfied that the requirements specified in subsection (2) are met, he shall pay to the employee out of the National Insurance Fund a sum calculated in accordance with section 168 but reduced by so much (if any) of the employer's payment as has already been paid.

(2) The requirements referred to in subsection (1) are—

(a) that the employee is entitled to the employer's payment, and

(b) that one of the conditions specified in paragraphs (a) and (b) of subsection (1) of section 166 is fulfilled,

and, in a case where the employer's payment is a payment such as is mentioned in subsection (2)(b) of that section, that the employee's right to the payment arises by virtue of a period of continuous employment (computed in accordance with the provisions of the agreement in question) which is not less than two years.

(3) Where under this section the Secretary of State pays a sum to an employee in respect of an employer's payment—

(a) all rights and remedies of the employee with respect to the employer's payment, or (if the Secretary of State has paid only part of it) all the rights and remedies of the employee with respect to that part of the employer's payment, are transferred to and vest in the Secretary of State, and

(b) any decision of an industrial tribunal requiring the employer's payment to be paid to the employee has effect as if it required that payment, or that part of it which the Secretary of State has paid, to be paid to the Secretary of State.

(4) Any money recovered by the Secretary of State by virtue of subsection (3) shall be paid into the National Insurance Fund.

168 Amount of payments

(1) The sum payable to an employee by the Secretary of State under section 167—

(a) where the employer's payment to which the employee's application under section 166 relates is a redundancy payment or a part of a redundancy payment, is a sum equal to the amount of the redundancy payment or part, and

(b) where the employer's payment to which the employee's application under section 166 relates is a payment which the employer is liable to make under an agreement in respect of which an order is in force under section 157, is a sum equal to the amount of the employer's payment or of the relevant redundancy payment, whichever is less.

(2) The reference in subsection (1)(b) to the amount of the relevant redundancy payment is to the amount of the redundancy payment which the employer would have been liable to pay to the employee on the assumptions specified in subsection (3).

(3) The assumptions referred to in subsection (2) are that—

(a) the order in force in respect of the agreement had not been made,

(b) the circumstances in which the employer's payment is payable had been such that the employer was liable to pay a redundancy payment to the employee in those circumstances,

(c) the relevant date, in relation to any such redundancy payment, had been the date on which the termination of the employee's contract of employment is treated as having taken effect for the purposes of the agreement, and

(d) in so far as the provisions of the agreement relating to the circumstances in which the continuity of an employee's period of employment is to be treated as broken, and the weeks which are to count in computing a period of employment, are inconsistent with the provisions of Chapter I of Part XIV, the provisions of the agreement were substituted for those provisions.

169 Information relating to applications for payments

(1) Where an employee makes an application to the Secretary of State under section 166, the Secretary of State may, by notice in writing given to the employer, require the employer—

(a) to provide the Secretary of State with such information, and

(b) to produce for examination on behalf of the Secretary of State documents in his custody or under his control of such description,

as the Secretary of State may reasonably require for the purpose of determining whether the application is well-founded.

(2) Where a person on whom a notice is served under subsection (1) fails without reasonable excuse to comply with a requirement imposed by the notice, he is guilty

of an offence and liable on summary conviction to a fine not exceeding level 3 on the standard scale.

(3) A person is guilty of an offence if—

(a) in providing any information required by a notice under subsection (1), he makes a statement which he knows to be false in a material particular or recklessly makes a statement which is false in a material particular, or

(b) he produces for examination in accordance with a notice under subsection (1) a document which to his knowledge has been wilfully falsified.

(4) A person guilty of an offence under subsection (3) is liable—

(a) on summary conviction, to a fine not exceeding the statutory maximum or to imprisonment for a term not exceeding three months, or to both, or

(b) on conviction on indictment, to a fine or to imprisonment for a term not exceeding two years, or to both.

170 References to industrial tribunals

(1) Where on an application made to the Secretary of State for a payment under section 166 it is claimed that an employer is liable to pay an employer's payment, there shall be referred to an industrial tribunal—

(a) any question as to the liability of the employer to pay the employer's payment, and

(b) any question as to the amount of the sum payable in accordance with section 168.

(2) For the purposes of any reference under this section an employee who has been dismissed by his employer shall, unless the contrary is proved, be presumed to have been so dismissed by reason of redundancy.

CHAPTER VII

SUPPLEMENTARY

Application of Part to particular cases

171 Employment not under contract of employment

(1) The Secretary of State may by regulations provide that, subject to such exceptions and modifications as may be prescribed by the regulations, this Part and the provisions of this Act supplementary to this Part have effect in relation to any employment of a description to which this section applies as may be so prescribed as if—

(a) it were employment under a contract of employment,

(b) any person engaged in employment of that description were an employee, and

(c) such person as may be determined by or under the regulations were his employer.

(2) This section applies to employment of any description which—

(a) is employment in the case of which secondary Class 1 contributions are payable under Part I of the Social Security Contributions and Benefits Act 1992 in respect of persons engaged in it, but

(b) is not employment under a contract of service or of apprenticeship or employment of any description falling within subsection (3).

(3) The following descriptions of employment fall within this subsection—

(a) any employment such as is mentioned in section 159 (whether as originally enacted or as modified by an order under section 209(1)),

(b) any employment remunerated out of the revenue of the Duchy of Lancaster or the Duchy of Cornwall,

(c) any employment remunerated out of the Queen's Civil List, and

(d) any employment remunerated out of Her Majesty's Privy Purse.

172 Termination of employment by statute

(1) The Secretary of State may by regulations provide that, subject to such exceptions and modifications as may be prescribed by the regulations, this Part has effect in relation to any person who by virtue of any statutory provisions—

(a) is transferred to, and becomes a member of, a body specified in those provisions, but

(b) at a time so specified ceases to be a member of that body unless before that time certain conditions so specified have been fulfilled,

as if the cessation of his membership of that body by virtue of those provisions were dismissal by his employer by reason of redundancy.

(2) The power conferred by subsection (1) is exercisable whether or not membership of the body in question constitutes employment within the meaning of section 230(5); and, where that membership does not constitute such employment, that power may be exercised in addition to any power exercisable under section 171.

173 Employees paid by person other than employer

(1) For the purposes of the operation of the provisions of this Part (and Chapter I of Part XIV) in relation to any employee whose remuneration is, by virtue of any statutory provision, payable to him by a person other than his employer, each of the references to the employer specified in subsection (2) shall be construed as a reference to the person by whom the remuneration is payable.

(2) The references referred to in subsection (1) are the first reference in section 135(1), the third reference in section 140(3), the first reference in section 142(3) and the first reference in section 143(2)(c) and the references in sections 142(2)(b), 143(4) and (5), 149(a) and (b), 150(3), 152(1)(b), 158(4), 162(6), 164 to 169, 170(1) and 214(5).

Death of employer or employee

174 Death of employer: dismissal

(1) Where the contract of employment of an employee is taken for the purposes of this Part to be terminated by his employer by reason of the employer's death, this Part has effect in accordance with the following provisions of this section.

(2) Section 138 applies as if—

(a) in subsection (1)(a), for the words "in pursuance" onwards there were substituted "by a personal representative of the deceased employer",

(b) in subsection (1)(b), for the words "either immediately" onwards there were substituted "not later than eight weeks after the death of the deceased employer", and

(c) in subsections (2)(b) and (6)(a), for the word "employer" there were substituted "personal representative of the deceased employer".

(3) Section 141(1) applies as if—

(a) for the words "before the end of his employment" there were substituted "by a personal representative of the deceased employer", and

(b) for the words "either immediately" onwards there were substituted "not later than eight weeks after the death of the deceased employer."

(4) For the purposes of section 141—

(a) provisions of the contract as renewed, or of the new contract, do not differ from the corresponding provisions of the contract in force immediately before the death of the deceased employer by reason only that the personal representative would be substituted for the deceased employer as the employer, and

(b) no account shall be taken of that substitution in determining whether refusal of the offer was unreasonable or whether the employee acted reasonably in terminating or giving notice to terminate the new or renewed employment.

(5) Section 146 has effect as if—

(a) subsection (1) were omitted, and

(b) in subsection (2), paragraph (a) were omitted and, in paragraph (b), for the word "four" there were substituted "eight".

(6) For the purposes of the application of this Part (in accordance with section 161(2)) in relation to an employee who was employed as a domestic servant in a private household, references in this section and sections 175 and 218(4) and (5) to a personal representative include a person to whom the management of the household has passed, otherwise than in pursuance of a sale or other disposition for valuable consideration, in consequence of the death of the employer.

175 Death of employer: lay-off and short-time

(1) Where an employee is laid off or kept on short-time and his employer dies, this Part has effect in accordance with the following provisions of this section.

(2) Where the employee—

(a) has been laid off or kept on short-time for one or more weeks before the death of the employer,

(b) has not given the deceased employer notice of intention to claim before the employer's death,

(c) after the employer's death has his contract of employment renewed, or is re-engaged under a new contract, by a personal representative of the deceased employer, and

(d) after renewal or re-engagement is laid off or kept on short-time for one or more weeks by the personal representative,

the week in which the employer died and the first week of the employee's employment by the personal representative shall be treated for the purposes of Chapter III as consecutive weeks (and references to four weeks or thirteen weeks shall be construed accordingly).

(3) The following provisions of this section apply where—

(a) the employee has given the deceased employer notice of intention to claim before the employer's death,

(b) the employer's death occurred before the end of the period of four weeks after the service of the notice, and

(c) the employee has not terminated his contract of employment by notice expiring before the employer's death.

(4) If the contract of employment is not renewed, and the employee is not re-engaged under a new contract, by a personal representative of the deceased employer before the end of the period of four weeks after the service of the notice of intention to claim—

(a) sections 149 and 152 do not apply, but

(b) (subject to that) Chapter III applies as if the employer had not died and the employee had terminated the contract of employment by a week's notice, or by the minimum notice which he is required to give to terminate the contract (if longer than a week), expiring at the end of that period.

(5) If—

(a) the contract of employment is renewed, or the employee is re-engaged under a new contract, by a personal representative of the deceased employer before the end of the period of four weeks after the service of the notice of intention to claim, and

(b) the employee was laid off or kept on short-time by the deceased employer for one or more of those weeks and is laid off or kept on short-time by the personal representative for the week, or for the next two or more weeks, following the renewal or re-engagement,

subsection (6) has effect.

(6) Where this subsection has effect Chapter III applies as if—

(a) all the weeks mentioned in subsection (5) were consecutive weeks during which the employee was employed (but laid off or kept on short-time) by the same employer, and

(b) the periods specified by section 150(3)(a) and (b) as the relevant period were extended by any week or weeks any part of which was after the death of the employer and before the date on which the renewal or re-engagement took effect.

176 Death of employee

(1) Where an employee whose employer has given him notice to terminate his contract of employment dies before the notice expires, this Part applies as if the contract had been duly terminated by the employer by notice expiring on the date of the employee's death.

(2) Where—

(a) an employee's contract of employment has been terminated by the employer,

(b) (by virtue of subsection (5) of section 145) a date later than the relevant date as defined by the previous provisions of that section is the relevant date for the purposes of certain provisions of this Act, and

(c) the employee dies before that date,

that subsection applies as if the notice to which it refers would have expired on the employee's death.

(3) Where—

(a) an employer has given notice to an employee to terminate his contract of employment and has offered to renew his contract of employment or to re-engage him under a new contract, and

(b) the employee dies without having accepted or refused the offer and without the offer having been withdrawn,

section 141(2) applies as if for the words "he unreasonably refuses" there were substituted "it would have been unreasonable on his part to refuse".

(4) Where an employee's contract of employment has been renewed or he has been re-engaged under a new contract—

(a) if he dies during the trial period without having terminated, or given notice to terminate, the contract, section 141(4) applies as if for paragraph (d) there were substituted—

"(d) it would have been unreasonable for the employee during the trial period to terminate or give notice to terminate the contract.", and

(b) if during that trial period he gives notice to terminate the contract but dies before the notice expires, sections 138(2) and 141(4) apply as if the notice had expired (and the contract had been terminated by its expiry) on the date of the employee's death.

(5) Where in the circumstances specified in paragraphs (a) and (b) of subsection (3) of section 136 the employee dies before the notice given by him under paragraph (b) of that subsection expires—

(a) if he dies before his employer has given him a notice such as is specified in subsection (2) of section 142, subsections (3) and (4) of that section apply as if the employer had given him such a notice and he had not complied with it, and

(b) if he dies after his employer has given him such a notice, that section applies as if the employee had not died but did not comply with the notice.

(6) Where an employee has given notice of intention to claim—

(a) if he dies before he has given notice to terminate his contract of employment and before the relevant period (as defined in subsection (3) of section 150) has expired, that section does not apply, and

(b) if he dies within the period of seven days after the service of the notice of intention to claim, and before the employer has given a counter-notice, Chapter III applies as if the employer had given a counter-notice within that period of seven days.

(7) Where a claim for a redundancy payment is made by a personal representative of a deceased employee—

(a) if the employee died before the end of the period of six months beginning with the relevant date, subsection (1) of section 164, and

(b) if the employee died after the end of the period of six months beginning with the relevant date but before the end of the following period of six months, subsection (2) of that section,

applies as if for the words "six months" there were substituted "one year".

Equivalent payments

177 References to industrial tribunals

(1) Where the terms and conditions (whether or not they constitute a contract of employment) on which a person is employed in employment of any description mentioned in section 171(3) include provision—

(a) for the making of a payment to which this section applies, and

(b) for referring to an industrial tribunal any question as to the right of any person to such a payment in respect of that employment or as to the amount of such a payment,

the question shall be referred to and determined by an industrial tribunal.

(2) This section applies to any payment by way of compensation for loss of employment of any description mentioned in section 171(3) which is payable in accordance with arrangements falling within subsection (3).

(3) The arrangements which fall within this subsection are arrangements made with the approval of the Treasury (or, in the case of persons whose service is for the purposes of pensions and other superannuation benefits treated as service in the civil service of the State, of the Minister for the Civil Service) for securing that a payment will be made—

(a) in circumstances which in the opinion of the Treasury (or Minister) correspond (subject to the appropriate modifications) to those in which a right to a redundancy payment would have accrued if the provisions of this Part (apart from section 159 and this section) applied, and

(b) on a scale which in the opinion of the Treasury (or Minister), taking into account any sums payable in accordance with—

(i) a scheme made under section 1 of the Superannuation Act 1972, or

(ii) the Superannuation Act 1965 as it continues to have effect by virtue of section 23(1) of the Superannuation Act 1972,

to or in respect of the person losing the employment in question, corresponds (subject to the appropriate modifications) to that on which a redundancy payment would have been payable if those provisions applied.

Other supplementary provisions

178 Old statutory compensation schemes

(1) The Secretary of State may make provision by regulations for securing that where—

(a) (apart from this section) a person is entitled to compensation under a statutory provision to which this section applies, and

(b) the circumstances are such that he is also entitled to a redundancy payment,

the amount of the redundancy payment shall be set off against the compensation to which he would be entitled apart from this section; and any statutory provision to which any such regulations apply shall have effect subject to the regulations.

(2) This section applies to any statutory provision—

(a) which was in force immediately before 6th December 1965, and

(b) under which the holders of such situations, places or employments as are specified in that provision are, or may become, entitled to compensation for loss of employment, or for loss or diminution of emoluments or of pension rights, in consequence of the operation of any other statutory provision referred to in that provision.

179 Notices

(1) Any notice which under this Part is required or authorised to be given by an employer to an employee may be given by being delivered to the employee, or left for him at his usual or last-known place of residence, or sent by post addressed to him at that place.

(2) Any notice which under this Part is required or authorised to be given by an employee to an employer may be given either by the employee himself or by a person authorised by him to act on his behalf, and (whether given by or on behalf of the employee)—

(a) may be given by being delivered to the employer, or sent by post addressed to him at the place where the employee is or was employed by him, or

(b) if arrangements have been made by the employer, may be given by being delivered to a person designated by the employer in pursuance of the arrangements, left for such a person at a place so designated or sent by post to such a person at an address so designated.

(3) In this section any reference to the delivery of a notice includes, in relation to a notice which is not required by this Part to be in writing, a reference to the oral communication of the notice.

(4) Any notice which, in accordance with any provision of this section, is left for a person at a place referred to in that provision shall, unless the contrary is proved, be presumed to have been received by him on the day on which it was left there.

(5) Nothing in subsection (1) or (2) affects the capacity of an employer to act by a servant or agent for the purposes of any provision of this Part (including either of those subsections).

(6) In relation to an employee to whom section 173 applies, this section has effect as if—

(a) any reference in subsection (1) or (2) to a notice required or authorised to be given by or to an employer included a reference to a notice which, by virtue of that section, is required or authorised to be given by or to the person by whom the remuneration is payable,

(b) in relation to a notice required or authorised to be given to that person, any reference to the employer in paragraph (a) or (b) of subsection (2) were a reference to that person, and

(c) the reference to an employer in subsection (5) included a reference to that person.

180 Offences

(1) Where an offence under this Part committed by a body corporate is proved—

(a) to have been committed with the consent or connivance of, or

(b) to be attributable to any neglect on the part of,

any director, manager, secretary or other similar officer of the body corporate, or any person who was purporting to act in any such capacity, he (as well as the body corporate) is guilty of the offence and liable to be proceeded against and punished accordingly.

(2) In this section "director", in relation to a body corporate established by or under any enactment for the purpose of carrying on under national ownership any industry or part of an industry or undertaking, being a body corporate whose affairs are managed by its members, means a member of that body corporate.

181 Interpretation

(1) In this Part—

"counter-notice" shall be construed in accordance with section 149(a),

"dismissal" and "dismissed" shall be construed in accordance with sections 136 to 138,

"employer's payment" has the meaning given by section 166,

"notice of intention to claim" shall be construed in accordance with section 148(1),

"obligatory period of notice" has the meaning given by section 136(4), and

"trial period" shall be construed in accordance with section 138(3).

(2) In this Part—

(a) references to an employee being laid off or being eligible for a redundancy payment by reason of being laid off, and

(b) references to an employee being kept on short-time or being eligible for a redundancy payment by reason of being kept on short-time,

shall be construed in accordance with sections 147 and 148.

PART XII

INSOLVENCY OF EMPLOYERS

182 Employee's rights on insolvency of employer

If, on an application made to him in writing by an employee, the Secretary of State is satisfied that—

(a) the employee's employer has become insolvent,

(b) the employee's employment has been terminated, and

(c) on the appropriate date the employee was entitled to be paid the whole or part of any debt to which this Part applies,

the Secretary of State shall, subject to section 186, pay the employee out of the National Insurance Fund the amount to which, in the opinion of the Secretary of State, the employee is entitled in respect of the debt.

183 Insolvency

(1) An employer has become insolvent for the purposes of this Part—

(a) where the employer is an individual, if (but only if) subsection (2) is satisfied, and

(b) where the employer is a company, if (but only if) subsection (3) is satisfied.

(2) This subsection is satisfied in the case of an employer who is an individual—

(a) in England and Wales if—

(i) he has been adjudged bankrupt or has made a composition or arrangement with his creditors, or

(ii) he has died and his estate falls to be administered in accordance with an order under section 421 of the Insolvency Act 1986, and

(b) in Scotland if—

(i) sequestration of his estate has been awarded or he has executed a trust deed for his creditors or has entered into a composition contract, or

(ii) he has died and a judicial factor appointed under section 11A of the Judicial Factors (Scotland) Act 1889 is required by that section to divide his insolvent estate among his creditors.

(3) This subsection is satisfied in the case of an employer which is a company—

(a) if a winding up order or an administration order has been made, or a resolution for voluntary winding up has been passed, with respect to the company,

(b) if a receiver or (in England and Wales only) a manager of the company's undertaking has been duly appointed, or (in England and Wales only) possession has been taken, by or on behalf of the holders of any debentures secured by a floating charge, of any property of the company comprised in or subject to the charge, or

(c) if a voluntary arrangement proposed in the case of the company for the purposes of Part I of the Insolvency Act 1986 has been approved under that Part of that Act.

184 Debts to which Part applies

(1) This Part applies to the following debts—

(a) any arrears of pay in respect of one or more (but not more than eight) weeks,

(b) any amount which the employer is liable to pay the employee for the period of notice required by section 86(1) or (2) or for any failure of the employer to give the period of notice required by section 86(1),

(c) any holiday pay—

(i) in respect of a period or periods of holiday not exceeding six weeks in all, and

(ii) to which the employee became entitled during the twelve months ending with the appropriate date,

(d) any basic award of compensation for unfair dismissal, and

(e) any reasonable sum by way of reimbursement of the whole or part of any fee or premium paid by an apprentice or articled clerk.

(2) For the purposes of subsection (1)(a) the following amounts shall be treated as arrears of pay—

(a) a guarantee payment,

(b) any payment for time off under Part VI of this Act or section 169 of the Trade Union and Labour Relations (Consolidation) Act 1992 (payment for time off for carrying out trade union duties etc.),

(c) remuneration on suspension on medical grounds under section 64 of this Act and remuneration on suspension on maternity grounds under section 68 of this Act, and

(d) remuneration under a protective award under section 189 of the Trade Union and Labour Relations (Consolidation) Act 1992.

(3) In subsection (1)(c) "holiday pay", in relation to an employee, means—

(a) pay in respect of a holiday actually taken by the employee, or

(b) any accrued holiday pay which, under the employee's contract of employment, would in the ordinary course have become payable to him in respect of the period of a holiday if his employment with the employer had continued until he became entitled to a holiday.

(4) A sum shall be taken to be reasonable for the purposes of subsection (1)(e) in a case where a trustee in bankruptcy, or (in Scotland) a permanent or interim trustee (within the meaning of the Bankruptcy (Scotland) Act 1985), or liquidator has been or is required to be appointed—

(a) as respects England and Wales, if it is admitted to be reasonable by the trustee in bankruptcy or liquidator under section 348 of the Insolvency Act 1986 (effect of bankruptcy on apprenticeships etc.), whether as originally enacted or as applied to the winding up of a company by rules under section 411 of that Act, and

(b) as respects Scotland, if it is accepted by the permanent or interim trustee or liquidator for the purposes of the sequestration or winding up.

185 The appropriate date

In this Part "the appropriate date"—

(a) in relation to arrears of pay (not being remuneration under a protective award made under section 189 of the Trade Union and Labour Relations (Consolidation) Act 1992) and to holiday pay, means the date on which the employer became insolvent,

(b) in relation to a basic award of compensation for unfair dismissal and to remuneration under a protective award so made, means whichever is the latest of—

(i) the date on which the employer became insolvent,

(ii) the date of the termination of the employee's employment, and

(iii) the date on which the award was made, and

(c) in relation to any other debt to which this Part applies, means whichever is the later of—

(i) the date on which the employer became insolvent, and

(ii) the date of the termination of the employee's employment.

186 Limit on amount payable under section 182

(1) The total amount payable to an employee in respect of any debt to which this Part applies, where the amount of the debt is referable to a period of time, shall not exceed—

(a) £210 in respect of any one week, or

(b) in respect of a shorter period, an amount bearing the same proportion to £210 as that shorter period bears to a week.

(2) The Secretary of State may vary the limit specified in subsection (1), after a review under section 208, by order made in accordance with that section.

187 Role of relevant officer

(1) Where a relevant officer has been, or is required to be, appointed in connection with an employer's insolvency, the Secretary of State shall not make a payment under section 182 in respect of a debt until he has received a statement from the relevant officer of the amount of that debt which appears to have been owed to the employee on the appropriate date and to remain unpaid.

(2) If the Secretary of State is satisfied that he does not require a statement under subsection (1) in order to determine the amount of a debt which was owed to the employee on the appropriate date and remains unpaid, he may make a payment under section 182 in respect of the debt without having received such a statement.

(3) A relevant officer shall, on request by the Secretary of State, provide him with a statement for the purposes of subsection (1) as soon as is reasonably practicable.

(4) The following are relevant officers for the purposes of this section—

- (a) a trustee in bankruptcy or a permanent or interim trustee (within the meaning of the Bankruptcy (Scotland) Act 1985),
- (b) a liquidator,
- (c) an administrator,
- (d) a receiver or manager,
- (e) a trustee under a composition or arrangement between the employer and his creditors, and
- (f) a trustee under a trust deed for his creditors executed by the employer.

(5) In subsection (4)(e) "trustee" includes the supervisor of a voluntary arrangement proposed for the purposes of, and approved under, Part I or VIII of the Insolvency Act 1986.

188 Complaints to industrial tribunals

(1) A person who has applied for a payment under section 182 may present a complaint to an industrial tribunal—

- (a) that the Secretary of State has failed to make any such payment, or
- (b) that any such payment made by him is less than the amount which should have been paid.

(2) An industrial tribunal shall not consider a complaint under subsection (1) unless it is presented—

- (a) before the end of the period of three months beginning with the date on which the decision of the Secretary of State on the application was communicated to the applicant, or
- (b) within such further period as the tribunal considers reasonable in a case where it is not reasonably practicable for the complaint to be presented before the end of that period of three months.

(3) Where an industrial tribunal finds that the Secretary of State ought to make a payment under section 182, the tribunal shall—

- (a) make a declaration to that effect, and
- (b) declare the amount of any such payment which it finds the Secretary of State ought to make.

189 Transfer to Secretary of State of rights and remedies

(1) Where, in pursuance of section 182, the Secretary of State makes a payment to an employee in respect of a debt to which this Part applies—

(a) on the making of the payment any rights and remedies of the employee in respect of the debt (or, if the Secretary of State has paid only part of it, in respect of that part) become rights and remedies of the Secretary of State, and

(b) any decision of an industrial tribunal requiring an employer to pay that debt to the employee has the effect that the debt (or the part of it which the Secretary of State has paid) is to be paid to the Secretary of State.

(2) Where a debt (or any part of a debt) in respect of which the Secretary of State has made a payment in pursuance of section 182 constitutes—

(a) a preferential debt within the meaning of the Insolvency Act 1986 for the purposes of any provision of that Act (including any such provision as applied by any order made under that Act) or any provision of the Companies Act 1985, or

(b) a preferred debt within the meaning of the Bankruptcy (Scotland) Act 1985 for the purposes of any provision of that Act (including any such provision as applied by section 11A of the Judicial Factors (Scotland) Act 1889),

the rights which become rights of the Secretary of State in accordance with subsection (1) include any right arising under any such provision by reason of the status of the debt (or that part of it) as a preferential or preferred debt.

(3) In computing for the purposes of any provision mentioned in subsection (2)(a) or (b) the aggregate amount payable in priority to other creditors of the employer in respect of—

(a) any claim of the Secretary of State to be paid in priority to other creditors of the employer by virtue of subsection (2), and

(b) any claim by the employee to be so paid made in his own right,

any claim of the Secretary of State to be so paid by virtue of subsection (2) shall be treated as if it were a claim of the employee.

(4) But the Secretary of State shall be entitled, as against the employee, to be so paid in respect of any such claim of his (up to the full amount of the claim) before any payment is made to the employee in respect of any claim by the employee to be so paid made in his own right.

(5) Any sum recovered by the Secretary of State in exercising any right, or pursuing any remedy, which is his by virtue of this section shall be paid into the National Insurance Fund.

190 Power to obtain information

(1) Where an application is made to the Secretary of State under section 182 in respect of a debt owed by an employer, the Secretary of State may require—

(a) the employer to provide him with such information as he may reasonably require for the purpose of determining whether the application is well-founded, and

(b) any person having the custody or control of any relevant records or other documents to produce for examination on behalf of the Secretary of State any such document in that person's custody or under his control which is of such a description as the Secretary of State may require.

(2) Any such requirement—

(a) shall be made by notice in writing given to the person on whom the requirement is imposed, and

(b) may be varied or revoked by a subsequent notice so given.

(3) If a person refuses or wilfully neglects to furnish any information or produce any document which he has been required to furnish or produce by a notice under this section he is guilty of an offence and liable on summary conviction to a fine not exceeding level 3 on the standard scale.

(4) If a person, in purporting to comply with a requirement of a notice under this section, knowingly or recklessly makes any false statement he is guilty of an offence and liable on summary conviction to a fine not exceeding level 5 on the standard scale.

(5) Where an offence under this section committed by a body corporate is proved—

(a) to have been committed with the consent or connivance of, or

(b) to be attributable to any neglect on the part of,

any director, manager, secretary or other similar officer of the body corporate, or any person who was purporting to act in any such capacity, he (as well as the body corporate) is guilty of the offence and liable to be proceeded against and punished accordingly.

(6) Where the affairs of a body corporate are managed by its members, subsection (5) applies in relation to the acts and defaults of a member in connection with his functions of management as if he were a director of the body corporate.

PART XIII

MISCELLANEOUS

CHAPTER I

PARTICULAR TYPES OF EMPLOYMENT

Crown employment etc.

191 Crown employment

(1) Subject to sections 192 and 193, the provisions of this Act to which this section applies have effect in relation to Crown employment and persons in Crown employment as they have effect in relation to other employment and other employees or workers.

(2) This section applies to—

(a) Parts I to III,

(b) Part V, apart from section 45,

(c) Parts VI to VIII,

(d) in Part IX, sections 92 and 93,

(e) Part X, apart from section 101, and
(f) this Part and Parts XIV and XV.

(3) In this Act "Crown employment" means employment under or for the purposes of a government department or any officer or body exercising on behalf of the Crown functions conferred by a statutory provision.

(4) For the purposes of the application of provisions of this Act in relation to Crown employment in accordance with subsection (1)—
(a) references to an employee or a worker shall be construed as references to a person in Crown employment,
(b) references to a contract of employment, or a worker's contract, shall be construed as references to the terms of employment of a person in Crown employment,
(c) references to dismissal, or to the termination of a worker's contract, shall be construed as references to the termination of Crown employment,
(d) references to redundancy shall be construed as references to the existence of such circumstances as are treated, in accordance with any arrangements falling within section 177(3) for the time being in force, as equivalent to redundancy in relation to Crown employment, and
(e) references to an undertaking shall be construed—
(i) in relation to a Minister of the Crown, as references to his functions or (as the context may require) to the department of which he is in charge, and
(ii) in relation to a government department, officer or body, as references to the functions of the department, officer or body or (as the context may require) to the department, officer or body.

(5) Where the terms of employment of a person in Crown employment restrict his right to take part in—
(a) certain political activities, or
(b) activities which may conflict with his official functions,

nothing in section 50 requires him to be allowed time off work for public duties connected with any such activities.

(6) Sections 159 and 160 are without prejudice to any exemption or immunity of the Crown.

192 Armed forces

(1) Section 191—
(a) applies to service as a member of the naval, military or air forces of the Crown but subject to the following provisions of this section, and
(b) applies to employment by an association established for the purposes of Part XI of the Reserve Forces Act 1996.

(2) The provisions of this Act which have effect by virtue of section 191 in relation to service as a member of the naval, military or air forces of the Crown are—
(a) Part I,
(b) in Part VI, sections 55 to 57,
(c) Parts VII and VIII,

(d) in Part IX, sections 92 and 93,
(e) Part X, apart from sections 100 to 103 and 134, and
(f) this Part and Parts XIV and XV.

(3) Her Majesty may by Order in Council—
(a) amend subsection (2) by making additions to, or omissions from, the provisions for the time being specified in that subsection, and
(b) make any provision for the time being so specified apply to service as a member of the naval, military or air forces of the Crown subject to such exceptions and modifications as may be specified in the Order in Council,

but no provision contained in Part II may be added to the provisions for the time being specified in subsection (2).

(4) Modifications made by an Order in Council under subsection (3) may include provision precluding the making of a complaint or reference to any industrial tribunal unless the person aggrieved has availed himself of the service redress procedures applicable to him.

(5) Where modifications made by an Order in Council under subsection (3) include provision such as is mentioned in subsection (4), the Order in Council shall also include provision designed to secure that the service redress procedures result in a determination, or what is to be treated under the Order in Council as a determination, in sufficient time to enable a complaint or reference to be made to an industrial tribunal.

(6) In subsections (4) and (5) "the service redress procedures" means the procedures, excluding those which relate to the making of a report on a complaint to Her Majesty, referred to in—
(a) sections 180 and 181 of the Army Act 1955,
(b) sections 180 and 181 of the Air Force Act 1955, and
(c) section 130 of the Naval Discipline Act 1957.

(7) No provision shall be made by virtue of subsection (4) which has the effect of substituting a period longer than six months for any period specified as the normal period for a complaint or reference.

(8) In subsection (7) "the normal period for a complaint or reference", in relation to any matter within the jurisdiction of an industrial tribunal, means the period specified in the relevant enactment as the period within which the complaint or reference must be made (disregarding any provision permitting an extension of that period at the discretion of the tribunal).

193 National security

(1) The provisions of this Act to which this section applies do not have effect in relation to any Crown employment in respect of which there is in force a certificate issued by or on behalf of a Minister of the Crown certifying that employment of a description specified in the certificate, or the employment of a particular person so specified, is (or, at a time specified in the certificate, was) required to be excepted from those provisions for the purpose of safeguarding national security.

(2) This section applies to—
(a) Part I, so far as it relates to itemised pay statements,
(b) Part III,

(c) in Part VI, sections 50 to 54,

(d) in Part VII, sections 64 and 65, and sections 69 and 70 so far as relating to those sections,

(e) in Part IX, sections 92 and 93, except where they apply by virtue of section 92(4),

(f) Part X, except so far as relating to a dismissal which is treated as unfair—

(i) by section 99(1) to (3), 100 or 103, or

(ii) by subsection (1) of section 105 by reason of the application of subsection (2), (3) or (6) of that section, and

(g) this Part and Parts XIV and XV (so far as relating to any of the provisions specified in paragraphs (a) to (f)).

(3) Any document purporting to be a certificate issued as mentioned in subsection (1)—

(a) shall be received in evidence, and

(b) unless the contrary is proved, shall be deemed to be such a certificate.

Parliamentary staff

194 House of Lords staff

(1) The provisions of this Act to which this section applies have effect in relation to employment as a relevant member of the House of Lords staff as they have effect in relation to other employment.

(2) This section applies to—

(a) Part I,

(b) Part III,

(c) in Part V, sections 44 and 47, and sections 48 and 49 so far as relating to those sections,

(d) Part VI, apart from sections 58 to 60,

(e) Parts VII and VIII,

(f) in Part IX, sections 92 and 93,

(g) Part X, apart from sections 101 and 102, and

(h) this Part and Parts XIV and XV.

(3) For the purposes of the application of the provisions of this Act to which this section applies in relation to a relevant member of the House of Lords staff references to an undertaking shall be construed as references to the House of Lords.

(4) Nothing in any rule of law or the law or practice of Parliament prevents a relevant member of the House of Lords staff from bringing before the High Court or a county court—

(a) a claim arising out of or relating to a contract of employment or any other contract connected with employment, or

(b) a claim in tort arising in connection with employment.

(5) Where the terms of the contract of employment of a relevant member of the House of Lords staff restrict his right to take part in—

(a) certain political activities, or

(b) activities which may conflict with his official functions, nothing in section 50 requires him to be allowed time off work for public duties connected with any such activities.

(6) In this section "relevant member of the House of Lords staff" means any person who is employed under a contract of employment with the Corporate Officer of the House of Lords.

(7) For the purposes of the application of—

(a) the provisions of this Act to which this section applies, or

(b) a claim within subsection (4),

in relation to a person continuously employed in or for the purposes of the House of Lords up to the time when he became so employed under a contract of employment with the Corporate Officer of the House of Lords, his employment shall not be treated as having been terminated by reason only of a change in his employer before or at that time.

195 House of Commons staff

(1) The provisions of this Act to which this section applies have effect in relation to employment as a relevant member of the House of Commons staff as they have effect in relation to other employment.

(2) This section applies to—

(a) Part I,

(b) Part III,

(c) in Part V, sections 44 and 47, and sections 48 and 49 so far as relating to those sections,

(d) Part VI, apart from sections 58 to 60,

(e) Parts VII and VIII,

(f) in Part IX, sections 92 and 93,

(g) Part X, apart from sections 101 and 102, and

(h) this Part and Parts XIV and XV.

(3) For the purposes of the application of the provisions of this Act to which this section applies in relation to a relevant member of the House of Commons staff—

(a) references to an employee shall be construed as references to a relevant member of the House of Commons staff,

(b) references to a contract of employment shall be construed as including references to the terms of employment of a relevant member of the House of Commons staff,

(c) references to dismissal shall be construed as including references to the termination of the employment of a relevant member of the House of Commons staff, and

(d) references to an undertaking shall be construed as references to the House of Commons.

(4) Nothing in any rule of law or the law or practice of Parliament prevents a relevant member of the House of Commons staff from bringing before the High Court or a county court—

(a) a claim arising out of or relating to a contract of employment or any other contract connected with employment, or

(b) a claim in tort arising in connection with employment.

(5) In this section "relevant member of the House of Commons staff" means any person—

(a) who was appointed by the House of Commons Commission or is employed in the refreshment department, or

(b) who is a member of the Speaker's personal staff.

(6) Subject to subsection (7), for the purposes of—

(a) the provisions of this Act to which this section applies,

(b) Part XI (where applicable to relevant members of the House of Commons staff), and

(c) a claim within subsection (4),

the House of Commons Commission is the employer of staff appointed by the Commission and the Speaker is the employer of his personal staff and of any person employed in the refreshment department and not appointed by the Commission.

(7) Where the House of Commons Commission or the Speaker designates a person to be treated for all or any of the purposes mentioned in subsection (6) as the employer of any description of staff (other than the Speaker's personal staff), the person so designated shall be treated for those purposes as their employer.

(8) Where any proceedings are brought by virtue of this section against—

(a) the House of Commons Commission,

(b) the Speaker, or

(c) any person designated under subsection (7),

the person against whom the proceedings are brought may apply to the court or industrial tribunal concerned to have some other person against whom the proceedings could at the time of the application be properly brought substituted for him as a party to the proceedings.

(9) For the purposes mentioned in subsection (6)—

(a) a person's employment in or for the purposes of the House of Commons shall not (provided he continues to be employed in such employment) be treated as terminated by reason only of a change in his employer, and

(b) (provided he so continues) his first appointment to such employment shall be deemed after the change to have been made by his employer for the time being.

(10) In accordance with subsection (9)—

(a) an employee shall be treated for the purposes mentioned in subsection (6) as being continuously employed by his employer for the time being from the commencement of his employment until its termination, and

(b) anything done by or in relation to his employer for the time being in respect of his employment before the change shall be so treated as having been done by or in relation to the person who is his employer for the time being after the change.

(11) In subsections (9) and (10) "employer for the time being", in relation to a person who has ceased to be employed in or for the purposes of the House of Commons, means the person who was his employer immediately before he ceased to be so employed, except that where some other person would have been his employer for the time being if he had not ceased to be so employed it means that other person.

(12) If the House of Commons resolves at any time that any provision of subsections (5) to (8) should be amended in its application to any member of the staff of that House, Her Majesty may by Order in Council amend that provision accordingly.

Excluded classes of employment

196 Employment outside Great Britain

(1) Sections 1 to 7 and sections 86 to 91 do not apply in relation to employment during any period when the employee is engaged in work wholly or mainly outside Great Britain unless—

(a) the employee ordinarily works in Great Britain and the work outside Great Britain is for the same employer, or

(b) the law which governs his contract of employment is the law of England and Wales or the law of Scotland.

(2) The provisions to which this subsection applies do not apply to employment where under the employee's contract of employment he ordinarily works outside Great Britain.

(3) Subsection (2) applies to—

(a) in Part I, sections 8 to 10,

(b) Parts II, III and V,

(c) Part VI, apart from sections 58 to 60,

(d) Parts VII and VIII,

(e) in Part IX, sections 92 and 93, and

(f) (subject to subsection (4)) Part X.

(4) Part X applies to employment where under her contract of employment the employee ordinarily works outside Great Britain if—

(a) section 84 applies to her dismissal, or

(b) she is treated as dismissed by section 96.

(5) For the purposes of subsections (2) and (4), a person employed to work on board a ship registered in the United Kingdom shall be regarded as a person who under his contract ordinarily works in Great Britain unless—

(a) the ship is registered at a port outside Great Britain,

(b) the employment is wholly outside Great Britain, or

(c) the person is not ordinarily resident in Great Britain.

(6) An employee—

(a) is not entitled to a redundancy payment if he is outside Great Britain on the relevant date unless under his contract of employment he ordinarily worked in Great Britain, and

(b) is not entitled to a redundancy payment if under his contract of employment he ordinarily works outside Great Britain unless on the relevant date he is in Great Britain in accordance with instructions given to him by his employer.

(7) Part XII does not apply to employment where, under the employee's contract of employment, he ordinarily works outside the territory of the member States of the European Communities and of Norway and Iceland.

197 Fixed-term contracts

(1) Part X does not apply to dismissal from employment under a contract for a fixed term of one year or more if—

(a) the dismissal consists only of the expiry of that term without its being renewed, and

(b) before the term expires the employee has agreed in writing to exclude any claim in respect of rights under that Part in relation to the contract.

(2) Subsection (1) does not prevent Part X from applying if the dismissal is regarded as unfair by virtue of section 101.

(3) An employee employed under a contract of employment for a fixed term of two years or more is not entitled to a redundancy payment in respect of the expiry of that term without its being renewed (whether by the employer or by an associated employer of his) if, before the term expires, the employee has agreed in writing to exclude any right to a redundancy payment in that event.

(4) An agreement such as is mentioned in subsection (1) or (3) may be contained—

(a) in the contract itself, or

(b) in a separate agreement.

(5) Where—

(a) an agreement such as is mentioned in subsection (3) is made during the currency of a fixed term, and

(b) the term is renewed,

the agreement shall not be construed as applying to the term as renewed; but this subsection is without prejudice to the making of a further agreement in relation to the renewed term.

198 Short-term employment

Sections 1 to 7 do not apply to an employee if his employment continues for less than one month.

199 Mariners

(1) Sections 1 to 7, Part II and sections 86 to 91 do not apply to a person employed as a seaman in a ship registered in the United Kingdom under a crew agreement the provisions and form of which are of a kind approved by the Secretary of State.

(2) Sections 8 to 10, Part III, sections 44, 45, 47, 50 to 57 and 61 to 63, Parts VII and VIII, sections 92 and 93 and (subject to subsection (3)) Parts X to XII do not apply to employment as master, or as a member of the crew, of a fishing vessel where the employee is remunerated only by a share in the profits or gross earnings of the vessel.

(3) Part X applies to employment such as is mentioned in subsection (2) if—

(a) section 84 applies to the employee's dismissal, or

(b) she is treated as dismissed by section 96,

and Part XI applies to employment such as is so mentioned if the employee is treated as dismissed by section 137.

(4) Sections 8 to 10 and 50 to 54 and Part XII do not apply to employment as a merchant seaman.

(5) In subsection (4) "employment as a merchant seaman"—

(a) does not include employment in the fishing industry or employment on board a ship otherwise than by the owner, manager or charterer of that ship except employment as a radio officer, but

(b) subject to that, includes—

(i) employment as a master or a member of the crew of any ship,

(ii) employment as a trainee undergoing training for the sea service, and

(iii) employment in or about a ship in port by the owner, manager or charterer of the ship to do work of the kind ordinarily done by a merchant seaman on a ship while it is in port.

(6) Section 196(6) does not apply to an employee, and section 197(3) does not apply to a contract of employment, if the employee is—

(a) employed as a master or seaman in a British ship, and

(b) ordinarily resident in Great Britain.

200 Police officers

(1) Sections 8 to 10, Part III, sections 44, 45, 47, 50 to 57 and 61 to 63, Parts VII and VIII, sections 92 and 93, Part X and section 137 do not apply to employment under a contract of employment in police service or to persons engaged in such employment.

(2) In subsection (1) "police service" means—

(a) service as a member of a constabulary maintained by virtue of an enactment, or

(b) subject to section 126 of the Criminal Justice and Public Order Act 1994 (prison staff not to be regarded as in police service), service in any other capacity by virtue of which a person has the powers or privileges of a constable.

Offshore employment

201 Power to extend employment legislation to offshore employment

(1) In this section "offshore employment" means employment for the purposes of activities—

(a) in the territorial waters of the United Kingdom,

(b) connected with the exploration of the sea-bed or subsoil, or the exploitation of their natural resources, in the United Kingdom sector of the continental shelf, or

(c) connected with the exploration or exploitation, in a foreign sector of the continental shelf, of a cross-boundary petroleum field.

(2) Her Majesty may by Order in Council provide that—

(a) the provisions of this Act, and

(b) any Northern Ireland legislation making provision for purposes corresponding to any of the purposes of this Act, apply, to such extent and for such purposes as may be specified in the Order (with or without modification), to or in relation to a person in offshore employment.

(3) An Order in Council under this section—

(a) may make different provision for different cases,

(b) may provide that all or any of the provisions referred to in subsection (2), as applied by such an Order in Council, apply—

(i) to individuals whether or not they are British subjects, and

(ii) to bodies corporate whether or not they are incorporated under the law of a part of the United Kingdom,

and apply even where the application may affect their activities outside the United Kingdom,

(c) may make provision for conferring jurisdiction on any court or class of court specified in the Order in Council, or on industrial tribunals, in respect of offences, causes of action or other matters arising in connection with offshore employment,

(d) may (without prejudice to subsection (2) and paragraph (a)) provide that the provisions referred to in subsection (2), as applied by the Order in Council, apply in relation to any person in employment in a part of the areas referred to in subsection (1)(a) and (b),

(e) may exclude from the operation of section 3 of the Territorial Waters Jurisdiction Act 1878 (consents required for prosecutions) proceedings for offences under the provisions referred to in subsection (2) in connection with offshore employment,

(f) may provide that such proceedings shall not be brought without such consent as may be required by the Order in Council,

(g) may (without prejudice to subsection (2)) modify or exclude the operation of any or all of sections 196, 199 and 215(2) to (6) or of any corresponding Northern Ireland legislation.

(4) Any jurisdiction conferred on a court or tribunal under this section is without prejudice to jurisdiction exercisable apart from this section by that or any other court or tribunal.

(5) In this section—

"cross-boundary petroleum field" means a petroleum field that extends across the boundary between the United Kingdom sector of the continental shelf and a foreign sector of the continental shelf,

"foreign sector of the continental shelf" means an area outside the territorial waters of any state, within which rights with respect to the sea-bed and subsoil and their natural resources are exercisable by a state other than the United Kingdom,

"petroleum field" means a geological structure identified as an oil or gas field by the Order in Council concerned, and

"United Kingdom sector of the continental shelf" means the area designated under section 1(7) of the Continental Shelf Act 1964.

CHAPTER II

OTHER MISCELLANEOUS MATTERS

Restrictions on disclosure of information

202 National security

(1) Where in the opinion of any Minister of the Crown the disclosure of any information would be contrary to the interests of national security—

(a) nothing in any of the provisions to which this section applies requires any person to disclose the information, and

(b) no person shall disclose the information in any proceedings in any court or tribunal relating to any of those provisions.

(2) This section applies to—

(a) Part I, so far as it relates to employment particulars,

(b) in Part V, sections 44 and 47, and sections 48 and 49 so far as relating to those sections,

(c) in Part VI, sections 55 to 57 and 61 to 63,

(d) in Part VII, sections 66 to 68, and sections 69 and 70 so far as relating to those sections,

(e) Part VIII,

(f) in Part IX, sections 92 and 93 where they apply by virtue of section 92(4),

(g) Part X so far as relating to a dismissal which is treated as unfair—

(i) by section 99(1) to (3), 100 or 103, or

(ii) by subsection (1) of section 105 by reason of the application of subsection (2), (3) or (6) of that section, and

(h) this Part and Parts XIV and XV (so far as relating to any of the provisions in paragraphs (a) to (g)).

Contracting out etc. and remedies

203 Restrictions on contracting out

(1) Any provision in an agreement (whether a contract of employment or not) is void in so far as it purports—

(a) to exclude or limit the operation of any provision of this Act, or

(b) to preclude a person from bringing any proceedings under this Act before an industrial tribunal.

(2) Subsection (1)—

(a) does not apply to any provision in a collective agreement excluding rights under section 28 if an order under section 35 is for the time being in force in respect of it,

(b) does not apply to any provision in a dismissal procedures agreement excluding the right under section 94 if that provision is not to have effect unless an order under section 110 is for the time being in force in respect of it,

(c) does not apply to any provision in an agreement if an order under section 157 is for the time being in force in respect of it,

(d) does not apply to any provision of an agreement relating to dismissal from employment such as is mentioned in section 197(1) or (3),

(e) does not apply to any agreement to refrain from instituting or continuing proceedings where a conciliation officer has taken action under section 18 of the Industrial Tribunals Act 1996, and

(f) does not apply to any agreement to refrain from instituting or continuing before an industrial tribunal any proceedings within section 18(1)(d) (proceedings under this Act where conciliation available) of the Industrial Tribunals Act 1996 if the conditions regulating compromise agreements under this Act are satisfied in relation to the agreement.

(3) For the purposes of subsection (2)(f) the conditions regulating compromise agreements under this Act are that—

(a) the agreement must be in writing,

(b) the agreement must relate to the particular complaint,

(c) the employee or worker must have received independent legal advice from a qualified lawyer as to the terms and effect of the proposed agreement and, in particular, its effect on his ability to pursue his rights before an industrial tribunal,

(d) there must be in force, when the adviser gives the advice, a policy of insurance covering the risk of a claim by the employee or worker in respect of loss arising in consequence of the advice,

(e) the agreement must identify the adviser, and

(f) the agreement must state that the conditions regulating compromise agreements under this Act are satisfied.

(4) In subsection (3)—

"independent", in relation to legal advice received by an employee or worker, means that the advice is given by a lawyer who is not acting in the matter for the employer or an associated employer, and

"qualified lawyer" means—

(a) as respects England and Wales, a barrister (whether in practice as such or employed to give legal advice), or a solicitor who holds a practising certificate, and

(b) as respects Scotland, an advocate (whether in practice as such or employed to give legal advice), or a solicitor who holds a practising certificate.

204 Law governing employment

(1) For the purposes of this Act it is immaterial whether the law which (apart from this Act) governs any person's employment is the law of the United Kingdom, or of a part of the United Kingdom, or not.

(2) Subsection (1) is subject to section 196(1)(b).

205 Remedy for infringement of certain rights

(1) The remedy of an employee for infringement of any of the rights conferred by section 8, Part III, Parts V to VIII, section 92, Part X and Part XII is, where provision is made for a complaint or the reference of a question to an industrial tribunal, by way of such a complaint or reference and not otherwise.

(2) The remedy of a worker in respect of any contravention of section 13, 15, 18(1) or 21(1) is by way of a complaint under section 23 and not otherwise.

General provisions about death of employer or employee

206 Institution or continuance of tribunal proceedings

(1) Where an employer has died, any tribunal proceedings arising under any of the provisions of this Act to which this section applies may be defended by a personal representative of the deceased employer.

(2) This section and section 207 apply to—

- (a) Part I, so far as it relates to itemised pay statements,
- (b) Part III,
- (c) Part V,
- (d) Part VI, apart from sections 58 to 60,
- (e) Parts VII and VIII,
- (f) in Part IX, sections 92 and 93, and
- (g) Parts X to XII.

(3) Where an employee has died, any tribunal proceedings arising under any of the provisions of this Act to which this section applies may be instituted or continued by a personal representative of the deceased employee.

(4) If there is no personal representative of a deceased employee, any tribunal proceedings arising under any of the provisions of this Act to which this section applies may be instituted or continued on behalf of the estate of the deceased employee by any appropriate person appointed by the industrial tribunal.

(5) In subsection (4) "appropriate person" means a person who is—

- (a) authorised by the employee before his death to act in connection with the proceedings, or
- (b) the widow or widower, child, parent or brother or sister of the deceased employee;

and in Part XI and the following provisions of this section and section 207 references to a personal representative include a person appointed under subsection (4).

(6) In a case where proceedings are instituted or continued by virtue of subsection (4), any award made by the industrial tribunal shall be—

- (a) made in such terms, and
- (b) enforceable in such manner,

as the Secretary of State may by regulations provide.

(7) Any reference in the provisions of this Act to which this section applies to the doing of anything by or in relation to an employer or employee includes a reference to the doing

of the thing by or in relation to a personal representative of the deceased employer or employee.

(8) Any reference in the provisions of this Act to which this section applies to a thing required or authorised to be done by or in relation to an employer or employee includes a reference to a thing required or authorised to be done by or in relation to a personal representative of the deceased employer or employee.

(9) Subsections (7) and (8) do not prevent a reference to a successor of an employer including a personal representative of a deceased employer.

207 Rights and liabilities accruing after death

(1) Any right arising under any of the provisions of this Act to which this section applies which accrues after the death of an employee devolves as if it had accrued before his death.

(2) Where an industrial tribunal determines under any provision of Part XI that an employer is liable to pay to a personal representative of a deceased employee—

(a) the whole of a redundancy payment to which he would have been entitled but for some provision of Part XI or section 206, or

(b) such part of such a redundancy payment as the tribunal thinks fit,

the reference in subsection (1) to a right includes any right to receive it.

(3) Where—

(a) by virtue of any of the provisions to which this section applies a personal representative is liable to pay any amount, and

(b) the liability has not accrued before the death of the employer,

it shall be treated as a liability of the deceased employer which had accrued immediately before his death.

Modifications of Act

208 Review of limits

(1) The Secretary of State shall in each calendar year review—

(a) the limits specified in section 31,

(b) the limit specified in section 186(1), and

(c) the limits imposed by subsection (1) of section 227 for the purposes specified in paragraphs (a) to (c) of that subsection,

and shall determine whether any of those limits should be varied.

(2) In making a review under subsection (1) the Secretary of State shall consider—

(a) the general level of earnings obtaining in Great Britain at the time of the review,

(b) the national economic situation as a whole, and

(c) such other matters as he thinks relevant.

(3) If on a review under subsection (1) the Secretary of State determines that, having regard to the considerations mentioned in subsection (2), any of the limits specified in subsection (1) should be varied, he shall prepare and lay before each House of Parliament the draft of an order giving effect to his decision.

(4) Where a draft of an order under this section is approved by resolution of each House of Parliament the Secretary of State shall make an order in the form of the draft.

(5) If, following the completion of a review under subsection (1), the Secretary of State determines that any of the limits referred to in that subsection should not be varied, he shall lay before each House of Parliament a report containing a statement of his reasons for that determination.

(6) The Secretary of State may at any time, in addition to the annual review provided by in subsection (1), conduct a further review of the limits specified in subsection (1) so as to determine whether any of them should be varied.

(7) Subsections (2) to (4) shall apply to a review under subsection (6) as if it were a review under subsection (1).

209 Powers to amend Act

(1) The Secretary of State may by order—

(a) provide that any provision of this Act, other than any to which this paragraph does not apply, which is specified in the order shall not apply to persons, or to employments, of such classes as may be prescribed in the order,

(b) provide that any provision of this Act, other than any to which this paragraph does not apply, shall apply to persons or employments of such classes as may be prescribed in the order subject to such exceptions and modifications as may be so prescribed, or

(c) vary, or exclude the operation of, any of the provisions to which this paragraph applies.

(2) Subsection (1)(a) does not apply to—

(a) Parts II and IV,

(b) in Part V, sections 45 and 46, and sections 48 and 49 so far as relating to those sections,

(c) in Part VI, sections 58 to 60,

(d) in Part IX, sections 87(3), 88 to 90, 91(1) to (4) and (6) and 92(6) to (8),

(e) in Part X, sections 95, 97(1) to (5), 98(1) to (4) and (6), 100, 101, 102, 103, 105, 107, 110, 111, 120(2), 124(1), (2) and (5), 125(7) and 134,

(f) in Part XI, sections 143, 144, 160(2) and (3), 166 to 173 and 177 to 180,

(g) in Part XIII, sections 196(1) and 197(1),

(h) Chapter I of Part XIV, or

(j) in Part XV, section 236(3) so far as relating to sections 120(2), 124(2) and 125(7).

(3) Subsection (1)(b) does not apply to—

(a) any of the provisions to which subsection (1)(a) does not apply,

(b) sections 1 to 7, or

(c) the provisions of sections 86 to 91 not specified in subsection (2).

(4) The provision which may be made by virtue of paragraph (b) of subsection (1) in relation to section 94 does not include provision for application subject to exceptions or modifications; but this subsection does not prejudice paragraph (a) of that subsection.

(5) Subsection (1)(c) applies to sections 29(2), 65(2), 86(5), 92(3), 108(1), 109(1), 159, 160(1), 196(2), (3) and (5) and 199(1), (2), (4) and (5).

(6) The Secretary of State may by order amend any of—
- (a) sections 84, 85, 97(6), 98(5) and 99(4),
- (b) sections 108(3), 109(2) and 110(2) so far as relating to section 84, and
- (c) sections 114(5), 115(4), 119(6), 127, 137(2), 145(7), 146(3), 156(2), 157(6), 162(7), 196(4), 199(3), 226(3)(a) and (5)(a) and 227(4)(a),

or modify the application of any of those provisions to any description of case.

(7) The Secretary of State may by order provide that, subject to any such modifications and exceptions as may be prescribed in the order, section 44, and any other provisions of this Act so far as relating to that section, shall apply to such descriptions of persons other than employees as may be so prescribed as to employees (but as if references to their employer were to such person as may be so prescribed).

(8) The provisions of this section are without prejudice to any other power of the Secretary of State to amend, vary or repeal any provision of this Act or to extend or restrict its operation in relation to any person or employment.

PART XIV

INTERPRETATION

CHAPTER I

CONTINUOUS EMPLOYMENT

210 Introductory

(1) References in any provision of this Act to a period of continuous employment are (unless provision is expressly made to the contrary) to a period computed in accordance with this Chapter.

(2) In any provision of this Act which refers to a period of continuous employment expressed in months or years—
- (a) a month means a calendar month, and
- (b) a year means a year of twelve calendar months.

(3) In computing an employee's period of continuous employment for the purposes of any provision of this Act, any question—
- (a) whether the employee's employment is of a kind counting towards a period of continuous employment, or
- (b) whether periods (consecutive or otherwise) are to be treated as forming a single period of continuous employment,

shall be determined week by week; but where it is necessary to compute the length of an employee's period of employment it shall be computed in months and years of twelve months in accordance with section 211.

(4) Subject to sections 215 to 217, a week which does not count in computing the length of a period of continuous employment breaks continuity of employment.

(5) A person's employment during any period shall, unless the contrary is shown, be presumed to have been continuous.

211 Period of continuous employment

(1) An employee's period of continuous employment for the purposes of any provision of this Act—

(a) (subject to subsections (2) and (3)) begins with the day on which the employee starts work, and

(b) ends with the day by reference to which the length of the employee's period of continuous employment is to be ascertained for the purposes of the provision.

(2) For the purposes of sections 155 and 162(1), an employee's period of continuous employment shall be treated as beginning on the employee's eighteenth birthday if that is later than the day on which the employee starts work.

(3) If an employee's period of continuous employment includes one or more periods which (by virtue of section 215, 216 or 217) while not counting in computing the length of the period do not break continuity of employment, the beginning of the period shall be treated as postponed by the number of days falling within that intervening period, or the aggregate number of days falling within those periods, calculated in accordance with the section in question.

212 Weeks counting in computing period

(1) Any week during the whole or part of which an employee's relations with his employer are governed by a contract of employment counts in computing the employee's period of employment.

(2) Any week (not within subsection (1)) during an employee's period of absence from work occasioned wholly or partly by pregnancy or childbirth after which the employee returns to work in accordance with section 79, or in pursuance of an offer described in section 96(3), counts in computing the employee's period of employment.

(3) Subject to subsection (4), any week (not within subsection (1)) during the whole or part of which an employee is—

(a) incapable of work in consequence of sickness or injury,

(b) absent from work on account of a temporary cessation of work,

(c) absent from work in circumstances such that, by arrangement or custom, he is regarded as continuing in the employment of his employer for any purpose, or

(d) absent from work wholly or partly because of pregnancy or childbirth,

counts in computing the employee's period of employment.

(4) Not more than twenty-six weeks count under subsection (3)(a) or (subject to subsection (2)) subsection (3)(d) between any periods falling under subsection (1).

213 Intervals in employment

(1) Where in the case of an employee a date later than the date which would be the effective date of termination by virtue of subsection (1) of section 97 is treated for certain purposes as the effective date of termination by virtue of subsection (2) or (4) of that section, the period of the interval between the two dates counts as a period of employment in ascertaining for the purposes of section 108(1) or 119(1) the period for which the employee has been continuously employed.

(2) Where an employee is by virtue of section 138(1) regarded for the purposes of Part XI as not having been dismissed by reason of a renewal or re-engagement taking effect after an interval, the period of the interval counts as a period of employment in ascertaining for the purposes of section 155 or 162(1) the period for which the employee has been continuously employed (except so far as it is to be disregarded under section 214 or 215).

(3) Where in the case of an employee a date later than the date which would be the relevant date by virtue of subsections (2) to (4) of section 145 is treated for certain purposes as the relevant date by virtue of subsection (5) of that section, the period of the interval between the two dates counts as a period of employment in ascertaining for the purposes of section 155 or 162(1) the period for which the employee has been continuously employed (except so far as it is to be disregarded under section 214 or 215).

214 Special provisions for redundancy payments

(1) This section applies where a period of continuous employment has to be determined in relation to an employee for the purposes of the application of section 155 or 162(1).

(2) The continuity of a period of employment is broken where—

- (a) a redundancy payment has previously been paid to the employee (whether in respect of dismissal or in respect of lay-off or short-time), and
- (b) the contract of employment under which the employee was employed was renewed (whether by the same or another employer) or the employee was re-engaged under a new contract of employment (whether by the same or another employer).

(3) The continuity of a period of employment is also broken where—

- (a) a payment has been made to the employee (whether in respect of the termination of his employment or lay-off or short-time) in accordance with a scheme under section 1 of the Superannuation Act 1972 or arrangements falling within section 177(3), and
- (b) he commenced new, or renewed, employment.

(4) The date on which the person's continuity of employment is broken by virtue of this section—

- (a) if the employment was under a contract of employment, is the date which was the relevant date in relation to the payment mentioned in subsection (2)(a) or (3)(a), and
- (b) if the employment was otherwise than under a contract of employment, is the date which would have been the relevant date in relation to the payment mentioned in subsection (2)(a) or (3)(a) had the employment been under a contract of employment.

(5) For the purposes of this section a redundancy payment shall be treated as having been paid if—

(a) the whole of the payment has been paid to the employee by the employer,

(b) a tribunal has determined liability and found that the employer must pay part (but not all) of the redundancy payment and the employer has paid that part, or

(c) the Secretary of State has paid a sum to the employee in respect of the redundancy payment under section 167.

215 Employment abroad etc

(1) This Chapter applies to a period of employment—

(a) (subject to the following provisions of this section) even where during the period the employee was engaged in work wholly or mainly outside Great Britain, and

(b) even where the employee was excluded by or under this Act from any right conferred by this Act.

(2) For the purposes of sections 155 and 162(1) a week of employment does not count in computing a period of employment if the employee—

(a) was employed outside Great Britain during the whole or part of the week, and

(b) was not during that week an employed earner for the purposes of the Social Security Contributions and Benefits Act 1992 in respect of whom a secondary Class 1 contribution was payable under that Act (whether or not the contribution was in fact paid).

(3) Where by virtue of subsection (2) a week of employment does not count in computing a period of employment, the continuity of the period is not broken by reason only that the week does not count in computing the period; and the number of days which, for the purposes of section 211(3), fall within the intervening period is seven for each week within this subsection.

(4) Any question arising under subsection (2) whether—

(a) a person was an employed earner for the purposes of the Social Security Contributions and Benefits Act 1992, or

(b) if so, whether a secondary Class 1 contribution was payable in respect of him under that Act,

shall be determined by the Secretary of State.

(5) Any legislation (including regulations) as to the determination of questions which under the Social Security Administration Act 1992 the Secretary of State is empowered to determine (including provisions as to the reference of questions for decision, or as to appeals, to the High Court or the Court of Session) apply to the determination of any question by the Secretary of State under subsection (4).

(6) Subsection (2) does not apply in relation to a person who is—

(a) employed as a master or seaman in a British ship, and

(b) ordinarily resident in Great Britain.

216 Industrial disputes

(1) A week does not count under section 212 if during the week, or any part of the week, the employee takes part in a strike.

(2) The continuity of an employee's period of employment is not broken by a week which does not count under this Chapter (whether or not by virtue only of subsection (1)) if during the week, or any part of the week, the employee takes part in a strike; and the number of days which, for the purposes of section 211(3), fall within the intervening period is the number of days between the last working day before the strike and the day on which work was resumed.

(3) The continuity of an employee's period of employment is not broken by a week if during the week, or any part of the week, the employee is absent from work because of a lock-out by the employer; and the number of days which, for the purposes of section 211(3), fall within the intervening period is the number of days between the last working day before the lock-out and the day on which work was resumed.

217 Reinstatement after military service

(1) If a person who is entitled to apply to his former employer under the Reserve Forces (Safeguard of Employment) Act 1985 enters the employment of the employer not later than the end of the six month period mentioned in section 1(4)(b) of that Act, his period of service in the armed forces of the Crown in the circumstances specified in section 1(1) of that Act does not break his continuity of employment.

(2) In the case of such a person the number of days which, for the purposes of section 211(3), fall within the intervening period is the number of days between the last day of his previous period of employment with the employer (or, if there was more than one such period, the last of them) and the first day of the period of employment beginning in the six month period.

218 Change of employer

(1) Subject to the provisions of this section, this Chapter relates only to employment by the one employer.

(2) If a trade or business, or an undertaking (whether or not established by or under an Act), is transferred from one person to another—
   (a) the period of employment of an employee in the trade or business or undertaking at the time of the transfer counts as a period of employment with the transferee, and
   (b) the transfer does not break the continuity of the period of employment.

(3) If by or under an Act (whether public or local and whether passed before or after this Act) a contract of employment between any body corporate and an employee is modified and some other body corporate is substituted as the employer—
   (a) the employee's period of employment at the time when the modification takes effect counts as a period of employment with the second body corporate, and
   (b) the change of employer does not break the continuity of the period of employment.

(4) If on the death of an employer the employee is taken into the employment of the personal representatives or trustees of the deceased—

(a) the employee's period of employment at the time of the death counts as a period of employment with the employer's personal representatives or trustees, and

(b) the death does not break the continuity of the period of employment.

(5) If there is a change in the partners, personal representatives or trustees who employ any person—

(a) the employee's period of employment at the time of the change counts as a period of employment with the partners, personal representatives or trustees after the change, and

(b) the change does not break the continuity of the period of employment.

(6) If an employee of an employer is taken into the employment of another employer who, at the time when the employee enters the second employer's employment, is an associated employer of the first employer—

(a) the employee's period of employment at that time counts as a period of employment with the second employer, and

(b) the change of employer does not break the continuity of the period of employment.

(7) If an employee of the governors of a school maintained by a local education authority is taken into the employment of the authority or an employee of a local education authority is taken into the employment of the governors of a school maintained by the authority—

(a) his period of employment at the time of the change of employer counts as a period of employment with the second employer, and

(b) the change does not break the continuity of the period of employment.

(8) If a person employed in relevant employment by a health service employer is taken into relevant employment by another such employer, his period of employment at the time of the change of employer counts as a period of employment with the second employer and the change does not break the continuity of the period of employment.

(9) For the purposes of subsection (8) employment is relevant employment if it is employment of a description—

(a) in which persons are engaged while undergoing professional training which involves their being employed successively by a number of different health service employers, and

(b) which is specified in an order made by the Secretary of State.

(10) The following are health service employers for the purposes of subsections (8) and (9)—

(a) Health Authorities established under section 8 of the National Health Service Act 1977,

(b) Special Health Authorities established under section 11 of that Act,

(c) National Health Service trusts established under Part I of the National Health Service and Community Care Act 1990,

(d) the Dental Practice Board, and

(e) the Public Health Laboratory Service Board.

219 Reinstatement or re-engagement of dismissed employee

(1) Regulations made by the Secretary of State may make provision—

(a) for preserving the continuity of a person's period of employment for the purposes of this Chapter or for the purposes of this Chapter as applied by or under any other enactment specified in the regulations, or

(b) for modifying or excluding the operation of section 214 subject to the recovery of any such payment as is mentioned in that section,

in cases where, in consequence of action to which subsection (2) applies, a dismissed employee is reinstated or re-engaged by his employer or by a successor or associated employer of that employer.

(2) This subsection applies to any action taken in relation to the dismissal of an employee which consists of—

(a) his making a claim in accordance with a dismissal procedures agreement designated by an order under section 110,

(b) the presentation by him of a relevant complaint of dismissal,

(c) any action taken by a conciliation officer under section 18 of the Industrial Tribunals Act 1996, or

(d) the making of a relevant compromise contract.

(3) In subsection (2)(b) "relevant complaint of dismissal" means—

(a) a complaint under section 111 of this Act,

(b) a complaint under section 63 of the Sex Discrimination Act 1975 arising out of a dismissal,

(c) a complaint under section 54 of the Race Relations Act 1976 arising out of a dismissal, or

(d) a complaint under section 8 of the Disability Discrimination Act 1995 arising out of a dismissal.

(4) In subsection (2)(d) "relevant compromise contract" means—

(a) an agreement or contract authorised by—

(i) section 203(2)(f) of this Act,

(ii) section 77(4)(aa) of the Sex Discrimination Act 1975,

(iii) section 72(4)(aa) of the Race Relations Act 1976, or

(iv) section 9(2)(b) of the Disability Discrimination Act 1995, or

(b) an agreement to refrain from instituting or continuing any proceedings before an industrial tribunal where the tribunal has jurisdiction in respect of the proceedings by virtue of an order under section 3 of the Industrial Tribunals Act 1996.

CHAPTER II

A WEEK'S PAY

Introductory

220 Introductory

The amount of a week's pay of an employee shall be calculated for the purposes of this Act in accordance with this Chapter.

Employments with normal working hours

221 General

(1) This section and sections 222 and 223 apply where there are normal working hours for the employee when employed under the contract of employment in force on the calculation date.

(2) Subject to section 222, if the employee's remuneration for employment in normal working hours (whether by the hour or week or other period) does not vary with the amount of work done in the period, the amount of a week's pay is the amount which is payable by the employer under the contract of employment in force on the calculation date if the employee works throughout his normal working hours in a week.

(3) Subject to section 222, if the employee's remuneration for employment in normal working hours (whether by the hour or week or other period) does vary with the amount of work done in the period, the amount of a week's pay is the amount of remuneration for the number of normal working hours in a week calculated at the average hourly rate of remuneration payable by the employer to the employee in respect of the period of twelve weeks ending—

- (a) where the calculation date is the last day of a week, with that week, and
- (b) otherwise, with the last complete week before the calculation date.

(4) In this section references to remuneration varying with the amount of work done includes remuneration which may include any commission or similar payment which varies in amount.

(5) This section is subject to sections 227 and 228.

222 Remuneration varying according to time of work

(1) This section applies if the employee is required under the contract of employment in force on the calculation date to work during normal working hours on days of the week, or at times of the day, which differ from week to week or over a longer period so that the remuneration payable for, or apportionable to, any week varies according to the incidence of those days or times.

(2) The amount of a week's pay is the amount of remuneration for the average number of weekly normal working hours at the average hourly rate of remuneration.

(3) For the purposes of subsection (2)—

(a) the average number of weekly hours is calculated by dividing by twelve the total number of the employee's normal working hours during the relevant period of twelve weeks, and

(b) the average hourly rate of remuneration is the average hourly rate of remuneration payable by the employer to the employee in respect of the relevant period of twelve weeks.

(4) In subsection (3) "the relevant period of twelve weeks" means the period of twelve weeks ending—

(a) where the calculation date is the last day of a week, with that week, and

(b) otherwise, with the last complete week before the calculation date.

(5) This section is subject to sections 227 and 228.

223 Supplementary

(1) For the purposes of sections 221 and 222, in arriving at the average hourly rate of remuneration, only—

(a) the hours when the employee was working, and

(b) the remuneration payable for, or apportionable to, those hours,

shall be brought in.

(2) If for any of the twelve weeks mentioned in sections 221 and 222 no remuneration within subsection (1)(b) was payable by the employer to the employee, account shall be taken of remuneration in earlier weeks so as to bring up to twelve the number of weeks of which account is taken.

(3) Where—

(a) in arriving at the average hourly rate of remuneration, account has to be taken of remuneration payable for, or apportionable to, work done in hours other than normal working hours, and

(b) the amount of that remuneration was greater than it would have been if the work had been done in normal working hours (or, in a case within section 234(3), in normal working hours falling within the number of hours without overtime),

account shall be taken of that remuneration as if the work had been done in such hours and the amount of that remuneration had been reduced accordingly.

Employments with no normal working hours

224 Employments with no normal working hours

(1) This section applies where there are no normal working hours for the employee when employed under the contract of employment in force on the calculation date.

(2) The amount of a week's pay is the amount of the employee's average weekly remuneration in the period of twelve weeks ending—

(a) where the calculation date is the last day of a week, with that week, and

(b) otherwise, with the last complete week before the calculation date.

(3) In arriving at the average weekly remuneration no account shall be taken of a week in which no remuneration was payable by the employer to the employee and

remuneration in earlier weeks shall be brought in so as to bring up to twelve the number of weeks of which account is taken.

(4) This section is subject to sections 227 and 228.

The calculation date

225 Rights during employment

(1) Where the calculation is for the purposes of section 30, the calculation date is—

(a) where the employee's contract has been varied, or a new contract entered into, in connection with a period of short-time working, the last day on which the original contract was in force, and

(b) otherwise, the day in respect of which the guarantee payment is payable.

(2) Where the calculation is for the purposes of section 53 or 54, the calculation date is the day on which the employer's notice was given.

(3) Where the calculation is for the purposes of section 56, the calculation date is the day of the appointment.

(4) Where the calculation is for the purposes of section 62, the calculation date is the day on which the time off was taken or on which it is alleged the time off should have been permitted.

(5) Where the calculation is for the purposes of section 69—

(a) in the case of an employee suspended on medical grounds, the calculation date is the day before that on which the suspension begins, and

(b) in the case of an employee suspended on maternity grounds, the calculation date is—

(i) where the day before that on which the suspension begins falls within either the employee's maternity leave period or the further period up to the day on which the employee exercises the right conferred on her by section 79, the day before the beginning of the maternity leave period, and

(ii) otherwise, the day before that on which the suspension begins.

226 Rights on termination

(1) Where the calculation is for the purposes of section 88 or 89, the calculation date is the day immediately preceding the first day of the period of notice required by section 86(1) or (2).

(2) Where the calculation is for the purposes of section 93, 117 or 125, the calculation date is—

(a) if the dismissal was with notice, the date on which the employer's notice was given, and

(b) otherwise, the effective date of termination.

(3) Where the calculation is for the purposes of section 119 or 121, the calculation date is—

(a) if the employee is taken to be dismissed by virtue of section 96(1), the last day on which the employee worked under her contract of employment immediately before the beginning of her maternity leave period,

(b) if by virtue of subsection (2) or (4) of section 97 a date later than the effective date of termination as defined in subsection (1) of that section is to be treated for certain purposes as the effective date of termination, the effective date of termination as so defined, and

(c) otherwise, the date specified in subsection (6).

(4) Where the calculation is for the purposes of section 147(2), the calculation date is the day immediately preceding the first of the four, or six, weeks referred to in section 148(2).

(5) Where the calculation is for the purposes of section 162, the calculation date is—

(a) if the employee is taken to be dismissed by virtue of section 137(1), the last day on which the employee worked under her contract of employment immediately before the beginning of her maternity leave period,

(b) if by virtue of subsection (5) of section 145 a date is to be treated for certain purposes as the relevant date which is later than the relevant date as defined by the previous provisions of that section, the relevant date as so defined, and

(c) otherwise, the date specified in subsection (6).

(6) The date referred to in subsections (3)(c) and (5)(c) is the date on which notice would have been given had—

(a) the contract been terminable by notice and been terminated by the employer giving such notice as is required by section 86 to terminate the contract, and

(b) the notice expired on the effective date of termination, or the relevant date,

(whether or not those conditions were in fact fulfilled).

Maximum amount of week's pay

227 Maximum amount

(1) For the purpose of calculating—

(a) a basic award of compensation for unfair dismissal,

(b) an additional award of compensation for unfair dismissal, or

(c) a redundancy payment,

the amount of a week's pay shall not exceed £210.

(2) The Secretary of State may vary the limits imposed by subsection (1), after a review under section 208, by order made in accordance with that section.

(3) Such an order may provide that it applies in the case of a dismissal—

(a) in relation to which the date which is the effective date of termination for the purposes of this subsection by virtue of section 97(2) or (4) falls after the order comes into force, or

(b) in relation to which the date which is the relevant date for the purposes of this subsection by virtue of section 145(5) falls after the order comes into force,

even if the date which is the effective date of termination, or the relevant date, for other purposes of this Act falls before the order comes into force.

(4) Subsection (3)—
 (a) does not apply to a case within section 96(1) or 137(1), but
 (b) is without prejudice to section 236(5).

Miscellaneous

228 New employments and other special cases

(1) In any case in which the employee has not been employed for a sufficient period to enable a calculation to be made under the preceding provisions of this Chapter, the amount of a week's pay is the amount which fairly represents a week's pay.

(2) In determining that amount the industrial tribunal—
 (a) shall apply as nearly as may be such of the preceding provisions of this Chapter as it considers appropriate, and
 (b) may have regard to such of the considerations specified in subsection (3) as it thinks fit.

(3) The considerations referred to in subsection (2)(b) are—
 (a) any remuneration received by the employee in respect of the employment in question,
 (b) the amount offered to the employee as remuneration in respect of the employment in question,
 (c) the remuneration received by other persons engaged in relevant comparable employment with the same employer, and
 (d) the remuneration received by other persons engaged in relevant comparable employment with other employers.

(4) The Secretary of State may by regulations provide that in cases prescribed by the regulations the amount of a week's pay shall be calculated in such manner as may be so prescribed.

229 Supplementary

(1) In arriving at—
 (a) an average hourly rate of remuneration, or
 (b) average weekly remuneration,

under this Chapter, account shall be taken of work for a former employer within the period for which the average is to be taken if, by virtue of Chapter I of this Part, a period of employment with the former employer counts as part of the employee's continuous period of employment.

(2) Where under this Chapter account is to be taken of remuneration or other payments for a period which does not coincide with the periods for which the remuneration or other payments are calculated, the remuneration or other payments shall be apportioned in such manner as may be just.

CHAPTER III

OTHER INTERPRETATION PROVISIONS

230 Employees, workers etc

(1) In this Act "employee" means an individual who has entered into or works under (or, where the employment has ceased, worked under) a contract of employment.

(2) In this Act "contract of employment" means a contract of service or apprenticeship, whether express or implied, and (if it is express) whether oral or in writing.

(3) In this Act "worker" (except in the phrases "shop worker" and "betting worker") means an individual who has entered into or works under (or, where the employment has ceased, worked under)—

(a) a contract of employment, or

(b) any other contract, whether express or implied and (if it is express) whether oral or in writing, whereby the individual undertakes to do or perform personally any work or services for another party to the contract whose status is not by virtue of the contract that of a client or customer of any profession or business undertaking carried on by the individual;

and any reference to a worker's contract shall be construed accordingly.

(4) In this Act "employer", in relation to an employee or a worker, means the person by whom the employee or worker is (or, where the employment has ceased, was) employed.

(5) In this Act "employment"—

(a) in relation to an employee, means (except for the purposes of section 171) employment under a contract of employment, and

(b) in relation to a worker, means employment under his contract;

and "employed" shall be construed accordingly.

231 Associated employers

For the purposes of this Act any two employers shall be treated as associated if—

(a) one is a company of which the other (directly or indirectly) has control, or

(b) both are companies of which a third person (directly or indirectly) has control;

and "associated employer" shall be construed accordingly.

232 Shop workers

(1) In this Act "shop worker" means an employee who, under his contract of employment, is or may be required to do shop work.

(2) In this Act "shop work" means work in or about a shop in England or Wales on a day on which the shop is open for the serving of customers.

(3) Subject to subsection (4), in this Act "shop" includes any premises where any retail trade or business is carried on.

(4) Where premises are used mainly for purposes other than those of retail trade or business and would not (apart from subsection (3)) be regarded as a shop, only such part of the premises as—

(a) is used wholly or mainly for the purposes of retail trade or business, or

(b) is used both for the purposes of retail trade or business and for the purposes of wholesale trade and is used wholly or mainly for those two purposes considered together,

is to be regarded as a shop for the purposes of this Act.

(5) In subsection (4)(b) "wholesale trade" means the sale of goods for use or resale in the course of a business or the hire of goods for use in the course of a business.

(6) In this section "retail trade or business" includes—

(a) the business of a barber or hairdresser,

(b) the business of hiring goods otherwise than for use in the course of a trade or business, and

(c) retail sales by auction,

but does not include catering business or the sale at theatres and places of amusement of programmes, catalogues and similar items.

(7) In subsection (6) "catering business" means—

(a) the sale of meals, refreshments or intoxicating liquor for consumption on the premises on which they are sold, or

(b) the sale of meals or refreshments prepared to order for immediate consumption off the premises;

and in paragraph (a) "intoxicating liquor" has the same meaning as in the Licensing Act 1964.

(8) In this Act—

"notice period", in relation to an opted-out shop worker, has the meaning given by section 41(3),

"opted-out", in relation to a shop worker, shall be construed in accordance with section 41(1) and (2),

"opting-in notice", in relation to a shop worker, has the meaning given by section 36(6),

"opting-out notice", in relation to a shop worker, has the meaning given by section 40(2), and

"protected", in relation to a shop worker, shall be construed in accordance with section 36(1) to (5).

233 Betting workers

(1) In this Act "betting worker" means an employee who, under his contract of employment, is or may be required to do betting work.

(2) In this Act "betting work" means—

(a) work at a track in England or Wales for a bookmaker on a day on which the bookmaker acts as such at the track, being work which consists of or includes dealing with betting transactions, and

(b) work in a licensed betting office in England or Wales on a day on which the office is open for use for the effecting of betting transactions.

(3) In subsection (2) "betting transactions" includes the collection or payment of winnings on a bet and any transaction in which one or more of the parties is acting as a bookmaker.

(4) In this section "bookmaker" means any person who—

(a) whether on his own account or as servant or agent to any other person, carries on (whether occasionally or regularly) the business of receiving or negotiating bets or conducting pool betting operations, or

(b) by way of business in any manner holds himself out, or permits himself to be held out, as a person who receives or negotiates bets or conducts such operations.

(5) Expressions used in this section and in the Betting, Gaming and Lotteries Act 1963 have the same meaning in this section as in that Act.

(6) In this Act—

"notice period", in relation to an opted-out betting worker, has the meaning given by section 41(3),

"opted-out", in relation to a betting worker, shall be construed in accordance with section 41(1) and (2),

"opting-in notice", in relation to a betting worker, has the meaning given by section 36(6),

"opting-out notice", in relation to a betting worker, has the meaning given by section 40(2), and

"protected", in relation to a betting worker, shall be construed in accordance with section 36(1) to (5).

234 Normal working hours

(1) Where an employee is entitled to overtime pay when employed for more than a fixed number of hours in a week or other period, there are for the purposes of this Act normal working hours in his case.

(2) Subject to subsection (3), the normal working hours in such a case are the fixed number of hours.

(3) Where in such a case—

(a) the contract of employment fixes the number, or minimum number, of hours of employment in a week or other period (whether or not it also provides for the reduction of that number or minimum in certain circumstances), and

(b) that number or minimum number of hours exceeds the number of hours without overtime,

the normal working hours are that number or minimum number of hours (and not the number of hours without overtime).

235 Other definitions

(1) In this Act, except in so far as the context otherwise requires—

"act" and "action" each includes omission and references to doing an act or taking action shall be construed accordingly, "basic award of compensation for unfair dismissal" shall be construed in accordance with section 118,

"business" includes a trade or profession and includes any activity carried on by a body of persons (whether corporate or unincorporated),

"childbirth" means the birth of a living child or the birth of a child whether living or dead after twenty-four weeks of pregnancy,

"collective agreement" has the meaning given by section 178(1) and (2) of the Trade Union and Labour Relations (Consolidation) Act 1992,

"conciliation officer" means an officer designated by the Advisory, Conciliation and Arbitration Service under section 211 of that Act,

"dismissal procedures agreement" means an agreement in writing with respect to procedures relating to dismissal made by or on behalf of one or more independent trade unions and one or more employers or employers' associations,

"employers' association" has the same meaning as in the Trade Union and Labour Relations (Consolidation) Act 1992,

"expected week of childbirth" means the week, beginning with midnight between Saturday and Sunday, in which it is expected that childbirth will occur,

"guarantee payment" has the meaning given by section 28,

"independent trade union" means a trade union which—

(a) is not under the domination or control of an employer or a group of employers or of one or more employers' associations, and

(b) is not liable to interference by an employer or any such group or association (arising out of the provision of financial or material support or by any other means whatever) tending towards such control,

"job", in relation to an employee, means the nature of the work which he is employed to do in accordance with his contract and the capacity and place in which he is so employed,

"maternity leave period" shall be construed in accordance with sections 72 and 73,

"notified day of return" shall be construed in accordance with section 83,

"position", in relation to an employee, means the following matters taken as a whole—

(a) his status as an employee,

(b) the nature of his work, and

(c) his terms and conditions of employment,

"redundancy payment" has the meaning given by Part XI,

"relevant date" has the meaning given by sections 145 and 153,

"renewal" includes extension, and any reference to renewing a contract or a fixed term shall be construed accordingly,

"statutory provision" means a provision, whether of a general or a special nature, contained in, or in any document made or issued under, any Act, whether of a general or special nature,

"successor", in relation to the employer of an employee, means (subject to subsection (2)) a person who in consequence of a change occurring (whether by virtue of a sale or other disposition or by operation of law) in the ownership of the undertaking, or of the part of the undertaking, for the purposes of which the employee was employed, has become the owner of the undertaking or part, "trade union" has the meaning given by section 1 of the Trade Union and Labour Relations (Consolidation) Act 1992,

"week"—

(a) in Chapter I of this Part means a week ending with Saturday, and

(b) otherwise, except in section 86, means, in relation to an employee whose remuneration is calculated weekly by a week ending with a day other than Saturday, a week ending with that other day and, in relation to any other employee, a week ending with Saturday.

(2) The definition of "successor" in subsection (1) has effect (subject to the necessary modifications) in relation to a case where—

(a) the person by whom an undertaking or part of an undertaking is owned immediately before a change is one of the persons by whom (whether as partners, trustees or otherwise) it is owned immediately after the change, or

(b) the persons by whom an undertaking or part of an undertaking is owned immediately before a change (whether as partners, trustees or otherwise) include the persons by whom, or include one or more of the persons by whom, it is owned immediately after the change,

as it has effect where the previous owner and the new owner are wholly different persons.

(3) References in this Act to redundancy, dismissal by reason of redundancy and similar expressions shall be construed in accordance with section 139.

(4) In sections 136(2), 154 and 216(3) and paragraph 14 of Schedule 2 "lock-out" means—

(a) the closing of a place of employment,

(b) the suspension of work, or

(c) the refusal by an employer to continue to employ any number of persons employed by him in consequence of a dispute,

done with a view to compelling persons employed by the employer, or to aid another employer in compelling persons employed by him, to accept terms or conditions of or affecting employment.

(5) In sections 91(2), 140(2) and (3), 143(1), 144(2) and (3), 154 and 216(1) and (2) and paragraph 14 of Schedule 2 "strike" means—

(a) the cessation of work by a body of employed persons acting in combination, or

(b) a concerted refusal, or a refusal under a common understanding, of any number of employed persons to continue to work for an employer in consequence of a dispute,

done as a means of compelling their employer or any employed person or body of employed persons, or to aid other employees in compelling their employer or any employed person or body of employed persons, to accept or not to accept terms or conditions of or affecting employment.

PART XV

GENERAL AND SUPPLEMENTARY

General

236 Orders and regulations

(1) Any power conferred by any provision of this Act to make any order (other than an Order in Council) or regulations is exercisable by statutory instrument.

(2) A statutory instrument made under any power conferred by this Act to make an Order in Council or other order or regulations, except—

(a) an Order in Council or other order to which subsection (3) applies,

(b) an order under section 35 or Part II of Schedule 2, or

(c) an order made in accordance with section 208,

is subject to annulment in pursuance of a resolution of either House of Parliament.

(3) No recommendation shall be made to Her Majesty to make an Order in Council under section 192(3), and no order shall be made under section 72(3), 73(5), 79(3), 120(2), 124(2) or 125(7) or (subject to subsection (4)) section 209, unless a draft of the Order in Council or order has been laid before Parliament and approved by a resolution of each House of Parliament.

(4) Subsection (3) does not apply to an order under section 209(1)(b) which specifies only provisions contained in Part XI.

(5) Any power conferred by this Act which is exercisable by statutory instrument includes power to make such incidental, supplementary or transitional provisions as appear to the authority exercising the power to be necessary or expedient.

237 Financial provisions

There shall be paid out of the National Insurance Fund into the Consolidated Fund sums equal to the amount of—

(a) any expenses incurred by the Secretary of State in consequence of Part XI, and

(b) any expenses incurred by the Secretary of State (or by persons acting on his behalf) in exercising his functions under Part XII.

Reciprocal arrangements

238 Reciprocal arrangements with Northern Ireland

(1) If provision is made by Northern Ireland legislation for purposes corresponding to any of the purposes of this Act, other than an excepted provision, the Secretary of State may, with the consent of the Treasury, make reciprocal arrangements with the appropriate Northern Ireland authority for co-ordinating the relevant provisions of this Act with the corresponding provisions of the Northern Ireland legislation so as to secure that they operate, to such extent as may be provided by the arrangements, as a single system.

(2) The following provisions of this Act are excepted provisions for the purposes of subsection (1)—

(a) in Part I, sections 1 to 7,

(b) Parts II and IV,

(c) in Part V, sections 45 and 46,

(d) in Part VI, sections 58 to 60,

(e) in Part IX, sections 86 to 91, and

(f) in Part X, sections 101 and 102.

(3) The Secretary of State may make regulations for giving effect to any arrangements made under subsection (1).

(4) Regulations under subsection (3) may make different provision for different cases.

(5) Such regulations may provide that the relevant provisions of this Act have effect in relation to persons affected by the arrangements subject to such modifications and adaptations as may be specified in the regulations, including provision—

(a) for securing that acts, omissions and events having any effect for the purposes of the Northern Ireland legislation have a corresponding effect for the purposes of this Act (but not so as to confer a right to double payment in respect of the same act, omission or event), and

(b) for determining, in cases where rights accrue both under this Act and under the Northern Ireland legislation, which of those rights is available to the person concerned.

(6) In this section "the appropriate Northern Ireland authority" means such authority as may be specified in the Northern Ireland legislation.

239 Reciprocal arrangements with Isle of Man

(1) If an Act of Tynwald is passed for purposes similar to the purposes of Part XI, the Secretary of State may, with the consent of the Treasury, make reciprocal arrangements with the appropriate Isle of Man authority for co-ordinating the provisions of Part XI with the corresponding provisions of the Act of Tynwald so as to secure that they operate, to such extent as may be provided by the arrangements, as a single system.

(2) For the purposes of giving effect to any arrangements made under subsection (1) the Secretary of State may, in conjunction with the appropriate Isle of Man authority, make any necessary financial adjustments between the National Insurance Fund and any fund established under the Act of Tynwald.

(3) The Secretary of State may make regulations for giving effect to any arrangements made under subsection (1).

(4) Regulations under subsection (3) may provide that Part XI has effect in relation to persons affected by the arrangements subject to such modifications and adaptations as may be specified in the regulations, including provision—

(a) for securing that acts, omissions and events having any effect for the purposes of the Act of Tynwald have a corresponding effect for the purposes of Part XI (but not so as to confer a right to double payment in respect of the same act, omission or event), and

(b) for determining, in cases where rights accrue both under this Act and under the Act of Tynwald, which of those rights is available to the person concerned.

(5) In this section "the appropriate Isle of Man authority" means such authority as may be specified in an Act of Tynwald.

Final provisions

240 Consequential amendments

Schedule 1 (consequential amendments) shall have effect.

241 Transitionals, savings and transitory provisions

Schedule 2 (transitional provisions, savings and transitory provisions) shall have effect.

242 Repeals and revocations

The enactments specified in Part I of Schedule 3 are repealed, and the instruments specified in Part II of that Schedule are revoked, to the extent specified in the third column of that Schedule.

243 Commencement

This Act shall come into force at the end of the period of three months beginning with the day on which it is passed.

244 Extent

(1) Subject to the following provisions, this Act extends to England and Wales and Scotland but not to Northern Ireland.

(2) The provisions of this Act which refer to shop workers and betting workers extend to England and Wales only.

(3) Sections 201 and 238 (and sections 236 and 243, this section and section 245) extend to Northern Ireland (as well as to England and Wales and Scotland).

(4) Sections 240 and 242 and Schedules 1 and 3 have the same extent as the provisions amended or repealed by this Act.

245 Short title

This Act may be cited as the Employment Rights Act 1996.

SCHEDULES

SCHEDULE 1

Section 240.

CONSEQUENTIAL AMENDMENTS

The Equal Pay Act 1970 (c. 41)

1 (1) Section 1 of the Equal Pay Act 1970 is amended as follows.

(2) In subsection (10A)—

(a) for "section 139 of the Employment Protection (Consolidation) Act 1978" substitute "section 195 of the Employment Rights Act 1996", and

(b) for "subsections (4) to (9)" substitute "subsections (6) to (12)".

(3) In subsection (10B)—

(a) for "section 139A of the Employment Protection (Consolidation) Act 1978" substitute "section 194 of the Employment Rights Act 1996", and

(b) for "subsection (6)" substitute "subsection (7)".

The Atomic Energy Authority Act 1971 (c. 11)

2 (1) Section 10 of the Atomic Energy Authority Act 1971 is amended as follows.

(2) In subsection (2)—

(a) in paragraph (a), for "the said sections 1 to 4" substitute "sections 1 to 7 of the Employment Rights Act 1996", and

(b) in paragraph (b)—

(i) for "section 5 of the said Act of 1978" substitute "the Employment Rights Act 1996", and

(ii) for "subsection (1) of that section" substitute "section 1 of that Act".

(3) In subsection (3)—

(a) for "the Employment Protection (Consolidation) Act 1978" substitute "the Employment Rights Act 1996", and

(b) for "sections 1 to 4" substitute "section 1".

(4) In subsection (4)—

(a) for "Schedule 13 to the said Act of 1978" substitute "Chapter I of Part XIV of the Employment Rights Act 1996", and

(b) for the words from "sub-paragraph (2)" to "that sub-paragraph" substitute "subsection (2) of section 218 of that Act, be taken to be such a transfer of an undertaking as is mentioned in that subsection".

The Attachment of Earnings Act 1971 (c. 32)

3 Paragraph 3 of Part I of Schedule 3 to the Attachment of Earnings Act 1971 shall continue to have effect with the substitution (originally made by paragraph 4 of Schedule 4 to the Wages Act 1986) of the following paragraph for paragraph (c)—

"(c) amounts deductible under any enactment, or in pursuance of a request in writing by the debtor, for the purposes of a superannuation scheme, namely any enactment, rules, deed or other instrument providing for the payment of annuities or lump sums—

(i) to the persons with respect to whom the instrument has effect on their retirement at a specified age or on becoming incapacitated at some earlier age, or

(ii) to the personal representatives or the widows, relatives or dependants of such persons on their death or otherwise,

whether with or without any further or other benefits."

The British Library Act 1972 (c. 54)

4 In paragraph 13(3)(a) of the Schedule to the British Library Act 1972, for "the Employment Protection (Consolidation) Act 1978" substitute "the Employment Rights Act 1996".

The Health and Safety at Work etc. Act 1974 (c. 37)

5 In section 80(2A) of the Health and Safety at Work etc. Act 1974, for "the Employment Protection (Consolidation) Act 1978 which re-enact" substitute "the Employment Rights Act 1996 or the Trade Union and Labour Relations (Consolidation) Act 1992 which derive from provisions of the Employment Protection (Consolidation) Act 1978 which re-enacted".

The Sex Discrimination Act 1975 (c. 65)

6 (1) The Sex Discrimination Act 1975 is amended as follows.

(2) In section 85A(2)—

(a) for "section 139 of the Employment Protection (Consolidation) Act 1978" substitute "section 195 of the Employment Rights Act 1996", and

(b) for "subsections (4) to (9)" substitute "subsections (6) to (12)".

(3) In section 85B(2)—

(a) for "section 139A of the Employment Protection (Consolidation) Act 1978" substitute "section 194 of the Employment Rights Act 1996", and

(b) for "subsection (6)" substitute "subsection (7)".

The Scottish Development Agency Act 1975 (c. 69)

7 In paragraph 6 of Schedule 3 to the Scottish Development Agency Act 1975, for "the Employment Protection (Consolidation) Act 1978" substitute "the Employment Rights Act 1996".

The Welsh Development Agency Act 1975 (c. 70)

8 In paragraph 7 of Schedule 2 to the Welsh Development Agency Act 1975, for "the Employment Protection (Consolidation) Act 1978" substitute "the Employment Rights Act 1996".

The Lotteries and Amusements Act 1976 (c. 32)

9 In section 23(1) of the Lotteries and Amusements Act 1976, for "meanings given by section 153(1) of the Employment Protection (Consolidation) Act 1978" substitute "same meanings as in the Employment Rights Act 1996".

The Race Relations Act 1976 (c. 74)

10 (1) The Race Relations Act 1976 is amended as follows.

(2) In section 75A(2)—

(a) for "section 139 of the Employment Protection (Consolidation) Act 1978" substitute "section 195 of the Employment Rights Act 1996", and

(b) for "subsections (4) to (9)" substitute "subsections (6) to (12)".

(3) In section 75B(2)—

(a) for "section 139A of the Employment Protection (Consolidation) Act 1978" substitute "section 194 of the Employment Rights Act 1996", and

(b) for "subsection (6)" substitute "subsection (7)".

(4) In paragraph 11(4) of Schedule 2, for paragraphs (a) and (c) substitute—

"(a) the Employment Rights Act 1996 except Part XI;

(b) the Trade Union and Labour Relations (Consolidation) Act 1992; and".

The Development of Rural Wales Act 1976 (c. 75)

11 In—

(a) paragraph 6 of Schedule 2, and

(b) paragraph 6 of Schedule 6,

to the Development of Rural Wales Act 1976, for "the Employment Protection (Consolidation) Act 1978" substitute "the Employment Rights Act 1996".

The New Towns (Scotland) Act 1977 (c. 16)

12 In section 3(6) of the New Towns (Scotland) Act 1977, for "Parts I, IV, V and VI of the Employment Protection (Consolidation) Act 1978" substitute "Parts I and IX to XI of the Employment Rights Act 1996".

The National Health Service (Scotland) Act 1978 (c. 29)

13 In section 12C(3) of the National Health Service (Scotland) Act 1978—

(a) for "Part VI of the Employment Protection (Consolidation) Act 1978" substitute "Part XI of the Employment Rights Act 1996", and

(b) for "Part VI of that Act" substitute "that Part of that Act".

The House of Commons (Administration) Act 1978 (c. 36)

14 In paragraph 1 of Schedule 2 to the House of Commons (Administration) Act 1978, for "section 139 of the Employment Protection (Consolidation) Act 1978" substitute "section 195 of the Employment Rights Act 1996".

The New Towns Act 1981 (c. 64)

15 In section 54(5) of the New Towns Act 1981, for "Schedule 13 to the Employment Protection (Consolidation) Act 1978" substitute "Chapter I of Part XIV of the Employment Rights Act 1996".

The Wildlife and Countryside Act 1981 (c. 69)

16 In paragraph 8(4) of Schedule 13 to the Wildlife and Countryside Act 1981, for the words from "Schedule" to "continuous)" substitute "Chapter I of Part XIV of the Employment Rights Act 1996".

The Hops Marketing Act 1982 (c. 5)

17 In section 2(7) of the Hops Marketing Act 1982, for "the Employment Protection (Consolidation) Act 1978" substitute "the Employment Rights Act 1996".

The Oil and Gas (Enterprise) Act 1982 (c. 23)

18 (1) In Schedule 3 to the Oil and Gas (Enterprise) Act 1982, after paragraph 45 add—

"The Employment Rights Act 1996

46 (1) For subsection (1) of section 201 of the Employment Rights Act 1996 (offshore employment) there shall be substituted the following subsection—

(1) In this section "offshore employment" means employment for the purposes of—

(a) any activities in the territorial waters of the United Kingdom, or

(b) any such activities as are mentioned in section 23(2) of the Oil and Gas (Enterprise) Act 1982 in waters within subsection (6) (b) or (c) of that section."

(2) Subsection (5) of that section shall be omitted.

(2) The paragraph inserted by sub-paragraph (1) is subject to section 38(2) of the Oil and Gas (Enterprise) Act 1982 (power to bring provisions into force by order).

The Local Government Finance Act 1982 (c. 32)

19 In paragraph 8(3) of Schedule 3 to the Local Government Finance Act 1982, for "the Employment Protection (Consolidation) Act 1978" substitute "the Employment Rights Act 1996".

The Administration of Justice Act 1982 (c. 53)

20 In section 10(d) of the Administration of Justice Act 1982—

(a) for "the Employment Protection (Consolidation) Act 1978" substitute "the Employment Rights Act 1996", and
(b) for "section 81" substitute "section 135".

The Health and Social Services and Social Security Adjudications Act 1983 (c. 14)

21 In paragraph 23 of Part II of Schedule 3 to the Health and Social Services and Social Security Adjudications Act 1983, for "the Employment Protection (Consolidation) Act 1978" substitute "the Employment Rights Act 1996".

The National Audit Act 1983 (c. 44)

22 In paragraph 2(3) of Schedule 2 to the National Audit Act 1983, for "the Employment Protection (Consolidation) Act 1978" substitute "the Employment Rights Act 1996".

The National Heritage Act 1983 (c. 47)

23 In—
(a) paragraph 5(5) of Part I of Schedule 1,
(b) paragraph 15(5) of Part II of Schedule 1,
(c) paragraph 25(5) of Part III of Schedule 1,
(d) paragraph 35(5) of Part IV of Schedule 1,
(e) paragraph 2(5) of Schedule 2, and
(f) paragraph 5(5) of Schedule 3,

to the National Heritage Act 1983, for "the Employment Protection (Consolidation) Act 1978" substitute "the Employment Rights Act 1996".

The National Heritage (Scotland) Act 1985 (c. 16)

24 In—
(a) paragraph 5(5) of Part I, and
(b) paragraph 16(5) of Part II,

of Schedule 1 to the National Heritage (Scotland) Act 1985, for "the Employment Protection (Consolidation) Act 1978" substitute "the Employment Rights Act 1996".

The Prosecution of Offences Act 1985 (c. 23)

25 (1) The Prosecution of Offences Act 1985 is amended as follows.

(2) In section 11(5), for "Schedule 13 to the Employment Protection (Consolidation) Act 1978" substitute "Chapter I of Part XIV of the Employment Rights Act 1996".

(3) In section 15(6), for the words from "be treated as" to "shall not be so treated" substitute "not be treated as transferred functions".

The Local Government Act 1985 (c. 51)

26 (1) The Local Government Act 1985 is amended as follows.

(2) In section 54(2), for "Schedule 13 to the said Act of 1978" substitute "Chapter I of Part XIV of the Employment Rights Act 1996".

(3) In section 105(1), for "the Employment Protection (Consolidation) Act 1978" substitute "the Employment Rights Act 1996".

The Trustee Savings Banks Act 1985 (c. 58)

27 In section 3(7) of the Trustee Savings Banks Act 1985, for "paragraph 17(3) of Schedule 13 to the Employment Protection (Consolidation) Act 1978" substitute "section 218(3) of the Employment Rights Act 1996".

The Housing (Consequential Provisions) Act 1985 (c. 71)

28 In paragraph 7(2)(b) of Schedule 4 to the Housing (Consequential Provisions) Act 1985, for "Schedule 13 to that Act" substitute "Chapter I of Part XIV of the Employment Rights Act 1996".

The Insolvency Act 1986 (c. 45)

29 In paragraph 13 of Schedule 6 to the Insolvency Act 1986, for sub-paragraph (2) substitute—

"(2) An amount falls within this sub-paragraph if it is—

(a) a guarantee payment under Part III of the Employment Rights Act 1996 (employee without work to do);

(b) any payment for time off under section 53 (time off to look for work or arrange training) or section 56 (time off for ante-natal care) of that Act or under section 169 of the Trade Union and Labour Relations (Consolidation) Act 1992 (time off for carrying out trade union duties etc.);

(c) remuneration on suspension on medical grounds, or on maternity grounds, under Part VII of the Employment Rights Act 1996; or

(d) remuneration under a protective award under section 189 of the Trade Union and Labour Relations (Consolidation) Act 1992 (redundancy dismissal with compensation)."

The Legal Aid (Scotland) Act 1986 (c. 47)

30 In paragraph 10(1) of Schedule 1 to the Legal Aid (Scotland) Act 1986, for "the Employment Protection (Consolidation) Act 1978" substitute "the Employment Rights Act 1996".

The Debtors (Scotland) Act 1987 (c. 18)

31 In section 73(3)(g) of the Debtors (Scotland) Act 1987, for "section 81(1) of the Employment Protection (Consolidation) Act 1978" substitute "the Employment Rights Act 1996".

The Pilotage Act 1987 (c. 21)

32 In section 25(6) of the Pilotage Act 1987, for "Schedule 13 to the Employment Protection (Consolidation) Act 1978" substitute "Chapter I of Part XIV of the Employment Rights Act 1996".

The Housing (Scotland) Act 1987 (c. 26)

33 In paragraph 10(2)(b) of Schedule 22 to the Housing (Scotland) Act 1987, for "Schedule 13 to that Act" substitute "Chapter I of Part XIV of the Employment Rights Act 1996".

The Consumer Protection Act 1987 (c. 43)

34 In section 22(5) of the Consumer Protection Act 1987, for "the Employment Protection (Consolidation) Act 1978" substitute "the Employment Rights Act 1996".

The Income and Corporation Taxes Act 1988 (c. 1)

35 (1) The Income and Corporation Taxes Act 1988 is amended as follows.

(2) In section 579—

(a) in subsections (3)(a) and (5)(a) and in subsection (4)(a) as it has effect for the purposes of corporation tax, for the words from "by which" to "rebate" substitute "of the redundancy payment or the corresponding amount of the other employer's payment", and

(b) in subsection (6), for "section 106 of the Employment Protection (Consolidation) Act 1978" substitute "section 166 of the Employment Rights Act 1996".

(3) In section 580(1)—

(a) in paragraph (a), for ", "employer's payment" and "rebate" have the same meaning as in the Employment Protection (Consolidation) Act 1978 ("the 1978 Act")" substitute "and "employer's payment" have the same meaning as in Part XI of the Employment Rights Act 1996",

(b) in paragraph (b), for the words "of the relevant redundancy payment" onwards substitute "which would have been payable as a redundancy payment had one been payable;", and

(c) in paragraph (c), for "the 1978 Act" substitute "the Employment Rights Act 1996".

(4) In—

(a) paragraph 19(a) of Part III of Schedule 9, and

(b) paragraph 2 of Schedule 10,

for "the Employment Protection (Consolidation) Act 1978" substitute "the Employment Rights Act 1996".

The Legal Aid Act 1988 (c. 34)

36 In paragraph 7(1) of Schedule 7 to the Legal Aid Act 1988, for "the Employment Protection (Consolidation) Act 1978" substitute "the Employment Rights Act 1996".

The Education Reform Act 1988 (c. 40)

37 (1) The Education Reform Act 1988 is amended as follows.

(2) In section 174(2), for "Schedule 13 to that Act" substitute "Chapter I of Part XIV of the Employment Rights Act 1996".

(3) In section 203(7), for "section 55 of the Employment Protection (Consolidation) Act 1978" substitute "Part X of the Employment Rights Act 1996".

(4) In section 221(2)(b), for "section 81 of the Employment Protection (Consolidation) Act 1978" substitute "section 135 of the Employment Rights Act 1996".

(5) In section 235—

(a) in subsection (1), for "the Employment Protection (Consolidation) Act 1978" substitute "the Employment Rights Act 1996", and

(b) in subsection (2)(f), for "section 81 of the Employment Protection (Consolidation) Act 1978" substitute "section 139 of the Employment Rights Act 1996".

The Local Government Finance Act 1988 (c. 41)

38 In paragraph 6(4) of Schedule 11 to the Local Government Finance Act 1988, for "the Employment Protection (Consolidation) Act 1978" substitute "the Employment Rights Act 1996".

The Housing (Scotland) Act 1988 (c. 43)

39 In paragraph 12(1) of Schedule 1 to the Housing (Scotland) Act 1988, for "the Employment Protection (Consolidation) Act 1978" substitute "the Employment Rights Act 1996".

The Health and Medicines Act 1988 (c. 49)

40 In section 18 of the Health and Medicines Act 1988, for "the Employment Protection (Consolidation) Act 1978" substitute "the Employment Rights Act 1996".

The Housing Act 1988 (c. 50)

41 In paragraph 10(1) of Schedule 5 to the Housing Act 1988, for "the Employment Protection (Consolidation) Act 1978" substitute "the Employment Rights Act 1996".

The Dock Work Act 1989 (c. 13)

42 In section 6(3) of the Dock Work Act 1989—

(a) for "the 1978 Act" substitute "the Employment Rights Act 1996",

(b) for "section 151 of, and Schedule 13 to," substitute "Chapter I of Part XIV of",

(c) for "paragraph 15 of Schedule 13" substitute "section 216 of that Act", and

(d) for "paragraph 4 of that Schedule" substitute "section 212(1) of that Act".

The Electricity Act 1989 (c. 29)

43 (1) The Electricity Act 1989 is amended as follows.

(2) In section 56(3), for "Schedule 13 to the said Act of 1978" substitute "Chapter I of Part XIV of the Employment Rights Act 1996".

(3) In—

(a) paragraph 4(1) of Schedule 14, and

(b) paragraph 4(1) of Schedule 15,

for the words from the beginning to "continuous" substitute "Chapter I of Part XIV of the Employment Rights Act 1996".

The Local Government and Housing Act 1989 (c. 42)

44 In section 10 of the Local Government and Housing Act 1989—

(a) in subsection (1), for "subsection (4) of section 29 of the Employment Protection (Consolidation) Act 1978" substitute "section 50(4) of the Employment Rights Act 1996", and

(b) in subsection (2)—

(i) for "the Employment Protection (Consolidation) Act 1978" substitute "the Employment Rights Act 1996", and

(ii) for "subsection (1) of section 29" substitute "subsection (2) of section 50".

The National Health Service and Community Care Act 1990 (c. 19)

45 (1) The National Health Service and Community Care Act 1990 is amended as follows.

(2) In section 7(3)—

(a) for "Part VI of the Employment Protection (Consolidation) Act 1978" substitute "Part XI of the Employment Rights Act 1996", and

(b) for "the said Part VI" substitute "that Part of that Act".

(3) In—

(a) section 20(6), and

(b) section 49(3)(b),

for "the Employment Protection (Consolidation) Act 1978" substitute "the Employment Rights Act 1996".

(4) In section 60(3)—

(a) for "Part VI of the Employment Protection (Consolidation) Act 1978" substitute "Part XI of the Employment Rights Act 1996", and

(b) for "the said Part VI" substitute "that Part of that Act".

The Enterprise and New Towns (Scotland) Act 1990 (c. 35)

46 In paragraph 17(1) of Schedule 1 to the Enterprise and New Towns (Scotland) Act 1990, for "the Employment Protection (Consolidation) Act 1978" substitute "the Employment Rights Act 1996".

The Environmental Protection Act 1990 (c. 43)

47 In paragraph 15 of Schedule 10 to the Environmental Protection Act 1990, for "the Employment Protection (Consolidation) Act 1978" substitute "the Employment Rights Act 1996".

The Natural Heritage (Scotland) Act 1991 (c. 28)

48 In paragraph 4 of Schedule 4 to the Natural Heritage (Scotland) Act 1991, for "the Employment Protection (Consolidation) Act 1978" substitute "the Employment Rights Act 1996".

The Coal Mining Subsidence Act 1991 (c. 45)

49 In section 30(7) of the Coal Mining Subsidence Act 1991—

(a) for "section 153(4) of the Employment Protection (Consolidation) Act 1978" substitute "section 231 of the Employment Rights Act 1996", and

(b) for "meaning given by section 153(1) of the Employment Protection (Consolidation) Act 1978" substitute "same meaning as in the Employment Rights Act 1996".

The Ports Act 1991 (c. 52)

50 In section 24(8) of the Ports Act 1991, for the words from the beginning to "continuous" substitute "Chapter I of Part XIV of the Employment Rights Act 1996".

The Social Security Contributions and Benefits Act 1992 (c. 4)

51 (1) The Social Security Contributions and Benefits Act 1992 is amended as follows.

(2) In section 6(5), for "section 81" onwards substitute "Part XI of the Employment Rights Act 1996 (redundancy payments) does not apply by virtue of section 199(2) or 209 of that Act."

(3) In—

(a) section 27(2)(b), and

(b) section 28(4),

for "section 81(2) of the Employment Protection (Consolidation) Act 1978" substitute "section 139(1) of the Employment Rights Act 1996".

(4) In section 112(3)—

(a) in paragraph (a), for "the Employment Protection (Consolidation) Act 1978" substitute "the Employment Rights Act 1996",

(b) in paragraph (b), after "that Act" insert "or the Trade Union and Labour Relations (Consolidation) Act 1992", and

(c) in paragraph (c), for "the Employment Protection Act 1975" substitute "the Trade Union and Labour Relations (Consolidation) Act 1992".

(5) In section 171(1), for "section 55(2) to (7) of the Employment Protection (Consolidation) Act 1978" substitute "Part X of the Employment Rights Act 1996".

The Further and Higher Education Act 1992 (c. 13)

52 (1) The Further and Higher Education Act 1992 is amended as follows.

(2) In section 35—

(a) in subsection (1)(c)—

(i) for "section 84 of the Employment Protection (Consolidation) Act 1978" substitute "section 138 of the Employment Rights Act 1996", and

(ii) for "Part VI" substitute "Part XI", and

(b) in subsection (2), for "Schedule 13 to" substitute "Chapter I of Part XIV of".

(3) In section 49(2)(b), for "section 81 of the Employment Protection (Consolidation) Act 1978" substitute "Part XI of the Employment Rights Act 1996".

(4) In section 90(1), for "the Employment Protection (Consolidation) Act 1978" substitute "the Employment Rights Act 1996".

The Timeshare Act 1992 (c. 35)

53 In section 1 of the Timeshare Act 1992—

(a) in subsection (3)(b), for "as defined in section 153 of the Employment Protection (Consolidation) Act 1978" substitute "within the meaning of the Employment Rights Act 1996", and

(b) in subsection (8)(b), for "section 153 of the Employment Protection (Consolidation) Act 1978" substitute "the Employment Rights Act 1996".

The Further and Higher Education (Scotland) Act 1992 (c. 37)

54 In section 33(3)(b) of the Further and Higher Education (Scotland) Act 1992, for "section 81 of the Employment Protection (Consolidation) Act 1978" substitute "section 135 of the Employment Rights Act 1996".

The Museums and Galleries Act 1992 (c. 44)

55 In section 1(7) of the Museums and Galleries Act 1992, for "paragraph 17(3) of Schedule 13 to the Employment Protection (Consolidation) Act 1978" substitute "section 218(3) of the Employment Rights Act 1996".

The Trade Union and Labour Relations (Consolidation) Act 1992 (c. 52)

56 (1) The Trade Union and Labour Relations (Consolidation) Act 1992 is amended as follows.

(2) In section 67(8)—

(a) in paragraph (a), for "paragraph 8(1)(b) of Schedule 14 to the Employment Protection (Consolidation) Act 1978" substitute "section 227(1)(a) of the Employment Rights Act 1996", and

(b) in paragraph (b), for "section 75" substitute "section 124(1)".

(3) In section 68(11), for "Part I of the Wages Act 1986" substitute "the Employment Rights Act 1996".

(4) In section 68A(4)—

(a) in paragraph (a), for "the Employment Protection (Consolidation) Act 1978" substitute "the Employment Rights Act 1996", and

(b) in paragraph (b), for "section 1(1) of the Wages Act 1986" substitute "section 13 of that Act".

(5) In section 88—

(a) in subsection (2), for "section 1 of the Wages Act 1986" substitute "section 13 of the Employment Rights Act 1996",

(b) in subsection (3), for "section 5 of the Wages Act 1986" substitute "section 23 of the Employment Rights Act 1996", and

(c) in subsection (4), for "section 5(2) of the Wages Act 1986" substitute "section 23(2) of the Employment Rights Act 1996".

(6) In section 140(4), for "section 75 of the Employment Protection (Consolidation) Act 1978" substitute "section 124(1) of the Employment Rights Act 1996".

(7) In—

(a) section 152(1), and

(b) section 153,

for "Part V of the Employment Protection (Consolidation) Act 1978" substitute "Part X of the Employment Rights Act 1996".

(8) In section 154, for "Section 64 of the Employment Protection (Consolidation) Act 1978 (qualifying period and upper age limit for unfair dismissal protection) does" substitute "Sections 108 and 109 of the Employment Rights Act 1996 (qualifying period and upper age limit for unfair dismissal protection) do".

(9) In section 156—

(a) in subsection (1), for "subsection (7A), (7B) or (9) of section 73 of the Employment Protection (Consolidation) Act 1978" substitute "section 122 of the Employment Rights Act 1996", and

(b) in subsection (2), for "subsection (7B)" substitute "subsection (2)".

(10) In section 157—

(a) in subsection (1), for "section 73(2) of the Employment Protection (Consolidation) Act 1978" substitute "section 121 of the Employment Rights Act 1996", and

(b) in subsection (2), for "section 71(2)(b) of the Employment Protection (Consolidation) Act 1978" substitute "section 117(3)(b) of the Employment Rights Act 1996".

(11) In section 158—

(a) in subsection (2), for "section 71(2)(a) of the Employment Protection (Consolidation) Act 1978" substitute "section 117(3)(a) of the Employment Rights Act 1996",

(b) in subsection (3), for "section 73(5) of the Employment Protection (Consolidation) Act 1978" substitute "section 119(4) of the Employment Rights Act 1996", and

(c) in subsection (7), for the words from the beginning to "Part" substitute—

"(7) Chapter II of Part XIV of the Employment Rights Act 1996 (calculation of a week's pay) applies for the purposes of this section with the substitution for section 226 of the following—

For the purposes of this Chapter".

(12) In section 167—

(a) in subsection (1), for "Part V of the Employment Protection (Consolidation) Act 1978" substitute "Part X of the Employment Rights Act 1996", and

(b) in subsection (2)—

(i) for "section 67 of the Employment Protection (Consolidation) Act 1978" substitute "section 111 of the Employment Rights Act 1996",

(ii) for "section 68(2) or 71(2)(a)" substitute "section 112(4) or 117(3)(a)", and

(iii) for "section 69" substitute "section 113".

(13) In section 176(6)—

(a) in paragraph (a), for "paragraph 8(1)(b) of Schedule 14 to the Employment Protection (Consolidation) Act 1978" substitute "section 227(1)(a) of the Employment Rights Act 1996", and

(b) in paragraph (b), for "section 75" substitute "section 124(1)".

(14) In section 190—

(a) in subsection (4)—

(i) for "Schedule 3 to the Employment Protection (Consolidation) Act 1978" substitute "sections 87 to 91 of the Employment Rights Act 1996", and

(ii) for "section 49(1)" substitute "section 86(1)", and

(b) in subsection (5)—

(i) for "Schedule 14 to the Employment Protection (Consolidation) Act 1978" substitute "Chapter II of Part XIV of the Employment Rights Act 1996",

(ii) for "Part II of that Schedule" substitute "that Chapter", and

(iii) for "paragraph 7(1)(k) or (l) of that Schedule" substitute "section 226(5)".

(15) In sections 237(1A) and 238(2A)—

(a) for "section 57A, 57AA or 60 of the Employment Protection (Consolidation) Act 1978 (dismissal in health and safety cases, employee representative and maternity cases)" substitute "section 99(1) to (3), 100 or 103 of the Employment Rights Act 1996 (dismissal in maternity, health and safety and employee representative cases)", and

(b) for "section 59" substitute "section 105(9)".

(16) In section 239—

(a) in subsection (1), for "Part V of the Employment Protection (Consolidation) Act 1978" substitute "Part X of the Employment Rights Act 1996",

(b) in subsection (2), for "section 67(2)" substitute "section 111(2)", and

(c) in subsection (3), for "sections 57 to 61 of the Employment Protection (Consolidation) Act 1978" substitute "sections 98 to 106 of the Employment Rights Act 1996".

(17) In section 278(6), for "Subsections (4) to (9) of section 139 of the Employment Protection (Consolidation) Act 1978" substitute "Subsections (6) to (12) of section 195 of the Employment Rights Act 1996".

(18) In section 282, for subsection (2) substitute—

"(2) Chapter I of Part XIV of the Employment Rights Act 1996 (computation of period of continuous employment), and any provision modifying or supplementing that Chapter for the purposes of that Act, apply for the purposes of this section."

(19) In section 298, for "section 55 of the Employment Protection (Consolidation) Act 1978" substitute "Part X of the Employment Rights Act 1996".

The Tribunals and Inquiries Act 1992 (c. 53)

57 In section 11(2) of the Tribunals and Inquiries Act 1992, for "Subsection (1)" substitute "This section".

The Social Security Act 1993 (c. 3)

58 In section 2(4)(b) of the Social Security Act 1993, for "sections 106(2) and 122(1) of the Employment Protection (Consolidation) Act 1978" substitute "sections 167(1) and 182 of the Employment Rights Act 1996".

The Education Act 1993 (c. 35)

59 In section 305(1) of the Education Act 1993, for "the Employment Protection (Consolidation) Act 1978" substitute "the Employment Rights Act 1996".

The Railways Act 1993 (c. 43)

60 (1) The Railways Act 1993 is amended as follows.

(2) In section 93(5), (6) and (12), for "the Employment Protection (Consolidation) Act 1978" substitute "the Employment Rights Act 1996".

(3) In paragraph 6 of Schedule 11, for sub-paragraphs (10) to (12) substitute—

"(10) Chapter I of Part XIV of the Employment Rights Act 1996, except section 218(6), shall apply for the purposes of this paragraph as it applies for the purposes of that Act."

The Pension Schemes Act 1993 (c. 48)

61 (1) The Pension Schemes Act 1993 is amended as follows.

(2) In section 123(3), for "the Employment Protection (Consolidation) Act 1978" substitute "the Employment Rights Act 1996".

(3) In section 124(4), for ", maternity pay under Part III" onwards substitute "and any payment such as is referred to in section 184(2) of the Employment Rights Act 1996".

(4) In section 165—

(a) in subsection (7), for "section 137 of the Employment Protection (Consolidation) Act 1978" substitute "section 201 of the Employment Rights Act 1996", and

(b) in subsection (8), for "section 144(5) of the Employment Protection (Consolidation) Act 1978" substitute "section 199(5) of the Employment Rights Act 1996".

The Finance Act 1994 (c. 9)

62 In paragraph 27 of Schedule 24 to the Finance Act 1994—

(a) for sub-paragraphs (9) to (11) substitute—

"(9) Chapter I of Part XIV of the Employment Rights Act 1996, except section 218(6), shall apply for the purposes of this paragraph as it applies for the purposes of that Act.", and

(b) in sub-paragraph (13), for "sub-paragraphs (11) and" substitute "sub-paragraph".

The Local Government (Wales) Act 1994 (c. 19)

63 (1) The Local Government (Wales) Act 1994 is amended as follows.

(2) In section 41—

(a) in subsection (1)—

(i) for "section 84 of the Employment Protection (Consolidation) Act 1978" substitute "section 138 of the Employment Rights Act 1996", and

(ii) for "Part VI" substitute "Part XI", and

(b) in subsection (2), for "Schedule 13 to the Act of 1978" substitute "Chapter I of Part XIV of the Employment Rights Act 1996".

(3) In section 43—

(a) in subsection (6), for "section 82(5) or (6) or 84(3) of the Employment Protection (Consolidation) Act 1978" substitute "section 138 or 141 of the Employment Rights Act 1996", and

(b) in subsection (7), for "Part VI of the Act of 1978" substitute "Part XI of the Employment Rights Act 1996".

(4) In section 44—

(a) in subsection (1), for "Part IV, V or VI of the Employment Protection (Consolidation) Act 1978" substitute "Part IX, X or XI of the Employment Rights Act 1996",

(b) in subsection (3), for "sections 101, 102, 108 and 119 of the Act of 1978" substitute "sections 164, 165, 170 and 179 of the Employment Rights Act 1996", and

(c) in subsection (4), for "sections 81(4), 82(1) and 101 of the Act of 1978, and in Schedule 4 to that Act," substitute "sections 155, 156, 162 and 164 of the Employment Rights Act 1996".

(5) In section 45(5), for "the Employment Protection (Consolidation) Act 1978" substitute "the Employment Rights Act 1996".

The Coal Industry Act 1994 (c. 21)

64 In paragraph 4(11) of Schedule 5 to the Coal Industry Act 1994, for the words from the beginning to "that Schedule" substitute "Chapter I of Part XIV of the Employment Rights Act 1996, except section 218(6),".

The Criminal Justice and Public Order Act 1994 (c. 33)

65 In section 126(2) of the Criminal Justice and Public Order Act 1994, for paragraph (a) substitute—

"(a) the Trade Union and Labour Relations (Consolidation) Act 1992 and the Employment Rights Act 1996;".

The Local Government etc. (Scotland) Act 1994 (c. 39)

66 (1) The Local Government etc. (Scotland) Act 1994 is amended as follows.

(2) In section 10—

(a) in subsection (1)—

(i) for "section 84 of the Employment Protection (Consolidation) Act 1978" substitute "section 138 of the Employment Rights Act 1996", and

(ii) for "Part VI" substitute "Part XI", and

(b) in subsection (2), for "Schedule 13 to the said Act of 1978" substitute "Chapter I of Part XIV of the Employment Rights Act 1996".

(3) In section 13—

(a) in subsection (5), for the words from "subsections" to "1978" substitute "section 138 or 141 of the Employment Rights Act 1996 (renewal of contract or re-engagement)", and

(b) in subsection (6), for "Part VI of the said Act of 1978" substitute "Part XI of the Employment Rights Act 1996".

(4) In section 14(1), for "Part VI of the Employment Protection (Consolidation) Act 1978" substitute "Part XI of the Employment Rights Act 1996".

The Jobseekers Act 1995 (c. 18)

67 (1) The Jobseekers Act 1995 is amended as follows.

(2) In—

(a) section 14(3)(b), and

(b) section 19(7),

for "section 81(2) of the Employment Protection (Consolidation) Act 1978" substitute "section 139(1) of the Employment Rights Act 1996".

(3) In paragraph 6(2)(a)(i) of Schedule 1, for "the Employment Protection (Consolidation) Act 1978" substitute "the Employment Rights Act 1996".

The Environment Act 1995 (c. 25)

68 In paragraph 3 of Schedule 2 to the Environment Act 1995—

(a) in sub-paragraph (6), for "section 84 of the Employment Protection (Consolidation) Act 1978" substitute "section 138 of the Employment Rights Act 1996", and

(b) in sub-paragraph (7), for "Schedule 13 to the Employment Protection (Consolidation) Act 1978" substitute "Chapter I of Part XIV of the Employment Rights Act 1996".

The Disability Discrimination Act 1995 (c. 50)

69 (1) The Disability Discrimination Act 1995 is amended as follows.

(2) In section 50(9)(a), for "the Employment Protection (Consolidation) Act 1978" substitute "the Employment Rights Act 1996".

(3) In section 65(2), for "section 139 of the Employment Protection (Consolidation) Act 1978" substitute "section 195 of the Employment Rights Act 1996".

SCHEDULE 2

Section 241.

TRANSITIONAL PROVISIONS, SAVINGS AND TRANSITORY PROVISIONS

PART I

TRANSITIONAL PROVISIONS AND SAVINGS

General transitionals and savings

1 The substitution of this Act for the provisions repealed or revoked by this Act does not affect the continuity of the law.

2 (1) Anything done, or having effect as done, (including the making of subordinate legislation) under or for the purposes of any provision repealed or revoked by this Act has effect as if done under or for the purposes of any corresponding provision of this Act.

(2) Sub-paragraph (1) does not apply to the making of any subordinate legislation to the extent that it is reproduced in this Act.

3 Any reference (express or implied) in this Act or any other enactment, or in any instrument or document, to a provision of this Act is (so far as the context permits) to be read as (according to the context) being or including in relation to times, circumstances and purposes before the commencement of this Act a reference to the corresponding provision repealed or revoked by this Act.

4 (1) Any reference (express or implied) in any enactment, or in any instrument or document, to a provision repealed or revoked by this Act is (so far as the context permits) to be read as (according to the context) being or including in relation to times, circumstances and purposes after the commencement of this Act a reference to the corresponding provision of this Act.

(2) In particular, where a power conferred by an Act is expressed to be exercisable in relation to enactments contained in Acts passed before or in the same Session as the

Act conferring the power, the power is also exercisable in relation to provisions of this Act which reproduce such enactments.

5 Paragraphs 1 to 4 have effect in place of section 17(2) of the Interpretation Act 1978 (but are without prejudice to any other provision of that Act).

Preservation of old transitionals and savings

6 (1) The repeal by this Act of an enactment previously repealed subject to savings (whether or not in the repealing enactment) does not affect the continued operation of those savings.

(2) The repeal by this Act of a saving made on the previous repeal of an enactment does not affect the operation of the saving in so far as it remains capable of having effect.

(3) Where the purpose of an enactment repealed by this Act was to secure that the substitution of the provisions of the Act containing that enactment for provisions repealed by that Act did not affect the continuity of the law, the enactment repealed by this Act continues to have effect in so far as it is capable of doing so.

Employment particulars

7 (1) In this paragraph "pre-TURERA employee" means an employee whose employment with his employer began before 30th November 1993 (the day on which section 26 of the Trade Union Reform and Employment Rights Act 1993 came into force), whether or not the provisions of sections 1 to 6 of the Employment Protection (Consolidation) Act 1978, as they had effect before the substitution made by that section, applied to him before that date.

(2) Subject to the following provisions of this paragraph, sections 1 to 7 of this Act do not apply to a pre-TURERA employee (but the provisions of sections 1 to 6 of the Employment Protection (Consolidation) Act 1978, as they had effect before the substitution made by section 26 of the Trade Union Reform and Employment Rights Act 1993, continue in force in his case).

(3) Where a pre-TURERA employee, at any time—

(a) on or after the day on which this Act comes into force, and

(b) either before the end of his employment or within the period of three months beginning with the day on which his employment ends,

requests from his employer a statement under section 1 of this Act, the employer shall (subject to section 5 and any other provision disapplying or having the effect of disapplying sections 1 to 4) be treated as being required by section 1 to give him a written statement under that section not later than two months after the request is made; and section 4 of this Act shall (subject to that) apply in relation to the employee after he makes the request.

(4) An employer is not required to give an employee a statement under section 1 pursuant to sub-paragraph (3)—

(a) on more than one occasion, or

(b) if he has already given him a statement pursuant to paragraph 3(3) of Schedule 9 to the Trade Union Reform and Employment Rights Act 1993.

(5) Where—

(a) on or after the day on which this Act comes into force there is in the case of a pre-TURERA employee a change in any of the matters particulars of which would, had he been given a statement of particulars on 30th November 1993 under section 1 of the Employment Protection (Consolidation) Act 1978 (as substituted by section 26 of the Trade Union Reform and Employment Rights Act 1993), have been included or referred to in the statement, and

(b) he has not previously requested a statement under sub-paragraph (3) or paragraph 3(3) of Schedule 9 to the Trade Union Reform and Employment Rights Act 1993,

subsections (1) and (6) of section 4 of this Act shall be treated (subject to section 5 and any other provision disapplying or having the effect of disapplying section 4) as requiring his employer to give him a written statement containing particulars of the change at the time specified in subsection (3) of section 4; and the other provisions of section 4 apply accordingly.

Monetary limits in old cases

8 In relation to any case in which (but for this Act) a limit lower than that set by Article 3 of the Employment Protection (Increase of Limits) Order 1995 would have applied in accordance with Article 4 of that Order, this Act has effect as if it reproduced that lower limit.

Shop workers and betting workers to whom old maternity provisions applied

9 (1) This paragraph applies where an employee exercised a right to return to work under Part III of the Employment Protection (Consolidation) Act 1978 at a time when the amendments of that Part made by the Trade Union Reform and Employment Rights Act 1993 did not have effect in her case (so that her right was a right to return to work in the job in which she was employed under the original contract of employment).

(2) Section 36(4) shall have effect as if for paragraph (b) there were substituted—

> "(b) under her original contract of employment, she was a shop worker, or a betting worker, but was not employed to work only on Sunday."

(3) If the employee was employed as a shop worker under her original contract of employment, she shall not be regarded as failing to satisfy the condition in section 36(2)(a) or (c) or 41(1)(c) merely because during her pregnancy she was employed under a different contract of employment by virtue of section 60(2) of the Employment Protection (Consolidation) Act 1978 (as it had effect before the commencement of section 24 of the Trade Union Reform and Employment Rights Act 1993) or otherwise by reason of her pregnancy.

(4) In this paragraph, and in section 36(4)(b) as substituted by sub-paragraph (2), "original contract of employment" has the meaning given by section 153(1) of the Employment Protection (Consolidation) Act 1978 as originally enacted.

Validity of provisions deriving from certain regulations

10 Any question as to the validity of any of sections 47, 61, 62, 63 and 103, which derive from the Collective Redundancies and Transfer of Undertakings (Protection of Employment) (Amendment) Regulations 1995 made under subsection (2) of section 2 of the European Communities Act 1972, shall be determined as if those provisions were contained in regulations made under that subsection.

Unfair dismissal

11 Part X does not apply to a dismissal from employment under a contract for a fixed term of two years or more (not being a contract of apprenticeship) if—

(a) the contract was made before 28th February 1972, and

(b) the dismissal consists only of the expiry of that term without its being renewed.

Redundancy payments

12 (1) Section 135 does not apply to an employee who immediately before the relevant date is employed under a contract for a fixed term of two years or more (not being a contract of apprenticeship) if the contract was made before 6th December 1965.

(2) Section 197(3) does not apply if the contract was made before 6th December 1965.

Periods of employment

13 (1) The reference in section 215(2)(b) to a person being an employed earner for the purposes of the Social Security Contributions and Benefits Act 1992 in respect of whom a secondary Class 1 contribution was payable under that Act (whether or not it was in fact paid) shall be construed—

(a) as respects a week of employment after 1st June 1976 and before 1st July 1992, as a reference to a person being an employed earner for the purposes of the Social Security Act 1975 in respect of whom a secondary Class 1 contribution was payable under that Act (whether or not it was in fact paid),

(b) as respects a week of employment after 6th April 1975 and before 1st June 1976, as a reference to a person being an employed earner for the purposes of the Social Security Act 1975, and

(c) as respects a week of employment before 6th April 1975, as a reference to a person being an employee in respect of whom an employer's contribution was payable in respect of the corresponding contribution week (whether or not it was in fact paid).

(2) For the purposes of the application of sub-paragraph (1) to a week of employment where the corresponding contribution week began before 5th July 1948, an employer's contribution shall be treated as payable as mentioned in that sub-paragraph if such a contribution would have been so payable had the statutory provisions relating to national insurance in force on 5th July 1948 been in force in that contribution week.

(3) The references in subsection (4) of section 215 to the Social Security Contributions and Benefits Act 1992 include the Social Security Act 1975; and that subsection applies to any question arising whether an employer's contribution was or would have been payable as mentioned in sub-paragraph (1) or (2).

(4) In this paragraph—

"employer's contribution" has the same meaning as in the National Insurance Act 1965, and

"corresponding contribution week", in relation to a week of employment, means a contribution week (within the meaning of that Act) of which so much as falls within the period beginning with midnight between Sunday and Monday and ending with Saturday also falls within that week of employment.

14 (1) Subject to paragraph 13 and sub-paragraphs (2) and (3) of this paragraph, Chapter I of Part XIV applies to periods before this Act comes into force as it applies to later periods.

(2) If, during the whole or any part of a week beginning before 6th July 1964, an employee was absent from work—

(a) because he was taking part in a strike, or

(b) because of a lock-out by his employer,

the week counts as a period of employment.

(3) Any week which counted as a period of employment in the computation of a period of employment for the purposes of the Employment Protection (Consolidation) Act 1978 counts as a period of employment for the purposes of this Act; and any week which did not break the continuity of a person's employment for the purposes of that Act shall not break the continuity of a period of employment for the purposes of this Act.

PART II

TRANSITORY PROVISIONS

Occupational pension scheme trustees

15 (1) If sections 42 to 46 of the Pensions Act 1995 have not come into force before the commencement of this Act, this Act shall have effect with the omission of sections 46, 58 to 60 and 102 until the relevant commencement date.

(2) The reference in sub-paragraph (1) to the relevant commencement date is a reference—

(a) if an order has been made before the commencement of this Act appointing a day after that commencement as the day on which sections 42 to 46 of the Pensions Act 1995 are to come into force, to the day so appointed, and

(b) otherwise, to such day as the Secretary of State may by order appoint.

Armed forces

16 (1) If section 31 of the Trade Union Reform and Employment Rights Act 1993 has not come into force before the commencement of this Act, this Act shall have effect until the relevant commencement date as if for section 192 there were substituted—

"192 Armed forces

"192 "192 Armed forces

Section 191—

(a) does not apply to service as a member of the naval, military or air forces of the Crown, but

(b) does apply to employment by an association established for the purposes of Part XI of the Reserve Forces Act 1996."

(2) The reference in sub-paragraph (1) to the relevant commencement date is a reference—

(a) if an order has been made before the commencement of this Act appointing a day after that commencement as the day on which section 31 of the Trade Union Reform and Employment Rights Act 1993 is to come into force, to the day so appointed, and

(b) otherwise, to such day as the Secretary of State may by order appoint.

17 (1) If Part XI of the Reserve Forces Act 1996 has not come into force before the commencement of this Act, section 192 of this Act shall have effect until the relevant commencement date as if for "Part XI of the Reserve Forces Act 1996" there were substituted "Part VI of the Reserve Forces Act 1980".

(2) The reference in sub-paragraph (1) to the relevant commencement date is a reference—

(a) if an order has been made before the commencement of this Act appointing a day after that commencement as the day on which Part XI of the Reserve Forces Act 1996 is to come into force, to the day so appointed, and

(b) otherwise, to such day as the Secretary of State may by order appoint.

Disability discrimination

18 (1) If paragraph 3 of Schedule 6 to the Disability Discrimination Act 1995 has not come into force before the commencement of this Act, this Act shall have effect with the omission of subsections (3)(d) and (4)(a)(iv) of section 219 until the relevant commencement date.

(2) The reference in sub-paragraph (1) to the relevant commencement date is a reference—

(a) if an order has been made before the commencement of this Act appointing a day after that commencement as the day on which paragraph 3 of Schedule 6 to the Disability Discrimination Act 1995 is to come into force, to the day so appointed, and

(b) otherwise, to such day as the Secretary of State may by order appoint.

SCHEDULE 3

Section 242.

REPEALS AND REVOCATIONS

PART I

REPEALS

Chapter	*Short title*	*Extent of repeal*
1963 c. 2.	The Betting, Gaming and Lotteries Act 1963.	Section 31A.
		In Schedule 5A, paragraphs 1 to 20 and 22.

Chapter	*Short title*	*Extent of repeal*
1969 c. 48.	The Post Office Act 1969.	In Schedule 9, paragraph 33.
1971 c. 11.	The Atomic Energy Authority Act 1971.	Section 10(1).
1976 c. 74.	The Race Relations Act 1976.	In Schedule 2, in paragraph 11, in sub-paragraph (1), the words "and the following" and sub-paragraphs (2), (3) and (5) and paragraphs 12 and 13.
1978 c. 44.	The Employment Protection (Consolidation) Act 1978.	Sections 1 to 6.
		Sections 8 to 22C.
		Sections 29 to 47.
		Sections 49 to 57A.
		Sections 59 to 61.
		Sections 63 to 93.
		Section 96.
		Sections 98 to 102.
		Sections 106 to 108.
		Sections 110 to 112.
		Sections 114 to 120.
		Section 122.
		Sections 124 to 127.
		Section 129.
		Section 137.
		Section 138(1) to (6), (7)(a) to (d) and (f) and (8).
		Section 139(1)(a) to (c) and (e) and (2) to (9).
		Section 139A(1), (2), (3)(b) and (4) to (6).
		Sections 140 to 142.
		Section 144.
		Section 146.
		Section 146A.
		Sections 148 to 160.
		Schedules 1 to 4.

Chapter	Short title	Extent of repeal
		Schedule 7.
		Schedule 8.
		Schedules 12 to 17.
1980 c. 20.	The Education Act 1980.	In Schedule 1, paragraph 30.
1980 c. 42.	The Employment Act 1980.	Section 6.
		Section 8(2).
		Section 9.
		Sections 12 to 14.
		Section 20.
		Section 21.
		In Schedule 1, paragraphs 1, 8, 11, 13, 20, 22, 23, 25, 31 and 33.
		Schedule 2.
1980 c. 43.	The Magistrates' Courts Act 1980.	In Schedule 7, paragraph 175.
1980 c. 48.	The Finance Act 1980.	In Schedule 19, paragraph 5(4).
1981 c. 64.	The New Towns Act 1981.	Section 54(6).
1982 c. 16.	The Civil Aviation Act 1982.	In Schedule 3, paragraphs 6 and 8(1).
1982 c. 23.	The Oil and Gas (Enterprise) Act 1982.	In Schedule 3, paragraph 40.
1982 c. 24.	The Social Security and Housing Benefits Act 1982.	In Schedule 2, paragraph 13.
1982 c. 46.	The Employment Act 1982.	Section 20.
		Section 21(1) and (3).
		In Schedule 2, paragraphs 1 to 5, 6(2), (4) and (5), 7(1) and (2) and 9.
		In Schedule 3, in Part I, paragraphs 1, 2, 4 and 6 and, in Part II, paragraphs 15, 21 to 23, 25, 26, 27(1) and 28 to 30.
		Schedule 4.
1983 c. 23.	The Water Act 1983.	In Schedule 2, in Part I, paragraph 8(1)(b).

Chapter	*Short title*	*Extent of repeal*
1983 c. 41.	The Health and Social Services and Social Security Adjudications Act 1983.	In Schedule 9, in Part I, paragraph 25.
1984 c. 36.	The Mental Health (Scotland) Act 1984.	Section 126(2)(c).
1985 c. 17.	The Reserve Forces (Safeguard of Employment) Act 1985.	In Schedule 4, paragraph 6.
1985 c. 51.	The Local Government Act 1985.	In section 53, subsection (5) and, in subsection (6), the words "Except as provided in subsection (5) above" and "a redundancy payment under Part VI of the said Act of 1978 or to".
		Section 55(3) to (5).
		Section 59(1) to (3).
1985 c. 65.	The Insolvency Act 1985.	Section 218.
		In Schedule 8, paragraph 31(1), (2) and (5).
1985 c. 66.	The Bankruptcy (Scotland) Act 1985.	In Schedule 7, in Part I, paragraph 14(1), (2) and (4).
1985 c. 71.	The Housing (Consequential Provisions) Act 1985.	In Schedule 4, paragraph 7(2)(a).
1986 c. 45.	The Insolvency Act 1986.	In Schedule 14, the entries relating to the Employment Protection (Consolidation) Act 1978.
1986 c. 47.	The Legal Aid (Scotland) Act 1986.	In Schedule 1, in paragraph 10(2)(a), the words "Part VI of the Employment Protection (Consolidation) Act 1978 shall not apply to him and".
1986 c. 48.	The Wages Act 1986.	Sections 1 to 11.
		Sections 28 to 33.
		Schedule 1.
		In Schedule 4, paragraph 4.
		Schedule 5.
		In Schedule 6, paragraph 10.
1986 c. 50.	The Social Security Act 1986.	In Schedule 10, in Part IV, paragraphs 76 and 81.

Chapter	*Short title*	*Extent of repeal*
1986 c. 59.	The Sex Discrimination Act 1986.	Section 3.
1987 c. 26.	The Housing (Scotland) Act 1987.	In Schedule 22, in Part II, paragraph 10(2)(a).
1988 c. 1.	The Income and Corporation Taxes Act 1988.	Section 150(b).
		In section 579, subsection (2)(a), in subsections (2)(b) and (3)(b) and in subsection (4)(b) as it has effect otherwise than for the purposes of corporation tax, the word "net" and, in subsection (5)(b), the words ", and the full amount of the rebate".
		Section 580(2).
1988 c. 4.	The Norfolk and Suffolk Broads Act 1988.	In Schedule 6, paragraph 19.
1988 c. 20.	The Dartford-Thurrock Crossing Act 1988.	In Schedule 5, in Part I, paragraph 2(2).
1988 c. 34.	The Legal Aid Act 1988.	In Schedule 7, in paragraph 7(3), the words "Part VI of the Employment Protection (Consolidation) Act 1978 shall not apply to him and".
1988 c. 40.	The Education Reform Act 1988.	In section 173, subsection (6) and, in subsection (7), the words "Except as provided in subsection (6) above" and "a redundancy payment under Part VI of the Act of 1978 mentioned above or to".
		Section 175(3) to (5).
		Section 178(1) and (2).
		In Schedule 12, in Part I, paragraph 23 and, in Part III, paragraph 80.
1988 c. 43.	The Housing (Scotland) Act 1988.	In Schedule 1, in paragraph 12(2), the words "Part VI of the Employment Protection (Consolidation) Act 1978 shall not apply to him and".
1988 c. 50.	The Housing Act 1988.	In Schedule 5, in paragraph 10(2), the words "Part VI of the Employment Protection

Chapter	*Short title*	*Extent of repeal*
		(Consolidation) Act 1978 shall not apply to him and".
1989 c. 13.	The Dock Work Act 1989.	Section 6(2).
		Section 7(4).
		In Schedule 2, paragraphs 6 and 7.
1989 c. 15.	The Water Act 1989.	In section 194(7)(d), the words "and the Employment Protection (Consolidation) Act 1978".
		In Schedule 25, paragraph 56.
1989 c. 29.	The Electricity Act 1989.	Section 56(2).
1989 c. 38.	The Employment Act 1989.	Sections 15 to 18.
		Section 19(1).
		In section 27(1), the words "and 16 to 19".
		In section 29(1), the definition of "the 1978 Act".
		Section 30(3)(f).
		In Schedule 6, paragraphs 21 to 25.
		In Schedule 9, paragraphs 3 to 5.
1989 c. 39.	The Self-Governing Schools etc. (Scotland) Act 1989.	In Schedule 10, paragraph 7.
1990 c. 19.	The National Health Service and Community Care Act 1990.	In Schedule 9, paragraph 20.
1990 c. 35.	The Enterprise and New Towns (Scotland) Act 1990.	In Schedule 1, in paragraph 17(2), the words "Part VI of the said Act of 1978 shall not apply to him and".
1990 c. 38.	The Employment Act 1990.	Section 13(1), (2) and (4).
		Section 16.
		In section 17, subsection (1) and, in subsection (2), the words "Apart from this section,".
		In Schedule 2, paragraph 1(1) and (3) to (6).
		Schedule 3.

Chapter	*Short title*	*Extent of repeal*
1990 c. 43.	The Environmental Protection Act 1990.	In Schedule 10, in paragraph 16, the words "Part VI of the Employment Protection (Consolidation) Act 1978 shall not apply to him and".
1991 c. 28.	The Natural Heritage (Scotland) Act 1991.	In Schedule 4, in paragraph 5, the words "Part VI of the Employment Protection (Consolidation) Act 1978 shall not apply to him and".
1992 c. 6.	The Social Security (Consequential Provisions) Act 1992.	In Schedule 2, paragraphs 51 and 74.
1992 c. 13.	The Further and Higher Education Act 1992.	In Schedule 8, in Part II, paragraph 89.
1992 c. 37.	The Further and Higher Education (Scotland) Act 1992.	In Schedule 9, paragraph 6.
1992 c. 52.	The Trade Union and Labour Relations (Consolidation) Act 1992.	In Schedule 2, paragraphs 11 to 14, 16 to 18, 21 to 23, 29(2), 30, 33 and 34(1) and (2).
1993 c. 19.	The Trade Union Reform and Employment Rights Act 1993.	Sections 23 to 26.
		Sections 28 to 31.
		In section 39, subsection (1) and, in subsection (2), the words ", the Wages Act 1986".
		Section 54(2)(a) to (e).
		Schedules 2 to 5.
		In Schedule 6, paragraph 3.
		In Schedule 7, paragraphs 2 to 5, 11, 13, 14 and 16.
		In Schedule 8, paragraphs 10 to 18, 21 to 27, 31, 32, 35 to 37 and 67.
		In Schedule 9, paragraph 3.
1993 c. 48.	The Pension Schemes Act 1993.	Section 164(6).
		In Schedule 8, paragraphs 11(1) and 45(a).

Chapter	*Short title*	*Extent of repeal*
1994 c. 10.	The Race Relations (Remedies) Act 1994.	Section 1(2).
1994 c. 18.	The Social Security (Incapacity for Work) Act 1994.	In Schedule 1, in Part II, paragraph 54.
1994 c. 20.	The Sunday Trading Act 1994.	In Schedule 4, paragraphs 1 to 20 and 22.
1994 c. 40.	The Deregulation and Contracting Out Act 1994.	Section 20(3) and (5).
		Section 36(1).
		Schedule 8.
1995 c. 17.	The Health Authorities Act 1995.	In Schedule 1, paragraph 103.
1995 c. 25.	The Environment Act 1995.	In Schedule 7, in paragraph 11(3), the words from the beginning to "but".
1995 c. 26.	The Pensions Act 1995.	Sections 42 to 46.
		In Schedule 3, paragraphs 1 to 7 and 10.
1995 c. 50.	The Disability Discrimination Act 1995.	In Schedule 6, paragraph 3.
1996 c. 14.	The Reserve Forces Act 1996.	In Schedule 10, paragraph 17.

PART II

REVOCATIONS

Number	*Title*	*Extent of revocation*
S.I. 1983/624.	The Insolvency of Employer (Excluded Classes) Regulations 1983.	The whole instrument.
S.I. 1993/2798.	The Sex Discrimination and Equal Pay (Remedies) Regulations 1993.	In the Schedule, in paragraph 1, the entry relating to the Employment Protection (Consolidation) Act 1978 and paragraph 2.
S.I. 1995/31.	The Employment Protection (Part-time Employees) Regulations 1995.	The whole instrument.

Number	*Title*	*Extent of revocation*
S.I. 1995/278.	The Insolvency of Employer (Excluded Classes) Regulations 1995.	The whole instrument.
S.I. 1995/2587.	The Collective Redundancies and Transfer of Undertakings (Protection of Employment) (Amendment) Regulations 1995.	Regulation 12(1), (2) and (4).
		Regulation 13(1), (2) and (4) to (6).
		Regulation 14.
S.I. 1996/593.	The Environment Act 1995 (Consequential Amendments) Regulations 1996.	In Schedule 1, paragraph 19.
S.I. 1996/973.	The Environment Act 1995 (Consequential and Transitional Provisions) (Scotland) Regulations 1996.	In the Schedule, paragraph 4.

Adapted and published by GRANGIS under the OGL Licence 3.0.

www.nationalarchives.gov.uk/doc/open-government-licence/version/3/

GRANGIS - UK PUBLISHING 2022.

Thank you for taking the time to leave us a review regarding this version

★★★★★

For further inquiries, contact us at:
www.grangis.com / contact@grangis.com

www.ingramcontent.com/pod-product-compliance
Lightning Source LLC
LaVergne TN
LVHW060212210926
848481LV00008B/2705